STREE

A postgraduate in journalism and a gold seal diploma holder in creative writing, **Lalitha Balasubramanian** has published hundreds of articles on health, education and travel in reputed newspapers and magazines. She is the author of seven books, including mythological travelogues and books for children. Her recent book, *On the Krishna Trail*, has won acclaim from readers and critics alike. Her writing journey is fuelled by her fascination for the timeless epics, the Ramayana and the Mahabharata, and her love for delving into spiritual literature.

With a master's in world history, **Jai Shukla** has a diverse professional background from defence to banking. His most acclaimed work, *Kaikeyi: The Warrior Queen of Koshala*, has been received well by readers and critics alike. Jai has also published several enchanting children's books, delving into mythological tales featuring Hanuman, Ganesha, and Brahma. Jai draws his inspiration from Hindu Pauranik literature and the timeless epics, the Ramayana and the Mahabharata. Tulsidas's *Ramacharitmanas* holds a special place in his heart.

STREE

THE WOMEN OF THE RAMAYANA

LALITHA BALASUBRAMANIAN | JAI SHUKLA

Om Books International

First published in 2024 by

Om Books International

Corporate & Editorial Office
A-12, Sector 64, Noida 201 301
Uttar Pradesh, India
Phone: +91 120 477 4100
Email: editorial@ombooks.com
Website: www.ombooksinternational.com

Sales Office
107, Ansari Road, Darya Ganj,
New Delhi 110 002, India
Phone: +91 11 4000 9000
Email: sales@ombooks.com
Website: www.ombooks.com

ISBN: 978-93-6395-119-8

Printed in India

10 9 8 7 6 5 4 3 2 1

Dedicated to

Maharshi Valmiki
Kavichakravarty Kamban
Goswami Tulsidas

Contents

Authors' Note

When Suhail Mathur, CEO of The Book Bakers, informed us that Om Books International, one of India's leading publishing houses, had commissioned a book on the women of the Ramayana, we were both thrilled and deeply honoured. As storytellers focused on Hindu mythological stories, but still early in our journey as authors, being entrusted with such a project was nothing short of a dream come true.

In much of Puranic literature, including the two greatest epics—the Ramayana and the Mahabharata—female characters often remain in the shadows, their voices subdued, and their roles limited. Even strong figures like Kaikeyi, Sita, and Surpanakha in the *Ramayana*, or Panchali, Revati, and Satyawati in the Mahabharata are given far less space than they deserve, despite being pivotal to the narrative.

The writing of this book offered us a rare opportunity to delve into the stories of these remarkable women, shedding light on their experiences that have often been overlooked or marginalised. We explored the depths of their struggles, triumphs, emotions, and despair, portraying them not as distant, idealised figures but as fully human, etched with their own extraordinary power and individuality.

Through this book, we aim to bring the women from the Ramayana, long relegated to the sidelines of the patriarchal narrative in ancient texts, to the forefront. By acknowledging their significance beyond traditional roles, our goal is to give them the attention they have long deserved. The stories may not follow a linear path, but they maintain a consistent reflection of the characters' lives and experiences.

Jai Shukla
Lalitha Balasubramanian

Chapter 1

SHATARUPA

Brahma parented a pair of *manas putra and putri* (mind-born son and daughter) and asked them to create humans. He designated them the rulers of the earth. The girl, Shatarupa, meaning 'the woman with one hundred beautiful forms', entered a long *tapasya* (penance) to get a suitable husband. On the advice of Brahma, she married Swayambhu Manu, meaning 'the primaeval self-born man of humans.' Though spiritually awakened, Manu and Shatarupa were aware of their earthly responsibilities of creating progeny as the first man and woman. They, as the king and queen, had the responsibility to frame moral and legal codes for the society and governance of the earth. With the help of these principles and laws, Manu and Shatarupa ruled the earth and brought order and justice to the people. To expand humanity, together they produced five children; two sons: Priyavrat and Uttanpad, and three daughters: Akuti, Devahuti and Prasuti. The Sanskrit word '*manav*', meaning 'human', is derived from the name of Manu, denoting all humans as the children of Manu.

Shatarupa was a virtuous woman, the brightest jewel of womanhood. She was beautiful, learned and a great devotee of Lord Vishnu. From her childhood, she was averse to the luxuries of life and worldly pleasures and had a natural inclination towards spirituality. This did not, however, digress her from being a dutiful wife and an ideal mother. Her husband, Manu, was a man of wisdom and learning. He was a great king who ruled the material world with compassion and religiosity. All beings, animate and inanimate, were happy under the rule of Manu, and the entire earth was prosperous.

Manu ruled the kingdom of the mortals for thousands of years. Shatarupa supported him dutifully, never neglecting her personal quest for self-enrichment, striving for the ultimate goal of her human birth—salvation or moksha. She strived to reach the ultimate purpose of her birth as a human—salvation or moksha. However, as a woman and mother, she harboured different desires. She had seen gods and goddesses incarnate as her descendants' children. She, too, longed to bear God in her womb and give Him birth, believing this would make her a complete woman and perfect mother. She decided to discuss this with her husband.

The progenitor had been trying for a long time to leave the throne to his son and take *sanyas* (asceticism). However, Priyavrat requested him not to do so as he wanted him to continue as long as he could.

Shatarupa told her husband about her newfound desire to become a God's mother, which surprised him. Throughout their lives, they had focused on attaining a transcendent state and achieving release from the cycles of birth and death.

Manu pointed out to his wife that they were far beyond the age of procreation, and it was not possible for her to bear another child. But Shatarupa was clear in her mind. She knew what she wanted. She must become the mother of Maha Vishnu; if not in this birth, in any other birth in a different *yuga* or *manvantara* or *kalpa* (dimensions of time according to Hindu mythology). Shatarupa would wait for as many births as required but wouldn't give up. The purpose of her life was not the moksha now, it was to ensure that Paratpar Brahman incarnated in the human form and played in her lap as her baby. Manu always knew how determined his queen was. But this had gone too far. Who could believe that someone didn't want salvation and freedom from the cycles of life and death? It was certainly possible to get any of the three great gods—Brahma, Vishnu and Mahesh—as a child. But was it possible to get eternal, formless Supreme Brahman as a son? The one who is indestructible even when the universe merged with the cosmos, bringing an end to all the gods and goddesses?

'Yes Manu, it is possible. You always say the power of *tapas* (penance) has no limits. One can achieve anything through tapasya,' Shatarupa said emphatically.

'I agree. But it may not apply to Parabrahman, who is formless and without senses. No one knows Him. The great gods and the Vedas can't have His glimpse. How can you have him as your son?' asked Manu.

'He is unmanifested Supreme Brahma–the eternal, spiritual energy that is the basis of all existence. But He may, if He desires, take all forms. He is the creator of qualities and so will not be under the control of qualities. He carries out all acts without hands, walks without legs, smells without a nose, tastes and speaks without a tongue, hears without ears and sees without eyes. If pleased with the faith, love and supreme devotion of His devotees, He could manifest in a personal form.'

'Priyavrat wouldn't allow us to leave everything and walk away to take sanyas. You know, how many times I have tried in the past, but he has always requested me to stay back for some more time.' Manu said.

'We have lost our entire life in the sensory pleasures of the material world and are already late. Let's not delay further. We must depart, for the powerful and righteous Priyavrat, who is ever protected by the Lord, can rule the earth. Why do you want to seek his permission? We will let him know as and when we are ready to leave. You don't speak to the prince; I'll do that myself.'

Manu conferred with the Brahmins and decided upon a day and time when he and Shatarupa would leave for the forest. The family and citizens tried to dissuade them but to no avail.

On an auspicious day, he installed Priyavrat as the king. They gave away thousands of cows, and heaps of gold, silver and gems to the Brahmins. Before leaving, Manu and Shatarupa performed all the rituals under the guidance of learned sages, as detailed in the scriptures. When the ceremonies were complete, the king and queen took off their royal garments and dressed like hermits in deerskin clothes. A moonj grass yagyopavit, recommended for the *sanyasis* (sages), replaced the holy cotton thread of Manu. The couple left the palace accompanied by many great rishis and celibates. Their relatives came to pay them obeisance before their departure. The minds of Manu and Shatarupa were filled with joy as they left the palace, never to return.

Accepting simple food of wild fruits and roots and water only once a day, walking on foot, they began their new life of pilgrimage to the holy places. The sages, who accompanied them, taught them about the life of a hermit. After many days of travel, they arrived at Naimisharanya (the forest of Naimisha). A pilgrimage to Naimish was one of the holiest pilgrimages since the beginning of the universe. It was a lush green forest with abundant water from the natural reservoirs, Chakra Tirtha and River Gomati, which originated here. Many trees, laden with excellent fruits and beautiful, fragrant flowers, grew in all seasons; peacocks, cuckoos, swans, *chakrawarkas* (ruddy goose) and other birds, all singing beautiful songs. The royal couple also saw numerous *siddhas* and *rishis* (sages) meditating on the banks of Gomati, their minds fixed on the Parabrahman.

Vyasdeva composed all the scriptures—four Vedas, eighteen Maha Puranas and six Shastras—in this forest. This is the place where Lord Satyanarayan *vrata* and puja, (fasting and worship) as described in the Skanda Purana, was, for the first time, narrated by Ved Vyas to Sage Suka Deva. He told the rituals and procedure of the puja and *katha* (story or narrative) to Shaunak, Sanakadi and other rishis. The Naimisharanya is one of the fifty-one shaktipithas (the centres of divine energy) of Goddess Sati who dwells here as Shri Lalita Devi. People believe that when Shiva went around the earth with the corpse of Mother Sati, her heart fell at this place. The Chakra Tirtha is a holy site where the celestial disc or Sudarshan Chakra of Vishnu fell. It created a sacred lake from the consecrated water coming out of Patal Lok (the netherworld).

Soon after they arrived at the Naimisharanya, the ageless rishis from the nearby places visited and blessed the holy couple. One day, Sage Narad came to bless the newly arrived Manu and Shatarupa. Manu told the wandering minstrel about the purpose of their tapasya and how his wife was adamant about getting Maha Vishnu, Paratpar Brahman as her son. An impossible dream for any woman! Sage Narad said, 'What Devi Shatarupa wants is nothing impossible. It is natural and perfectly in line with her boon during her previous birth when she was Mother Aditi and you were Sage Kashyap, her husband.'

The revelation surprised Shatarupa. She requested the sage to elaborate. 'Yes, that is true. During your previous birth, in another kalp, you were born as Aditi, the daughter of Prajapati Daksha. Married to Sage Kashyap, you gave birth to the Adityas. You had Indra, Surya, Varuna and many other gods as your sons. Your husband, Sage Kashyap, had twelve other wives. Diti, your sister, was one of such co-wives who was the mother of the *daityas* (demons). Once, Daitya King Bali became extremely powerful. He tormented your sons and wanted to capture heaven, their kingdom, and its capital Indralok. Your sons requested you for help. You, as Aditi, entered a long penance and received the boon from Lord Vishnu that he would take birth as your son and help the gods.

'Lord Vishnu incarnated as Vaman to become your son. Vaman sought a donation of three paces of land from Bali. He measured the three worlds, earth, heaven and the netherworld in his three strides and restored heaven to the gods. Before Trivikrama or the God of Three Strides, left for his abode, he once again asked you to seek a boon. You requested him to take birth as your son once again, but not alone.

Mother Sita, the great goddess, and Lakshman, the incarnation of Adishesha, must also accompany the Lord.' With that, Narad left the ashram of Shatarupa. The royal couple was more determined now to seek God.

The forest was filled with the sounds of Vedic recitations and the chanting of the Lord's holy name. The entire region was as holy and serene as the Brahma-Lok (the abode of Lord Brahma). The sounds of mantras from the Vedas were soothing and delightful to the mind. Manu and Shatarupa attended the discourses of the learned Brahmins and felt soulful joy in their company. They gradually started enjoying living in the forest and preferred it to the luxury of the palace and the onerous duties of a king and the queen. They were happy to live a simple life of spirituality, seeking the Lord's pleasure. All the time they recited the Dwadas Akshar Mantra (the twelve lettered holy mantra of Lord Vaasudev)—*Om namo bhagwate vasudevay.*

Over time, they gradually abandoned their diet of fruits and roots, relying solely on water for survival. Eventually, they gave up water as well and sustained themselves on air for thousands of years. Manu and Shatarupa stood on one leg, and eventually, they even stopped breathing. Lord Brahma was first to approach them. He asked the royal couple to express their wish, but they refused. Vishnu was next. Again, both had nothing to say. Lord Mahadev came with Gauri. Mother Gauri repeatedly asked Shatarupa to speak her mind, but she sought nothing. They offered them the kingdom of the three worlds or Indra's throne or the longest ever life, but they were firm in their devotion. Their unyielding determination impressed the Great God and Goddess and they returned appreciating their steadfastness and devotion.

They repeated it millions and millions of times, over and over. The gods came and offered them boons but Manu and Shatarupa refused to seek anything. The increasing difficulties and physical hardships did not impede their mountain-like resolve. They were reduced to skin and bones, but their minds remained fully engaged in chanting the Dwadas Akshar Mantra. The holy couple knew that one day their prayers would be answered. Generations passed, but their penance continued unhindered. Most people forgot about their existence.

After the longest ever penance of twenty-three thousand years, one morning they heard the celestial sound from the seventh heaven: 'O Shatarupa, O Manu, please wake up from your meditation and listen to me. I am the one you seek. I am pleased with your rigorous and long tapas. No one undertook a more impassioned penance in the past. Your single-minded resolve achieved the impossible. It is the belief of Mother Shatarupa that won over me. I can give you everything. Nothing is beyond me. Please seek the boon of your choice.'

As the solemn and sobering voice that could bring back the dead to life, sailing through the ears, reached their hearts, the couple became as attractive, healthy and pristine as they were when they had just arrived in the forest from their palace. After bowing down with the folded hands, they requested, 'If you are pleased with us, O Lord of the lords, please be gracious and allow us to see your beautiful Maha Vishnu form as visualized by Brahma, Vishnu, Shiva and other gods. We want nothing else but your holy *darshan* (holy espial) with four arms and divine decorations accompanied by the Mother of the Universe.'

When Manu and Shatarupa opened their eyes, they saw the graceful form of Narayana, with his four arms holding a conch shell, Sudarshan disc, Kaumudi club and lotus flower. The countenance of the Lord was like an autumn full moon in indigo colour. His eyes possessed the exquisite beauty of fresh-blown lotuses, and his lovely glance captivated the heart. His shoulders were like that of a lion and arms like the trunk of an elephant. The lotus feet of the Lord were beyond description. After some moments, that four-armed form of Vishnu changed to Ram's two-armed form, from which all other forms of godhood emanated. On the left side of Ram stood Sita, His primordial energy, who was a storehouse of unbounded beauty and the source of the universe. The couple with tears of devotion in their eyes prostrated with reverence to the holy feet of Ram and Sita. They fell flat on the ground, clasping His feet with their hands.

The gracious Lord touched their heads with His lotus hands and lifted them up. Addressing Shatarupa, the effulgent Ram said, 'I am the knower of all, but it's my desire to listen to it from your mouth. Please tell me what boon you seek for which you undertook such an arduous tapasya. Keep nothing with you. I am ready to offer you anything unreservedly within the universe and beyond. There is nothing which I would not give you.'

Shatarupa folded her palms in reverence and said, 'O Lord, you are the protector of the pious and perfected beings, and destroyer of the non-believers and imperfect. I offer my obeisance unto you as you are the ultimate sanctuary. Knowing everything, you are all that is knowable. You, as the large-hearted one, may offer me everything, but I am too small to ask for what I really wish. I feel as if I will lose my voice and cannot speak in your august presence.'

The Lord smiled gracefully and said, 'Mother, you don't remember. In another Kalp and during my earlier incarnation as Vamana, you were my mother, Aditi. Your husband, King Manu, was my father Sage Kashyap. Like your sons Indra, Surya, Bhaga, Varuna and many more, I too have my regards for you as my mother. So, don't hesitate for a moment and speak to me as a mother speaks to her child.'

'I want a son like you and a daughter-in-law like the great goddess by your side,' said Shatarupa, in a low, almost inaudible voice.

Ram's gentle smile was pleasing to the couple. He said, 'But where shall I go to find an equal. It will be difficult for me to search for another Ram who could be your son. I would rather be your son instead if you agree, mother.'

Shatarupa closed her eyes, tears rolling down her cheeks. She bowed repeatedly, expressing her ecstatic emotions without uttering a word.

Ram then looked at Manu and asked him to express his desire. 'Please bless us with what the virtuous queen has asked.

That is my wish too. However, there is another request. When You be our son, my life must be subservient to Your presence. Like a fish dependent on water for its life and a cobra couldn't live without a nag-mani on its hood, my life may also depend on you and end with your separation,' said Manu, his voice soft, rich and clear.

'Let it be so,' said the Lord in a reassuring voice.

'There is something else I request You to bless me with. When You take birth as my son, let me not know your real self. After knowing the actuality, I could never treat you as my son and the love and bonding of a father and son would be lost.'

The Lord was pleased to grant him that, too. No such request came from Shatarupa. A son was a son, whether a mortal or Paratpar Brahma. She would always be a mother to him.

Ram looked lovingly at Manu and Shatarupa and said, 'Now is the time when both of you must dwell in the capital of Indra. Live there long enough and enjoy the fruits of your tapasya. Mother, you shall be born as Kaushalya, the daughter of King Bhanumant of Koshala. Your husband shall take birth as Dashrath, the king of Ayodhya. Both of you will once again be husband and wife, the king and queen of Koshala.'

'Voluntarily assuming the human guise, I will manifest Myself as your son Ram with My other partial incarnations. My primordial energy, that has brought forth the universe, will manifest Herself as Sita.'

Chapter 2

KAUSHALYA

Bhanumant had made lavish preparations for the *swayamvar* (self-selection of a groom by the bride) of his daughter Kaushalya. They arranged the ceremony in a large auditorium. It was a three-story oval-shaped building constructed like an arena. The ground floor of the building was used to showcase the major state events, whereas the first and second floors had tiered seating plans for the spectators. Bright gems sparkled on all sides of the spacious hall. The walls were inlaid with exquisite carvings depicting the gods and their consorts. They arranged hundreds of ivory and gold thrones encrusted with jewels around the hall for many monarchs and princelings who came contending for the princess's hand. There were another three rows of chairs behind the thrones for the accompanying personal and security attendants of the kings and princes sitting in the front rows. The contenders came on horseback and chariots wearing gaudy decorations and carrying imposing arms to impress the princess. Costly rugs were spread wall to wall on the pink marble floors.

Kaushalya was the younger daughter of King Bhanumant. His first daughter, Vershini, was married to Rompad, the king of Angdesh. Kaushalya had attained marriageable age and her father looked for a suitable bridegroom for her. Dashrath, a Suryavanshi king of Awadh, was a close friend of Rompad. He suggested Dashrath as the future spouse of Kaushalya to his father-in-law. But owing to the tradition of the Koshala royal family, they held a swayamvar, giving the princess a fair opportunity to choose her life partner. Queen Vershini, with her husband Rompad, also came to attend the swayamvar of Kaushalya. Dashrath, recently crowned as the king of Ayodhya, after the death of his father Aja, accompanied his friend to solicit the hand of the Koshala princess.

The day started with the elaborate puja, fire sacrifices and socio-religious ceremonies performed by the royal priests, Brahmins and the family elders. At the appointed hour, Kaushalya entered the arena and looked around, sending all the young hearts racing. She looked gorgeous in her coral-red bridal gown. She was svelte, less than medium height, but not too short. Her lotus-like eyes were sparkling black, her lips were full and rosy, and her smile was heart-warming. Vershini, her sister, her young, unmarried, gorgeous friends, and beautiful maids escorted the bride, tossing flowers on the bride as she walked past unhurriedly before the guests. With a beautiful garland of gold petals and fresh flowers strewn with bright gems in her hands, she went around majestically looking at each guest, her fawn-like eyes lowered. She looked for Dashrath among the kings and princes. Kaushalya had heard so much about the young and handsome prince of Ayodhya from her elder sister that she almost knew him. The Koshala princess had already decided to garland the king of Awadh.

Kaushalya glanced straight at Dashrath. Their eyes met for a moment and in that instant, he poured out his heart to her. He told her she was the most beautiful woman he ever met. He told her he loved her and wanted to be with her forever. It further confirmed the bond that had developed in their previous encounter during Vershini's marriage. Dashrath attended the marriage of his friend Rompad and had then met a teenage Kaushalya as the younger sister of the bride. Kaushalya completed the customary round, walking in a steady elegance, like a baby elephant, to ensure that all the suitors had a good look at her. She, too, saw them before deciding on any.

The unthinkable happened then. Ravan came with a large contingent of his warriors and, without warning, surrounded the venue of the swayamvar. He arrested all the kings and princes before they or their soldiers could raise their arms. Ravan kidnapped Kaushalya and took her to Lanka (now Sri Lanka), and ordered his men to search for Dashrath and kill him immediately.

***

After reaching Lanka, when Ravan was about to execute Kaushalya, his queen Mandodari asked him not to do so. She wanted to know from him why he wanted to kill such a pretty harmless damsel. Ravan said, 'I must kill her because she will cause my death. While coming back from Kailash after the darshan (holy espial) of Mahadev and Gauri, I met the four-headed Lord Brahma. Out of simple curiosity, I wanted him to tell me the cause of my death. You know Mandodari, what Prajapati told me? He told me that the son of Kaushalya and Dashrath will kill me. So, I thought it prudent to end the young woman's life before she could give birth to a son. Atikaya, our son, has gone to Ayodhya to hunt down Dashrath.'

Mandodari replied, 'You are a mighty warrior whose name sends shivers down the spine of the greatest warriors in the three worlds. You have defeated all the gods, demi-gods, humans, Gandharvas and others who serve you as menial labourers. Wouldn't this act of killing an unarmed virgin woman make you an universal laughing stock and bring disgrace to you? The mighty Dashanan is afraid of an innocent girl. Who would believe it?'

Ravan reflected on her virtuous wife's words. He agreed with her words of wisdom and spared Kaushalya's life. Why should he stain his hands with the blood of a woman? What could she do without Dashrath?

Mandodari was deeply concerned on hearing the prophecy of the creator. She said, 'I am a chaste woman and wield enormous divine powers. I curse this woman not to become the mother of a son through the seed of her husband.'

Ravan took the princess to the deserted island of Timingil in the middle of the sea north of Lankan island and left her to die for the want of food and water. He returned to Lanka and waited for the news of Dashrath's death.

***

Bhanumant was furious at seeing her daughter being kidnapped. He ordered his commanders to attack the *rakshasa*s (demons) and slaughter them. Dashrath also supported the king. They fought bravely with Ravan's soldiers, but could not hold long against the mighty rakshasas. Atikaya, the leader of the rakshasa army, killed Bhanumant. With the death of their king, the Koshala troops fled in all directions to save their lives.

Dashrath and his Prime Minister Sumantra escaped from the battlefield. Before returning to Ayodhya, Dashrath wanted to track down Kaushalya and get her freed from the custody of the Rakshasa. The rakshasa's army marched to Ayodhya and, not finding Dashrath there, besieged the city. Led by Atikaya and Subahu, they ransacked the city, massacred people, burnt houses and looted property. They assaulted young women and teenage girls and took many of them as slaves.

The kidnapping of the princess worried Dashrath. Ravan was notorious for his inhuman and violent treatment towards women. The story of the ill-treatment of Vedavati, a young and beautiful Brahmin widow, by Ravan and her subsequent suicide, was known all over the Jambudwip. While Dashrath and Sumantra searched for Kaushalya, they met a group of fishermen who were going to the market to sell their day's hunt. The fishermen informed Dashrath they saw the rakshasa king going with a woman towards Timingil island. Dashrath and Sumantra arranged a boat, and on reaching that barren island, found Kaushalya unconscious because of the lack of food and water. The two men lifted her into the boat and returned to Koshala.

Fearing Ravan might attack them again, Dashrath and Kaushalya immediately married as the Gandharvas did, and became husband and wife. Dashrath and Rompad performed the last rites of their father-in-law and divided the kingdom of Koshala into two halves. While the North Koshala went to the Anga king, South Koshala became an integral part of the kingdom of Awadh. Kaushalya came to Ayodhya with her husband as the queen consort of Dashrath.

Kaushalya was doubly blessed. She found a soulmate in Dashrath who loved her beyond words. Soon after her marriage, she became a mother. Her lovely daughter was almost six now.

Sage Vashisth, their family priest and the *rajguru* (the royal head priest) named her Shanta, the one who would bring peace and prosperity to her parents. Looking at her birth chart, the seer predicted the girl would indeed bring cheer to her parents if they kept her happy. But she wouldn't live in Ayodhya for long. Her stars would take her to another kingdom.

The pretty, playful girl was an apple of Kaushalya's eyes. There were many maids to take care of the mother and daughter, but the queen preferred to rear her child herself. Shanta was, like any other child of her age, fond of listening to the stories of kings and queens. Kaushalya told her the tales of the glorious past of their great ancestors, the unbelievable stories of Harishchandra, Bhagirath, Trishanku, Kukustha, and many more. It was a bedtime routine for the little girl, and Kaushalya wouldn't leave Shanta to the care of her maids till she was fast asleep.

King Dashrath felt aggrieved by the birth of a daughter as his first-born child, as he desired sons who could avenge the rakshasas. Despite Guru Vashisth's assurances, Dashrath remained indifferent, hoping Kaushalya would soon bear a son. As his impatience grew, he began to neglect his daughter, Shanta, and Kaushalya.

When King Rompad and his wife Vershini visited Ayodhya, Dashrath, without consulting Kaushalya, offered Shanta for adoption to them. Rompad and Vershini, unable to have children, were grateful for Dashrath's generous gesture. Upon learning about Shanta's adoption, Kaushalya confronted her husband, who justified his decision, believing that Shanta would remain within the larger family and that this act of generosity would soon bring them a son.

That was not to happen. Kaushalya remembered the curse of Mandodari and was sure that the words of a chaste woman could never go wrong. She had not disclosed to her husband that she would never become the mother of his son. She protested, 'Shanta is very close to me and wouldn't live without me, even for a day. She is our first-born child. She is my life. Let us wait for the second child. To honour your words, we may send her to Angdesh thereafter.'

'I have committed to Rompad. He has travelled all the way, hoping to get Shanta. Do you want your husband to back out from his promise? And what do I tell Vershini? Should I tell her Kaushalya does not want to part with her daughter?'

For the first time in her life, Kaushalya felt like a deprived woman. She left the royal bedchamber and went to the adjoining room of her daughter. She asked Shanta's nanny to go away and lay down with her, embracing her closely.

The next morning, after the holy darshan and worship at the Shrirangji Temple, she asked her charioteer to take her to the ashram of Guru Vashisth. The guru looked at Kaushalya, her ever-smiling bright and bubbly face had turned ashen white. Her sparkling eyes swelled because of sleeplessness. She was meek and restless. Vashisth took her inside the family cottage where he lived with his wife, Arundhati. Kaushalya told them about her husband's decision. She begged them for guidance and to help her find peace.

Vashisth said, 'The emperor has asked me to prepare for the adoption ceremony, so I know about your daughter going to Angdesh with King Rompad and Vershini. He, however, did not tell me he hadn't spoken to you in this matter. As a mother, you have first right on your child and without your consent and participation, I will not complete the religious ceremony. If you feel so strongly against giving away your daughter, I'll certainly speak to the king.'

'You know gurudev, with Shanta gone I may never have another child with me.'

'Yes, I know about the curse of Mandodari. But the ways of Brahma are not so simple to understand. My calculations reveal something different. Notwithstanding the curse, you will be the mother of one son.'

'How is that possible, gurudev? The two things don't match.'

'No, my child, at this stage I can tell you only this much. You shall be the mother of a son who will rule the world. People will regard him as God for his acts of wisdom, the emancipation of the week, bravery and religiosity. But before that, you will face unthought-of miseries and may feel like ending your life. But be courageous and face what comes your way because, at the end, for aeons, people will remember you as the mother of a God. Let Shanta go to Angdesh. Lord Brahma wants her to return to Ayodhya with her husband when we need her most. Their arrival will herald a new bright morning to a fading dusk sky of Koshala.'

The kind and prophetic words of Vashisth assuaged Kaushalya. The impending displacement disconcerted the child. Vershini had developed a good understanding with Shanta by telling her about amazing things that were found in Angdesh, but not in Ayodhya. She promised her niece a parrot that mimicked the human voice and the dolls, which danced at the pull of invisible strings. Vershini was a wonderful storyteller. Many times, the little girl went to her room to listen to the fascinating stories from her aunt and slept with her. Shanta was excited to accompany her Mausi to a wonderland, though she wanted her mother to accompany them too.

It relieved Kaushalya of a substantial burden of her heart. Her sister would take good care of Shanta, that was for sure. But the pangs of separation from her only child were unbearable. She felt cheated by her husband. He should have taken her into confidence. On such occasions, she recalled the comforting words of Guru Vashisth. There will be a morning after the dark night. She prepared herself for the days ahead when she would face worse days than the present. After the religious ceremonies and fire sacrifices at a *shubh-muhurat*, (auspicious time) Kaushalya and Dashrath gave away their daughter Shanta in adoption to Vershini and Rompad. But she would never forgive her husband for depriving her of motherhood. The kings of Angdesh and Koshala gave Brahmins and the poor lavish charities.

The nightmare predicted by the great sage came a bit too early. Kaushalya was hardly out of the trauma of the separation of her child when Dashrath revealed to her his intention to marry again. One evening after the meals, he said, 'Kaushalya, I have waited for almost seven years for you to give the people of Koshala a successor to the throne of Ikshvaku. But you have disappointed them. The minister's council and elders of Ayodhya have repeatedly requested me to remarry. It was my love for you that did not permit me to agree to their request. With each passing day, their demand is gaining strength. Tell me, my love, what do you have to say?' Dashrath's face was composed and unsmiling.

Sarangi, the personal maid of Kaushalya, who came with her from Koshala, had told her master about the talk of Dashrath's second marriage with a princess from Kashi. A priest came with a message from the king of Kashi. It was rumoured that he brought a marriage proposal for the king of Awadh, but this could not be confirmed.

'It is for you to decide. Your responsibilities as the king are more important than your love for me. I leave it to your superior wisdom and sense of justice,' said Kaushalya, her voice solemn with the effort to permit herself no sound of emotion.

She sat with her head bowed. Her husband could not bear to look at her. Dashrath waited for a few moments. Then, without looking at her, he drew his head slightly backwards and drawled defiantly, 'You would better tell me now. Don't create problems for the new bride later on. As a part of the crown, you must be as much responsive to the will of people of this kingdom as I am.'

It devastated Kaushalya. Dashrath was the only man she ever loved. She knew him since they first met during the marriage of Vershini. She wanted to live her whole life with him and could not fathom the idea that she would have to share her husband with another woman.

With the arrival of Sumitra, Dashrath's new wife, Kaushalya lost her smile forever. Even when she smiled, it looked dazed. It was as if she was somewhere else, lost in her own world. Gradually she became more and more reserved, distancing herself from others. Most of the time, she remained isolated in her room. She lost self-confidence and was unsure of herself. Sarangi was the only one she spoke to. Occasionally she went on pilgrimages but, not finding peace there also, returned hurriedly. She now regularly visited the ashram of Vashisth and found solace in the company of the guru-mother. Arundhati never forgot to cheer her up by repeating the prophecy of Vashisth. As the queen consort, she took part in all the socio-religious ceremonies, but her indifference on such occasions was clear to all those present.

Chapter 3

SHANTA

Little Shanta was the cynosure of all eyes as she was the first-born of Dashrath and Kaushalya. She was the apple of Kaushalya's eyes.

'She is so beautiful,' she thought to herself.

The look on Dashrath's face, however, seemed to reflect his disappointment. He had always wanted a male offspring to carry on his lineage and rule over his beloved kingdom of Ayodhya. Kaushalya saw his expression and a wave of sorrow stormed through her body. He had always mentioned his wish. But what could she do except accept the gift of the girl child from God? Another glance at her daughter however revived her spirits.

'The child was too beautiful to be ignored. Her father would not be able to do that,' she thought.

Dashrath was disappointed but he did participate in the celebrations of his newborn daughter. He held her in his arms and seeing her serene and lovable face, the royal couple named her Shanta.

A few years passed. Shanta grew up to be a beautiful little girl and was being well trained in all forms of arts. She spent the rest of her time playing with her friends and companions in the palace. But there was a longing in her heart always for some words of affection from her father, which never came. Dashrath was fixated on male heirs. He never gave attention to Shanta, though she was his daughter. Kaushalya tried to make up for this discrepancy on Dashrath's part. But Shanta's longing for recognition and love from her father whom she loved so much remained unfulfilled. She started having the feeling that for her beloved father, her existence was immaterial.

Once, the king of Angdesh, Rompad, and his wife Vershini paid a prolonged visit to Ayodhya. Vershini was the elder sister of Kaushalya and they had no children even after so many years of marriage. They poured their affection over the bubbling, vivacious and adorable little Shanta. The girl too loved playing with her aunt and uncle. When the time came for Rompad to return to his Angdesh, Vershini told Kaushalya that Dashrath had kindly allowed them to adopt Shanta and bring her up as their child. Kaushalya was flabbergasted. She had not expected such a statement from her sister. Kaushalya could not believe her ears. She was stunned. Her mind was in turmoil. How could her husband decide to part with their first-born child, her beloved Shanta, without even asking her? Had she no right over her daughter? And even now, she was hearing about the impending adoption from her sister, not her husband. Her grief led her to the doors of Maharshi Vashisth, who was also stunned by the fact that she had not been consulted about such a momentous decision regarding her daughter. He refused to conduct the adoption ritual if Kaushalya was not in agreement. However, he also consoled her saying that through his divine foresight, he could foresee that she would be a mother to a son who would win over the hearts of everyone in the world. He went to the extent of saying that that son would be considered as God by his people. Kaushalya was not fully convinced but she knew her husband's rigid penchant for keeping to his word. So even though her mind was disturbed at the impending parting from her beloved daughter, she had to give in. Her only solace was that she was giving her to her sister, whom she knew would take care of her as her daughter. She spent the entire night embracing her beloved daughter. Thus, Shanta, Dashrath's firstborn, was given in adoption to King Rompad and his wife Vershini.

The adoption had a significant impact on young Shanta. She loved her mother and had never spent a day without her till then. She loved her father too, and was devastated that her father whom she adored had decided to abandon her. There were unshed tears in her eyes, as Shanta left with her adopted parents to her new home. Rompad and Vershini brought her up lovingly as the princess of Angdesh. Her exceptional beauty coupled with extraordinary intelligence led to her being trained in warfare, Vedas, and all the fine arts. Her adopted parents doted on her. Rompad admired her wisdom and intelligence. It was a completely new experience for Shanta who had longed for some recognition of her presence by her biological father, to interact with her adopted father on matters of the land.

Once when King Rompad was discussing something seriously with Shanta, a Brahmin came to ask for help for cultivating his fields in the rainy season. Rompad was so engrossed in his discussion with Shanta that he apparently did not pay attention to the visiting Brahmin. Though the error was unintentional, the Brahmin went away disappointed. This Brahmin was a devotee of Lord Indra. When Indra came to know that his devotee had been slighted by King Rompad, he stopped the rains that brought water to the kingdom. The impending drought was severe. King Rompad was struggling to find a remedy. He invited many learned scholars, some of whom mentioned that only the advent of a celibate ascetic into the kingdom could bring relief to the drought-hit Angdesh.

'Who could be this celibate ascetic?' King Rompad thought aloud.

'There is a sage who is performing penance in the nearby forest. His name is Rishya Shringa. He is the son of the great Sage Vibhandaka and is a celibate. If you succeed in bringing him to Anga somehow, the power of his austerities will enable the country to receive rains as before,' said one scholar.

'Who is Sage Vibhandaka?' asked the king.

'Sage Vibhandaka is the son of Sage Kashyap. He was guided by his father to become a hermit and he was doing great penance near a river. His austerities reached a point when Lord Indra became scared of the power of his austerities and sent the divine apsara, Urvashi, to disturb his meditation.

'Urvashi had to obey Lord Indra and therefore approached Sage Vibhandaka, who was momentarily mesmerized by her beauty and left his penance to enjoy her company. Indra was happy that he had succeeded in disengaging the sage from his penance. After a few months, Urvashi was pregnant with the child of the sage. Their son was born and was named Rishya Shringa. But, as soon as Rishya Shringa was born, Indra sent a message to Urvashi that her work on earth was over and she should return to her duties at Devalok (heaven). Unwillingly, Urvashi had to part with her son. She left him in his father's arms, explained her situation and went away to her heavenly abode. Sage Vibhandaka was distraught to know that he had been temporarily distracted from his powerful penance by the charms of a woman. He started holding the entire womenfolk responsible for this and vowed that he would not allow his son Rishya Shringa to ever set his eyes on a woman. He brought him up carefully in the forest that bordered the kingdom of Angdesh and initiated him into the education of the Vedas and performance of penance. Time passed, and the boy grew up to be a man who was absolutely unaware of the existence of a woman. This celibacy had increased his powers exponentially.'

King Rompad listened to the entire tale from the learned scholar and though he was scared of Sage Vibhandaka's power and anger, he knew there was no other way to ease the situation of extreme drought and suffering in his kingdom than to somehow bring Sage Rishya Shringa to Angdesh. Hence, he called for the most beautiful courtesans in the kingdom and instructed them to attract and bring the Sage Rishya Shringa to the palace. These courtesans were scared of incurring the wrath of Sage Vibhandaka, but they set out to do their task for the love of their land.

They reached the forest and saw Rishya Shringa in deep meditation. They carefully chose a time when his father was not around to approach him.

The pleasant aroma of the women whiffed past his nostrils and his eyes fluttered. Rishya Shringa had never seen a woman before and he thought these girls to be strange men. He invited them into the hermitage and offered to wash their feet and give them food to eat. The women were scared that Sage Vibhandaka would come back, and so they went away without accepting his offer.

But Rishya Shringa could forget neither their beautiful forms nor the strange feeling that they had induced in him. His concentration wavered. When Sage Vibhandaka returned, he was surprised to see his son in a state of distraction. He inquired about the cause of his distraction and Rishya Shringa described the whole incident. He warned his son that they were evil creatures and that he should stay away from them. Rishya Shringa nodded in agreement but was not at all convinced.

Meanwhile, the courtesans returned to Angdesh. They recounted what had happened at the hermitage of Rishya Shringa. Shanta, who was listening avidly to their narrative, decided to go and try to convince the young Sage. Her adopted parents were concerned. But the kingdom's fate was at stake and they had no option but to allow their beloved daughter to give it a try.

She then set out to complete her mission. Though the courtesans accompanied her in the boat, they left her alone near the shore. She waded through the waters and arrived alone at the hermitage. Rishya Shringa was in deep meditation. She stepped back a few steps but fell into the water which she had waded through to reach the hermitage. Hearing the sound of someone falling in the water, the young sage woke up from his meditation. He was surprised to see Shanta in the water. Her clothes were ballooning around her and she seemed to have lost consciousness.

But the next moment, when she woke up, she was lying on land with Rishya Shringa sitting beside her to administer some herbal concoction to her wound. His virile male form stirred strange feelings in her mind. But his next words made her feel confused.

'Kumara, what happened? Are you better now?'

She nodded. But Shanta was flummoxed. This man did not even know that the female gender existed. How would she be able to seduce him? But thinking of the poor people of Angdesh, she decided to at least try talking to him.

'My dear Kumara, why did you not leave me to die? Why did you rescue me?' she asked plaintively.

'I have been taught by my father that saving a life is the noblest deed one can perform,' he replied with a smile. Shanta smiled back. She adjusted her wet clothing to cover her breasts. The action invited his surprised glance.

'You look different from the people who live here. Are you from another land?' he asked curiously.

She was happy that the difference in form had been noted by him.

'I am different from you,' she said and touched him gently on his shoulder. It stirred some strange emotions in him. He remembered the group of five or six people who had come to his hermitage earlier and the way his father had counselled him that they were bad. But, to him, this was a lone *kumara* who seemed to be so soft and friendly.

Shanta could see from his expression that he was in a confused state of mind. She said, 'Kumara, I am not a man, but a woman. We are completely different in our physical form as you have already noticed. You are unaware that there are so many things on this earth beyond the meditation and penance that you are performing for Brahma Gyan (knowledge of supreme being).'

Her words seemed to pull him out of a dilemma. He had always been told by his father that Brahma Gyaan was the aim of his existence. Shanta succeeded in drawing him into a conversation. She then decided to tell him about the desperate fate of the people of Angdesh. She told him how some were emaciated from hunger, some dying from thirst, the lack of rains and how it was affecting her people. He wept with sorrow as he heard her. She appealed to him that only his presence in Angdesh can save her people. Rishya Shringa was moved. He was also drawn by her beauty and intelligence. He decided to go with her to Angdesh. They held hands and walked back from the hermitage to Angdesh, rejoicing in each other's company. The arrow of Kama, the God of love, had struck successfully.

Within no time, they reached the realm of Angdesh. The sight of princess Shanta arriving with the young Sage with matted hair and dressed in a sole bark garment was a strange sight. No sooner had the Sage set foot on its soil, than Lord Indra was appeased and Angdesh was blessed with rains. The people were happy and so was King Rompad. He respectfully invited chaste Sage Rishya Shringa into his palace and offered his beautiful adopted daughter, Shanta in marriage to the hermit. This was what was ordained and it happened. The entire kingdom of Anga was relieved and grateful to their young princess and Sage Rishya Shringa for bringing rains to their kingdom. When Sage Vibhandaka heard about his son's marriage to Shanta, he was furious. He went to Angdesh but on seeing the beautiful and intelligent Shanta as his son's wife and the immense respect given to his son, he ended up blessing them. Rishya Shringa stayed on with Shanta at Angdesh, at an open hermitage and not at the palace. He needed no riches or luxury, and Shanta admired him for it.

Meanwhile, call it the act of destiny or karma, after giving away Shanta in adoption to King Rompad and his Queen Vershini, King Dashrath could not father any more children for a long time. Neither Kaushalya, Sumitra nor Kaikeyi (whom Dashrath married later) could bear him any further progeny. Years passed by, and King Dashrath still longed to have a male child. He requested advice from his Raj Guru, Vashisth Maharshi, who suggested that he perform the Putra Kameshti Yajna.

When the king asked him to arrange for the Yajna, Sage Vashisth declined as he felt that he was not the proper person to guide Dashrath in this particular Yajna. Guru Vashisth also said that there was only one person who was capable of performing the Putra Kameshti Yajna and that was Sage Rishya Shringa.

The king summoned his trusted minister Sumanthra to search for the whereabouts of Sage Rishya Shringa. Wise Sumanthra had been witness to all the previous events at Ayodhya. He was also aware of the entire happenings of Angdesh where Shanta lived and told the entire story of Sage Vibhandaka and his son, Rishya Shringa, to King Dashrath. He also cited the power of the penance of Rishya Shringa and the arrival of rains in the drought-hit Angdesh. He then went on to say that King Rompad had offered Shanta's hand in marriage to Rishya Shringa. Dashrath and his three wives immediately wanted to set out with a huge army, cavalry, elephants and palanquins to request Sage Rishya Shringa to perform the Yajna. But Sage Vashisth stopped them and advised that there was no need to make a show of pomp and strength.

'You are going to request the Sage to perform the Putra Kameshti Yajna. So in all humility, you and your queens will have to travel barefoot and sincerely make the request. Only then will you be able to convince that knowledgeable Sage,' said Vashisth.

Dashrath understood his point and they proceeded to humbly approach the Sage. It is said that at the request of his wife, Shanta, Rishya Shringa agreed to perform the Puthra Kameshti Yajna for Dashrath.

Again the irony of the situation comes to the fore. The girl who was given away in adoption, just because she happened to be a girl child by Dashrath, was the one driven by compassion for her biological parents, to induce her husband to perform the powerful Yajna. This helped Dashrath beget the sons that he longed for to continue his lineage.

Almost everyone familiar with the epic Ramayana knows what happened next. The Yajna was performed with Sage Rishya Shringa at the helm. Hundreds of holy men participated in that Yajna. From the sacrificial fire, rose Lord Agni with a pot of sacred kheer. He handed over the Kheer to Dashrath, who divided it equally between Kaushalya and Kaikeyi. Both of them gave a portion from their portions to Sumitra. Nine months later, Kaushalya gave birth to Lord Ram, Kaikeyi to Bharat, and Sumitra to Lakshman and Shatrughna.

Valmiki Ramayana does not mention Shanta as Ram's sister. There is just a passing reference to Shanta as the wife of Rishya Shringa. However, in Mahabharata, we learn of King Rompad adopting the daughter of Dashrath. It is in the Oriya Ramayana that King Rompad is said to have given his beautiful adopted daughter in marriage to Sage Rishya Shringa, whose great penance and celibacy had caused a drought in Angdesh. The marriage is said to have brought rains back to the parched land. Again, two versions describe the advent of Rishya Shringa into Angdesh. One goes that Rompad sent his best courtesans to attract the Sage. Another says that Shanta herself volunteers to go and bring the Sage to the palace. In this version, Shanta is described as a sensuous woman, who succeeds in using her beauty, intelligence and seductive skills to attract the celibate Sage.

Shanta's story does not end here. Tales of Shanta are more in folklore and have orally been passed down to generations. When Ram is banished to the forest, she is said to have reached the deathbed of her father to console him. But to her sorrow, Dashrath did not even recognize her. There are Telugu folktales and songs that mention Shanta as the beloved sister-in-law of Sita, and describe her as being furious on hearing that Sita was abandoned in the forest by her righteous brother and that too when she was pregnant. There are tales that Shanta was the only one to protest and abstain from attending the Ashwamedha Yajna performed by her brother as she felt that the golden statue of Sita which was installed for the purpose was an insult to her dear Sita. The character of Shanta, Ram's sister, can thus be described as the epitome of compassion, courage, intelligence and righteousness. There is a temple at Kigga, a town near Shringeri in Karnataka, where Goddess Shanta and Rishya Shringa are worshipped. Another temple dedicated to them exists in Kullu, Himachal Pradesh.

Chapter 4

SUMITRA

'Champa, don't disturb me. First, let me complete my lessons. I can't go out with you to play in the garden unless I am ready with tomorrow's lessons,' said Sumitra, admonishing her friend.

Her teacher left long back, but Sumitra was engrossed in the books preparing for the next day's lessons. The pre-adolescence girl surprised her teachers and parents alike with her intelligence and aptitude for learning. Unlike her elder brother Prince Suketu, who was interested only in weaponry and warcraft, she was keen to learn theology, statecraft, astrology, ancient scriptures, ayurveda and astronomy. She simultaneously learnt sixteen art forms and practised classical music and dance for hours. Her father, Kashiraj Sunit, arranged for a Gandharva guru to train her in singing and dancing.

Sumitra did not confine her studies to the palace. She dressed as a common girl and went around Kashi, and many times joined the classes of eminent scholars, unnoticed and unidentified. Kashi was the globally renowned centre of learning. The students came from far and wide to gain the knowledge of literature, art, and culture. Sumitra wanted to excel in these fields and become a learned person like Gargi, Lopamudra, and Arundhati. She wanted to join *gurukul* (residential school headed by a guru) where her brother went to study academics and weapons. But they did not admit girls, even from a royal family, in the ashrams.

Like any other day, Champa wanted her to go out and play with other children. Sumitra, not willing to leave her studies, delayed. Her impatient friend waited for her to finish. Sumitra knew Champa wouldn't go out without her, and after some time, she yielded to the demand of her stubborn friend. Champa was the daughter of Nagar Seth Arthkamik. She was very close to the princess. A couple of years younger than Sumitra, Champa mostly lived in the palace with the royal family. The king and queen loved her as their own daughter.

Kashi is a city as old as the creation itself. It is the oldest living city on the planet earth. The city is abode of one of the twelve Jyotirlingas (twelve most sacred lingams of Shiva) and one among the fifty-one Shaktipithas (the abode of Shakti), a rare presence of Shiva and Shakti in one centre of pilgrimage. Mahadev, in his form of Vishweswara, the Lord of the Universe, built the city as his capital. The lord is the king of Kashi and to keep the evils away, He always keeps his favourite city on the tip of his trident. Kashi is older than history, older than tradition and culture, and older than legends. The rulers of Kashi don't consider themselves as the king and act as the regents of Vishweswara and rule on His behalf. The practice started at the time of the first King Divodas. Lord Brahma selected Rudrasaras or Rudra Sarovar in Kashi, the holiest among the holy places in the triple world, to perform the Ashwamedh Yajna. After the Creator successfully performed ten Yajnas, he renamed the place Dasashwamedh (ten horse sacrifices). When King Bhagirath, the great scion of Suryavanshi Emperor Ikshvaku, brought the Ganga on earth and the river goddess passed through the city of Kashi to please Shiva, the Rudra Sarovar became Dasashwamedh Ghat.

Kashi is the place where truthful Harishchandra, an ancestor of King Dashrath of Ayodhya, worked in the cremation grounds as the servant of a chandala. He gave away his kingdom, sold his wife Shaivya and child Rohitashva and agreed to be a slave of a chandala to uphold the values of truth and dharma. The cremation ghat was thereafter called Harishchandra Ghat. Kashi has a special place in the heart of Mahadev, also known as the lord of annihilation. Here, he takes the form of a benevolent ruler. His basic act of destruction continues, but here he destroys the adversities and calamities and wards off the sins and distress of his subjects. As a ruler, He provides them four objects of human pursuits–*arth* (wealth), *dharma* (righteousness), *kam (pleasure)*, and *moksha* (liberation). If one dies in Kashi, he or she gets moksha, howsoever great sinner one must be. Shiva himself welcomes the departing soul and whispers the name of Rama in his ears.

The royal palace of the Kashiraj or the king of Kashi was outside the main city area. It was a grand edifice on the bank of the Ganga at a height of one hundred and eight steps from the stream. During the rainy season, the Janhavi submerged more than half of the steps in her violently flowing muddy water. But the stream never breached into the palace or the gardens outside, in the living memory. A thoroughfare connected the palace to Dasashwamedh Ghat and the temple of Lord Vishweswara. A large garden, full of ever blossoming trees, adorned the palace. The mild fragrance of the lotus pollens filled the air. In the centre of the garden, there was a large pond filled with the lotuses and lilies. Swans, karandavas (geese) and chakrawarkas (ruddy ducks) swam merrily across its surface. The periphery of the pond was lined with marble slabs. On all sides of the pond, there were beautiful flowers shivering in the gentle breeze arriving after kissing the holy water of the Ganga in the north. Before commencing his day, the king distributed charity to thousands of the Brahmins and the needy. He fed them with fine food and gave them *dakshina*, (a token of gift to a Brahmin, priest or guru) invoking their blessings.

The boys and girls waited for Sumitra and Champa when they walked through the manicured lawns and flower beds. They played hide and seek, or kho-kho, both team games, depending on the availability of the children. That day, many children had gathered, and they played kho-kho. The game demanded highest degree of brisk movements, great reflexes and tremendous stamina. Because of her dance practice and wonderful reflexes, the team led by Sumitra always won. By the time the game ended, a maid came to the garden looking for the princess and Champa. Sumitra was happy to get rid of the immature boys and girls who still wanted to continue.

Time moved pensively like a mahatma, twirling his prayer beads between his thumb and forefinger. Sumitra was two months away from her sixteenth birthday. The last one-year had robbed her of the little girl years. She cared little about her clothes and make-up. Although she looked gorgeous in her small and delicate features, her true beauty reflected in her intelligent eyes. A thin, bony girl was, almost overnight, transformed into a well-shaped, beautiful young woman with the perfect contours.

Soon, Sumitra was of marriageable age and her mother was concerned about this. She decided to take this matter up with her husband, King Sunit. King Sunit didn't give a thought about this earlier as he always remained absorbed in the governance of his country and attending to the holy men. King Sunit loved the company of the learned Brahmins. The greatest rishis of the world—Narad, Vashisth, Bhrigu, Angira, Kashyap and others—came to Kashi for the holy darshan of Vishweswara. The king welcomed them in his palace and discussed the spiritual knowledge. He also ensured that all the pilgrims coming to Kashi got adequate food and comfortable shelter.

Sumitra was not ready for marriage. The princess was well versed in the Vedas, Upanishads, politics, music, dance, art and literature, and wanted to pursue her studies further. Marriage could wait. She had journeyed to wonderful places with her parents across Bharat. She regularly attended conferences and religious gatherings in Kashi and elsewhere, experiencing a different world of wisdom and virtue. But it did not satiate her hunger for higher learning. There were many untouched places she had heard about in her growing years and wanted to visit them. She was certainly not against the institution of marriage, but right now, it was not her priority. She wanted to learn something new every day, every moment. Knowledge is what the universe is all about. No surprise that they equate knowledge with the god. Sumitra was the seeker of knowledge and marriage would restrain her urge. Who knew, after marriage, whether her husband would support her in her academic pursuits.

Shravan, the fifth month of the Hindu Lunar calendar, is very important for the Shaivites, the worshippers of Shiva. For the people of Kashi, it is like a month- long religious festival. People from all over Jambudwip come here for the darshan of Vishweswara and to perform His *abhishekam* (pouring of) with the holy water of the Ganga. The devotees of Shiva believe that to save the creation from the extinction, Lord Mahadev consumed Kalkut poison. He contained the venom in his throat and that turned his neck blue. To heal the burning caused by that deadly poison, the gods and demons offered the Lord water from the sacred Ganga. Ever since, the devotees offered Ganga-jal to show their devotion and gratitude to Neelkanth, or the blue-necked one, as Lord Mahadev is also known as, for saving the universe.

Each ashram, temple and household in Kashi made special arrangements for the festivities, penance and austerities of their inmates and visitors. The king spent the month living like a celibate sage in a hut on the Dasashwamedh Ghat. He fasted for the entire month and lived on the diet of fruits and roots. On Mondays, more auspicious than other days, he had only the Ganga-jal and a single piece of *bel* leaf. During the mornings and evenings, he took part in religious discourses. Sumitra was always a part of such gatherings since she remembered.

Maharshi Vashisth, one of the seven founders of the Vedic religion, was the guest of honour that day. He sat on the higher pedestal covered with black deerskin. The king sat on a simple mat of kusha (halfa) grass placed on a wooden platform slightly raised from the ground, with his daughter by his side. Vashisth spoke about a variety of subjects. His line of preaching made up several commandments on the duties and responsibilities of the kingship. The sage was well versed in every aspect of Vedic teachings. Vashisth explained, 'The kingship must aim at keeping the people toward progressive spiritualism that ultimately led to the life's goal of the moksha. A king must ensure that the citizens were fully protected and had all their genuine material needs fulfilled.'

As Vashisth completed his sermons, Sumitra, with folded palms, asked the foremost of the rishis, 'O great Maharshi, please tell me when the study of scriptures, possession of the wealth and a marriage are successful?'

'The study of scriptures is successful when it lead to humbleness and honourable conduct. To become successful, wealth must be enjoyed and given to charity. A marriage is successful when husband and wife mutually love and respect each other and produce offspring.'

Sumitra asked many more questions, and the sage satisfied her with his knowledge and wisdom. His words made sense to her. In a fructified marriage, a wife must bear her husband's son, who would carry forward the lineage of their ancestors. The girl child was unwanted by the patriarchal society of the Aryans.

The sage looked at the girl with renewed interest. He had met her a few years ago at the palace of the Kashiraj. But now she was a gorgeous teenage girl of above medium height, with a curvy sensuous figure, fair colour, large sparkling eyes, pert nose and full rose-red lips. The guru of Ayodhya's royal family was looking for a second bride for King Dashrath. His first wife, Kaushalya, had been unsuccessful in begetting a male child. It was over ten years now since she gave birth to a girl. The chances of her bearing another child were diminishing with each passing year. Whether a second wife would give a successor to continue Dashrath's royal dynasty was a question discussed in Ayodhya. This young woman sitting before him was suitable for the king. She was young and beautiful. Her knowledge of scriptures was better than many eminent sages and Brahmins. When she played veena with her eyes half closed, she looked like a celestial being. People claimed that she was like an incarnation of Goddess Saraswati herself.

To know more about her, the sage requested Sunit to bring her again in the evening. He asked the princess to come with her veena and sing few bhajans after the congregation.

After others left, Vashisth told Sunit about getting Sumitra married to King Dashrath. The proposal from the sage pleasantly surprised the king. The queen was after him and wanted their daughter to be married at the earliest. But he hadn't given it a serious thought yet. Sumitra was still a child to him, and he wanted her to enjoy her life to the fullest before she got shackled in a marriage. But this was an excellent proposal, a godsent opportunity. After the merger of the southern Koshala with the kingdom of Awadh, King Dashrath and the country of Koshala became powerful. Kashi was a small principality in its comparison. Dashrath performing the Rajsuya Yajna and him becoming a Chakravarti Samrat were already a matter of serious discussion among the kings of the Aryavart.

One month after Vashisth had left Kashi, her parents summoned Sumitra.

King Sunit said, 'My lovely daughter Sumi, we have received a proposal from King Dashrath of Ayodhya. He wants to marry you.'

The information stunned Sumitra. She kept quiet as if they expected no reply from her. Her strained smile concealed her inner conflict.

'Maharshi Vashisth, the knower of the past, present and future, has spoken to me. Dashrath is the most suitable king to marry you. Any princess in Jambudwip will be happy to be his wife,' added the king.

'Dashrath is already married to the princess of Koshala,' her mother said with a questioning look.

'That's true. He married Kaushalya, the daughter of Koshala King Bhanumant. Kshatriya kings marry many times, though personally I don't consider it a virtue. Dashrath has noble intensions to remarry. After ten years of his first marriage, the queen has not given him a successor to the throne of Ikshvaku.'

'How old he must be? Sumitra is not even seventeen,' the queen asked earnestly.

Sumitra had not spoken a word. The conversation between her parents sounded well-rehearsed and what they said to each other was only to inform and persuade her.

'The Koshala king is young, very young, but I do not know about his exact age. At the time of his first marriage, he was hardly twenty.' The king turned to Sumitra and said in a reassuring voice, 'Sumi, the decision is entirely yours. Take your time. I have given no commitment to the Maharshi. Whatever be your decision, we shall stand by you.'

The marriage of Sumitra and Dashrath took place in early winter. She saw her husband for the first time during the marriage ceremonies that were presided over by Sage Vamdev, supported by Vashisth himself. Dashrath was a handsome man of medium height with a warm and kind smile. He looked strong with a muscular body, broad lion-like shoulders, strong knee length arms and steel-grey eyes. The Koshala king looked much younger to his years and a perfect match for Sumitra. Dashrath and other guests from Ayodhya stayed in Kashi for about a month. In an auspicious muhurta, the Princess of Kashi left the bank of Ganga and went over to her new home on the bank of Sarayu. Sunit gave away vast quantities of gold, gems, silk, horses, chariots, and cows to his son-in-law. He also gave away many young and enticing maids and male servants. Sumitra wanted Champa to accompany her. She might return after Sumitra had settled into her new home and the new environment. Dashrath distributed sizeable sums of money, food, and clothing to the poor who came from far and wide, hoping to get rich donations. Both the kings distributed thousands of cows, their horns covered with gold and hoofs with silver, among the Brahmins and sages.

It took three days for the marriage party to reach Ayodhya from Kashi, one day extra, because on their way they stopped at Prayagraj to seek darshan of Rishi Bharadwaj and take a bath at the Triveni Sangam, a confluence of the Ganga, Yamuna and Saraswati rivers. After taking a holy dip at the Triveni, they went to the ashram of Bharadwaj, a little upstream on the bank of Ganga. The sage welcomed the newly wedded princess, and to the great joy of her husband blessed her: 'Princess, the gods are pleased with you in every way. You will be the mother of two illustrious sons. They will be noble and mighty warriors who will remain unconquered against the greatest of the enemies.'

Listening to the words of Bharadwaj, Dashrath and Sumitra were exuberant. The purpose of his remarriage was to get a son. Dashrath repeatedly bowed and prostrated before the great sage. Sumitra reached Ayodhya with her husband and Champa. Guru-mother Arundhati and Queen Kaushalya welcomed her. In the absence of Dashrath's mother, Arundhati performed the post-marriage rituals.

Sumitra waited for years, but prophesy of the great sage did not come true. To her utter dismay, Dashrath gradually started losing interest in her. It all began with her friend Champa. Dashrath, in the beginning, treated her as his sister-in-law, the younger sister of his wife. Within the social fabric of Awadh region, men could take verbal liberties while dealing with their wife's younger sister and elder brother's wife.

What began with the indecorous jokes and off-hand obscene comments took the vulgar turn leading to disastrous physical relationships. The affiliation between Champa and Dashrath was one such relationship. Champa never wanted to betray her friend and cross the threshold of decency. Champa was now a beautiful young woman and whenever she saw Dashrath and Sumitra together, her body ached for the company of a man. She was so enamoured of the young and handsome king that it completely shattered her defences in his presence. Dashrath took advantage of her youthful innocence and married her as the Gandharvas did. In an open defiance to Sumitra, she became a *bavata* or sub-wife of Dashrath. This was just the beginning. The perverse excursions of Dashrath that began with Champa turned him into the slave of his unending desires. He was not happy and contended with a woman for long and always yearned for the younger women to satisfy his unquenchable thirst.

In many smaller kingdoms of the Aryavart, the kings had four types of wives. The first duly wedded wife was Mahishi, or the queen consort. Next came Parivrata. They too were formally wedded and could be one or more. A Bavata was a woman accepted as a wife through non-Vedic marriages such as Gandharva-vivah, kidnapping, elopement, and others. The fourth type of wife was Palakali. They were maids and slaves who had been with the king on one or more occasions. The kings pursued a life of uninhibited pleasure with woman, wine, possessions, and material comforts.

It was no surprise that Dashrath found Sumitra less and less interesting. He left her alone, ignored her, spending all his time with newer and younger women. Kaushalya was the Rajmahishi (the queen consort) and must remain by her husband's side on all occasions–official, social, or religious, requiring a wife. Such occasions did not mandate Sumitra's presence. After initial deprivation and loneliness, she went back to her studies. She was a woman of absolute, uncompromising idealism and compassion. Her studies made her a strong-willed woman who never felt despondent. She saw the beacon at the end of a dark tunnel in the prophetic words of Sage Bharadwaj and waited for the birth of her sons. She now spent more and more time at the ashram of Sage Vashisth in the company of Guru-mother Arundhati.

Chapter 5

ARUNDHATI

'What brings you here to this desolate place? Aren't you Smriti, the wife of the great Sage Angiras?' asked Agni Adbhut, the God of fire. He was surprised by the presence of the wife of a sage all alone in the solitary forest.

'I am here to seek your company. Not only I, but we, the seven *rishikas* (female sages), will come one by one to be with you. Don't you too want to meet us?' said Swaha, who had taken the form of Smriti, the wife of Maharshi Angiras.

'What made you think I will accept you? You are a married woman, the wife of one of the greatest sages on earth. I haven't even spoken to you.'

'We have seen this desire in your ruby-coloured eyes. Women have a sixth sense men are oblivious of. It empowers us to sense the unknown when related to finding love, hate, and danger to self and our offspring. You are the most attractive person in the triple world, and we want you as much as you want any of us. Don't forget, apart from being rishikas, we are women too.'

Agni could never fathom that these innocent-looking virtuous women would attract him so easily. He was even more surprised to know they were willing for his courtship. While he was with Smriti (Swaha), he repeatedly asked when Arundhati was likely to come, the most beautiful among the rishikas.

The Saptarishis performed a great yagna at the ashram of Maharshi Vashisth. It lasted for a month. Arundhati, as the wife of the host and head priest, Vashisth, was actively involved in all the proceedings. She was a perfect homemaker and, with the help of Nandini, made elaborate preparations for the comfortable stay and necessities of hundreds of sages, their wives, and disciples. As the knower of the scriptures, she put together intricate preparations for the successful completion of the yajna. The participating sages and their wives were engaged in a strict protocol. Following celibacy, they had to live on fruits, roots, milk and honey and had to sleep on the earthen floor covered with kusha grass. Many times, the rishikas didn't go to their thatched huts and stayed overnight in the *yajna-mandapam* (yajna-enclosure). They pronounced the holy names of God, recited prayers and didn't sleep through the night. Because of the absence of any male, they were unmindful of their clothes and bodies.

While they sleepily rolled on their prayer mats, their tousled clothes and hair made them even more attractive. Their faces were calm and, with low, even breathing, their chest rhythmically moved up and down. Even during their sleep, they wore a gentle smile on their slightly parted lips. The rishikas, while in sleep, had completely lost control of their bodies. Some of them, with significant efforts, tried to keep themselves awake in the open space. They squeezed their bleary eyes, then opened them wide to stay awake. They yawned uncontrollably and stretched and shook their beautiful limbs repeatedly. Fire God Agni, living in the yajna-pit, watched these women day and night. Forgetting that they were married and chaste rishikas, he lost his self-control for them.

Agni knew his limitations and had no courage to express his feelings. He understood these chaste women would not, even in their dreams, think of any other man. A wife who held in her heart desirable thoughts of a man who was not her husband was as unfaithful as a woman who courted with such a man. But Agni was burning with lust. He found no remedy and at the end of yajna, went to the forest thinking of self-immolation.

Next day, Swaha took the form of Kshama, the wife of Sage Pulaha, and returned to dwell with Agni. He again asked about Arundhati and again Swaha's reply was the same. This happened for the next six days when Swaha came to see Agni as Puloma, Anasuya, Havirbhu, and Santati. But she could never take the form of the wife of Vashisth to his disappointment. Agni was upset. He met with six out of the seven wives of the Saptarishis, but not Arundhati. His desire would not get satiated without courting Arundhati.

Swaha told him the truth. 'You can't have Devi Arundhati. She is so chaste and virtuous that if I took her form and you touched me, you would be charred to cinders. As I love you, I will not take that chance. Now please listen to the truth. I am Swaha, the daughter of Prajapati Daksha and Prasuti. I fell in love with you since I first saw you in thc yajna of the Saptarishis and have since been pursuing you. But you never noticed my love. During the yajna rituals, the centre of your attraction was always the rishikas.'

'And the women who came to me in the last six days?'

'Only I came to meet you, no one else. I took the form of different rishikas.'

'How did you know that? No one else noticed that I had an eye for the sages' wives,' asked Agni with consternation.

'Because they concentrated on the holy rituals, making resolutions, with their eyes closed. But I could not take my eyes off your effulgence and beauty. The more I looked at you, the more passionate I became about you. When you left for the jungle in a hurry burning with desire, I came to comfort you with my presence.'

'So, every time you came as a different woman, and I couldn't make out.'

'That is true. You were under the influence of kama. This also proved that you never wanted these women. You just needed a woman, and I am that woman for you.'

The sages living in the forest engaged in invoking gods saw the wives of the seven sages except Arundhati going to Agni. They conveyed the rishikas' questionable conduct to the Saptarishis who, without checking the veracity of the charge, abandoned them. Swaha and Agni explained the truth, which had no effect on the angry sages. Arundhati met the six sages with her husband and told them that their wives were as pure as herself. They were always with her and did not leave the ashram. Then how was it possible for them to meet Agni? The entire world venerated Arundhati and appreciated her truthfulness, wisdom, and chastity. So, believing her word, the sages accepted their wives back into their ashrams.

Sumitra sat with Arundhati. The guru-mother finished the story of Swaha and Agni. Sumitra often came to the ashram and stayed there overnight. Her married life was in complete disarray, as Dashrath was involved elsewhere. For the last six months, he was not in Ayodhya. He led an expedition to the western borders to quell the uprising by the rakshasas. He was the guest of Kaikeya King Ashwapati when the reports last came in. The princess of Kashi found solace in her studies and resumed from where she left at the time of her marriage. Arundhati guided her in her study of scriptures and one day, like her, Sumitra too wished to compose the verses of the Vedas. Vashisth was not in the ashram because Dashrath requested, through a messenger, his immediate presence in Kaikeya. Arundhati had all the time for the queen.

Sumitra asked the guru-mother, 'Mother, what exactly happened at the time of Lord Shiva's marriage with Goddess Parvati. How did you convince Mother Maina to come out of the *kop-bhavan* (a room in the backside of the palace where a queen enters to express dissatisfaction or annoyance) and accept Mahadev as her daughter's husband when all others failed?'

'Sumitra, you must understand one thing. Only women can value the emotions of other women and understand their pain and anxieties. First to go into the kop-bhavan to persuade Maina was her husband, Himachal, followed by Narad and Vishnu. They expounded at great length how great Shiva was and how fortunate her daughter was to have him as her husband. No one spoke about her daughter's virtues, talents and beauty. She was a girl who would be accepted by anyone in the triple world—humans, gods or demons. When I spoke to her from Girija 's (another name of Parvati) point, I was able to convince her, and she came out of the Kop Bhavan.'

'Mother, why don't you tell me the story from the beginning?' Sumitra insisted on listening to the whole story whimpering like a child.

Arundhati said, 'Himachal has invited all the sages, kings, Gandharvas, mountains, rivers, lakes and others with their families for the marriage of his daughter Parvati. Shiva on his side invited not only all the gods and demons but also ghosts, goblins and all the creatures. The women gathered on the balcony of Himachal's palace waiting for the marriage procession. A sceptical Maina was eager to see the bridegroom. At the advice of Vishnu, they arranged the marriage procession in groups. At the head of the procession came the handsome Gandharvas, richly dressed, riding in their vehicles with flags and banners. Groups of singing and dancing heavenly nymphs accompanied them. Then came the Yakshas. When Maina saw Manigriva, their lord, she took him to be Shiva. She was told by Narad he was only an attendant of Shiva. When the next god surrounded by his retinue came within her sight, twice as splendid as Manigriva, she was similarly mistaken.'

Sumitra knew the story, but coming from the cast of this divine play, she listened on keenly.

The escalating splendour of each successive deity, including the king of gods, Indra, and Lord Brahma, mesmerized Maina thirteen times. Last to arrive was Shri Hari Vishnu, accompanied by his consort Lakshmi and thousands of his *parshadas* (attendants). Maina's happiness and pride knew no bounds. It became almost unbearable until Narad announced the arrival of Shiva. His Ganas (followers) of wondrous shapes and forms preceded and surrounded the Lord. The *bhoota*s and *preta*s, elementals and ghosts accompanying Shiva dispelled the pride and anticipation of Maina. The faces of the Ganas were frightful, horrid and fierce, and belonged to the animals, reptiles or insects. When Maina saw Shiva in their midst, she trembled.'

Sumitra smiled, listening to the mischief of the Great Lord and how he tested his devotees. The story swept away Arundhati's emotions as it happened yesterday.

'I was aghast, looking at Shiva. Before going to Himachal's palace, we, the Saptarishis and their wives, went to see Mahadev. With great difficulty, I persuaded him to dress like a prince for the occasion. I arranged for a beautiful silk dress and jewellery and prepared him for the occasion. But the handsome bridegroom adorned with gems and jewellery had mysteriously disappeared. The Lord of the lords had transformed himself back into his usual self, an ugly looking aghori with a skull garland, unkempt hair and cremation ash smeared all over his body. Alarmed, trembling, and stuck with misery, Maina fell to the ground and became unconscious. When brought back to her senses, she cried in anguish, cursing her fate and that of Parvati. She felt her daughter was deceived by such an ugly reward for her long and severe austerities. She wanted to slice Parvati's throat and commit self-immolation. The words of Narad, my husband Vashisth, and other rishis failed to assuage her.

'Parvati tried to dissuade her disconsolate mother, but it had no effect on a stubborn Maina. Finally, Parvati told her mother that she had wooed Shiva after years of tapasya and would marry him otherwise remain unmarried forever. Maina was even angrier listening to her daughter. She removed her jewellery and fine clothes and entered the kop-bhavan in a single coarse clothing.

'Her husband tried to pacify her that her anger was misplaced as she had not seen the actual appearance of Shiva. But she did not come out. Lord Vishnu, Narad and the Saptarishis went to her and lauded Shiva, who, when pleased, showed his most enchanting beauty. But her husband's pleas did not satisfy Maina. My husband asked me to speak to her and try to convince her. After entering the small windowless dimly lit room, I told Maina, "Let us think of Parvati. Do you think she will be happy if she marries someone else? She underwent long and difficult tapasya to seek Shiva as her husband. She loves Shiva, and he loves her too. That is why he agreed to the marriage. If you don't allow this marriage, how do you think

Parvati will feel? Let us think of the girl and her happiness. Your two unmarried daughters, Kritika and Kutila, have left home, never to return. Do you wish same fate for Parvati?"'

Maina ceased ranting when I said her Shiva had many forms, both hideous and handsome. However, she agreed to give her daughter to him only if he appeared as a handsome bridegroom. Consequently, Shiva revealed himself in his divine, compassionate form, elegantly adorned, just as my friends and I had prepared him for the occasion.'

Sumitra never wanted to ask about the most tragic event of Arundhati's life. In a single day, an arrogant king killed her hundred sons; their only crime—they were the sons of Arundhati and Vashisth.

The nightmare started with a casual visit to King Kaushik of Chedi. During his marches around the earth to become a Chakravarti Samrat, he came upon a hermit's ashram. The king was so impressed by its beauty and serenity that he said to his commanders, 'Whose hermitage is this that combined so much scenic beauty and the aura of spirituality?'

'It is the ashram of Maharshi Vashisth.'

Kaushik had heard much about the great sage, but never met him. He said, 'I must pay him my respect while I am near his place. Let the army stay where it is. I'll go alone and seek his blessings.'

Vashisth came to the entrance of the ashram to receive the Kshatriya king. After a brief meeting when the king rose to leave, he said, 'It was a pleasure meeting the greatest sage on earth in his own ashram filled with the aura of spiritual essences. Please allow me to leave now.'

What happened next was a defining moment in the annals of humankind. The sage, instead of telling, 'Thank you so much for your imperial visit,' said to the king, 'This is lunchtime, and we are straight headed for our meals. I'll request you to be my guest.'

'When outside Suktimati, our capital, I prefer taking meals with my troops. They must not wait for me. I have accepted your invite and will come once again to enjoy that offer. But I must go now.'

'Let them also join us. It will be Arundhati's pleasure to arrange a feast for them. We don't get such a royal opportunity every day.'

'They are more than a hundred thousand and pardon me great sage, soldiers can't fight with fruits and roots in their stomach.'

'Their large number is not a problem for us and who told you we'll offer them hermit's food. They can have whatever they wish.'

'How will you arrange it?' The king was curious to see the confidence of Vashisth.

'First, let them join us. You will see for yourself.'

Kaushik sent for his army. The troops poured in and settled wherever they found the place. No sooner had they taken their seats than all kinds of food in golden bowls were served. The feast satiated the hunger of the king and his followers. Kaushik suddenly felt worried by the astounding power of the sage. He asked earnestly, 'O greatest among sages, please forgive my curiosity. But I must know how you performed this miracle?'

Vashisth sensed the brewing trouble. He said, 'You are my guest, and your pleasure is my satisfaction. Leave it to the homemaker regarding how she managed it. Please tell me if you or any of your soldiers want anything else.'

'You provided me and my legion with everything we wanted. But this grand feast will be worth nothing unless you tell me how you managed it?'

When Vashisth saw he couldn't stave off the king, he asked him to follow. Amid lush green surroundings, there stood a milky white animal with the head of a lovely woman. Vashisth went near her and fondly rubbing her head said, 'She is Nandini. My wife Arundhati lovingly calls her Sabala.' Then, addressing the divine cow, he said, 'Nandini, meet our guest, son of Gadhi, the great King Kaushik.'

Nandini replied, 'I hope we could please you with our services, king.'

'Do you say you arranged the splendid feast?'

Vashisth informed the king that he officiated as the high priest on the occasion of the great churning of the Kshir Sagar by the devas and asuras to get the elixir of immortality. 'The gods gave me Nandini as my dakshina. She is the daughter of Kamdhenu, the wish fulfilling divine cow. Whatever I ask, she provides for me.'

Kaushik was proud of his might: wealthy, powerful and feared by all kings on the earth. But he had nothing like Nandini. He requested the sage, 'She belongs to a king's palace, not this open field. Let her go with me.'

He was the lord of the world, and everything belonged to him, including this cow. It did not amuse the king when Vashisth said, 'She is a gift of the gods to me. I have no right to give her to anyone else. When unable to keep her, I'll rather return her to the gods.'

Kaushik was not used to listening to a 'no'. He said, 'She must go with me. I march to the most difficult terrains on the earth with my legion and many times live without food and water. With Nandini around, I don't have to worry. I have the power to take her by force. But you are a well-known sage with no strength to defend. How can I offend an unarmed sage? Let the world not raise an accusing finger at me for taking away your possession by force.'

'Remember who are you talking to, Kaushik,' said Vashisth.

'I am offering you a million cows, gold in a heap, a golden chariot and whatever else you want, only let Sabala go.'

'You want me to surrender what is god-gifted and accept riches from a mortal.'

The arrogant monarch muttered under his breath, 'Let me see how this unarmed sage could stop me from taking away the cow!'

He beckoned one of his commanders. 'Get ten soldiers and drive this animal to our palace. Don't be rough and don't use force.'

The king's men seized hold of Nandini and dragged her away. The cow turned to the sage as if seeking his permission to retaliate. After getting a nod from her master, she bristled and shook her coat. Out of her falling hair, appeared ten fierce looking warriors who, with little effort, slew her perpetrators. The king was furious. He ordered one hundred men to come forward and take Sabala. A hundred warriors emerged from the cow and killed the king's soldiers. Kaushik ordered all his troops to attack at once, but Sabala's soldiers destroyed them like insects coming near a fire.

'Are you satisfied now after losing hundreds of thousands of lives? Please go back to your capital and never challenge a sage blessed by the gods,' said the sage in a calm and controlled voice, standing with folded arms, watching the happenings with detachment.

Kaushik was in deep thought. He said, 'I had the mightiest army on the earth some time back that has turned to dust now. Please tell me the source of your power and I promise to go away.'

'As a teacher, it is my duty to answer the question of an inquirer, so please listen. My power comes from my inner strength. God is within all of us and needs to be invoked through meditation and austerities. Sabala is only a personification of that godhood.'

'I will practise greater austerities than you and will not rest until I gain more powers than you possess. I will return one day with a new army and divine strength to seek revenge,' said the king.

He asked his son Ashtaka to return to the capital and rule the kingdom. He took off his royal costumes and jewellery and symbolically gave away his sword to Ashtaka. After cladding himself in a loincloth, he went to the Himalayas for tapasya. Lord Brahma answered his prayers and asked him to seek his desired boon. Kaushik asked for an inexhaustible army equipped with the subtlest weapons. He requested Brahma, 'I want to match my strength with Vashisth in all aspects. I must possess the best knowledge of archery and know about all the bows on earth. Please give me your ultimate weapon, the Brahmastra.'

Kaushik returned to his capital. He mustered a large army and equipped it with the latest weapons and missiles he had gained from Brahma and marched to Vashisth's ashram ranting war cries. Inmates of the ashram were panic-stricken, but Vashisth went about as if nothing was happening. Kaushik's warriors tried to storm the gate and fired fire-shafts and missiles, causing devastation in the ashram. Vashisth planted his staff in the middle of the ashram's entrance and went back to his hut. This simple-looking staff neutralised every arrow and divine missile fired by Kaushik and fell well short of the hermitage. No soldier could get past it. Finally, deranged with hate and revenge, the king employed the Brahmastra by invoking appropriate incantations and shot it at the one hundred sons of Vashisth and Arundhati.

The Brahmastra went towards the sky, emitting flames and returned to the entrance, multiplying its force and heat. The quiet-going hermits saw a million suns approaching the ashram. Lord Brahma's weapon came face to face with the staff and generated so much heat that the triple world was scorching. The agitated gods appeared in the sky and asked the king to withdraw this weapon of ultimate destruction. But in his vindictive vexation, the king forgot the right incantations. The gods then prayed to the Brahmarshi to remove the staff and save the creation from getting consumed by its energy. King Kaushik had aimed the Brahmastra at the sons of Vashisth, and if he removed the staff, they would certainly die. He must speak to Arundhati before making a decision. Without replying to the gods, he went to his hut.

Vashisth told Arundhati about his predicament. But Arundhati had no such misgivings. With no hesitation, she said, 'Vashisth, you always said that the entire creation was our family, and all the creatures were like our children. To save our one hundred sons, how can we allow millions and millions of lives to be destroyed? Before your arrival, I spoke to them, and they are happy to sacrifice their lives to save the three worlds. After all, they are our children and know the value of sacrifice.'

His wife's words didn't convince the sage. That was like infanticide. Arundhati could read her husband's mind and said, 'Our children have withdrawn their senses within and are meditating right now. They are ready to release their soul from their body without effort. Your duty as a Brahmarshi is far greater than your role as a father.'

Vashisth went to the entrance, and with teary eyes and shaking hands, removed the staff. Instantly, the Brahmastra killed all their sons. The Brahmastra went back to Lord Brahma.

When Vashisth returned to the hermitage, he saw his wife was preparing for a long journey. She told him, 'I have lost interest in the family life and decided to go to the Badrinath for austerities. What are we doing here in this ashram when our children are no more?'

Vashisth agreed with her. After bidding farewell to his disciples, he asked Nandini to go to Lord Indra in heaven. The wife and husband then left for Badrikashram (ancient name of Badrinath).

But no sooner they stepped out, Lord Brahma met them on the way. The Creator said, 'Your time to give up family life has not arrived yet. You must not grieve the loss of your children because you both are the Brahma-Gnanis, the knowers of the Brahman. Your sons were the Gandharvas born as humans because of the curse of Sage Durvasa. They were born as mortals to live here for a short period.'

'We don't find any purpose to continue here and would rather become ascetics. We must find Paratpar Brahman before it was too late,' said Arundhati.

'Arundhati, my child, don't get desperate. You will find the company of Paratpar Brahman in your family life. Maha Vishnu will incarnate as Ram and take birth in Ayodhya as the son of King Dashrath and Queen Kaushalya. Your husband will be the Rajguru of Ayodhya royal family and the teacher of Ram. You will be the guardian angel to the women of the royal family. Your son will be a close friend of Ram. Wouldn't you like to be associated with Maha Vishnu in his human form? Now go to Ayodhya and wait for Brahman to incarnate on the earth and bless you with his darshan.'

While on a military expedition to the northwest frontiers of his kingdom, King Dashrath was enchanted by Surupa, the teenage daughter of Ashwapati, the king of Kaikeya. Dashrath wanted his guru to speak with the king and help him in getting the hand of the princess. The geographical and social history of Jambudwip and Aryavart was about to see a great churning—whether for good or bad only time would tell.

Chapter 6

KAIKEYI

'O the Princess of Kaikeya, you have done what no other woman in the long history of the Aryavart has ever done. You saved the life of the emperor of Sapta Sindhu and won the battle against the mighty asuras. People will remember the tales of your bravery and sacrifice for many millennia. Lord Indra has asked me to convey his thanks and heartfelt greetings to you. In this open court and invoking the celestials, I shall grant you two boons of your choice at the time and place decided by you. Let the king of the gods be the witness.'

The investiture ceremony took place on the expansive palace grounds, a venue that took over three months to prepare for the grand occasion. The event was designed to accommodate ten thousand guests seated in a semi-circle beneath a massive canopy. The seating was arranged in gently sloping terraces to ensure unobstructed views for everyone.

Following the ceremony, the emperor hosted a lavish feast for the community. Dashrath's servants distributed charity to the poor who had travelled from distant lands to witness the event. Among the notable guests were friendly kings from Aryavart and relatives and friends of the emperor from Angdesh, Mithila, Kashi, Gidham and Kaikeya, all arriving with lavish gifts for the royal family. Kaikeya presented the most impressive gift: ten thousand well-bred horses.

Dashrath and Kaushalya's eldest daughter, Shanta, arrived with her adoptive parents, Rompad and Vershini. The emperor had arranged for guests to stay in luxurious white marble multi-storied mansions. Vershini and Shanta preferred to live with Kaushalya, while Ashwapati chose to stay with his daughter Surupa. Kaikeyi took this opportunity to catch up on all that had transpired in the years since her marriage.

The grandstand faced Shrirang-ji temple, with the royal throne positioned prominently in the centre of the podium. To the left of the king's throne were three jewel-encrusted gold thrones for the queens, while a gold settee covered with black deerskin was reserved for Rajguru Vashisth. The Brahmins conducted fire sacrifices in the Vishnu temple, and the harmonious chants from the Sam Veda resonated throughout the arena.

Before the main ceremony, actors and dancers entertained the audience, who had arrived ahead of the scheduled start. When the emperor arrived, the sound of hundreds of trumpets and resounding kettledrums filled the air. The Brahmins greeted him with conch shell blasts and shanti-path chants. The queens followed closely behind, with Kaikeyi making her entrance first and receiving a hero's welcome from the enthusiastic crowd. Sumantra, the Prime Minister, and General Balashali, the commander of the Koshala Army, extended their warmest welcomes to her. The other two queens arrived shortly thereafter and took their seats. Kaushalya, as the queen consort, sat beside the emperor. The final arrival was Vashisth, accompanied by his wife Arundhati and other sages. The king and queens honoured the holy couple with bows of reverence.

The Koshala Army had returned from the Dandaka Forest after their victorious campaign in the Dev-Asura battle. The victory celebrations had been postponed due to the king's life-threatening battle injury and Queen Kaikeyi's serious abdominal wound. With both having fully recovered now, today marked the first public appearance of Emperor Dashrath. The citizens of Koshala had multiple reasons to celebrate: their triumph over the asuras, the recovery of their king and queen, and renewed hopes for a successor to the throne. The prospect of the Ikshvaku dynasty's end had been a looming concern, and they were grateful to the youngest queen, who had risked her life to save the king.

The state administration had planned the event to honour and reward the brave soldiers who had distinguished themselves in battle. The gathering also paid tribute to those who had made the ultimate sacrifice and could not return to their families.

Kaikeyi did not expect such a gift from her husband. She had performed the duties of a soldier, a queen and a wife. That is what her elder brother Yudhajit, who was also her teacher in warcraft, had taught her. Her father, Ashwapati, was her teacher in charioting. But Sumantra, who was the best charioteer in the Aryavart, polished her skills. Kaikeyi's immediate concern was different—whether she could bear children after her abdomen injury. Koshala nurtured high hopes from her, but so far nothing had materialized. Her father waited impatiently for her son to arrive in this world. Sage Vamdev, an eminent physician in his own right, had told after examining her, 'There is nothing to worry about, princess. Your abdomen injury has healed completely. There is apparently no damage to your internal procreative organs, which are in the lower abdomen. I don't find a reason you shouldn't become a mother soon.'

After meeting the sages in Chitrakoot, Kaikeyi was even more determined to have a son. As soon as she recovered from the injuries, she visited Guru Vashisth. She was curious to know how far the sages involved him in the dream of the Akhand Bharat, so passionately nurtured by the great sages. To her relief, Vashisth was a member of the core council along with sages Atri, Agastya, Vishwamitra and Sutikshana. With the support of Guru Vashisth, her task was likely to become less difficult. She had no use for the boons because the purpose of her life had changed after meeting the sages. If the sages found him suitable, Kaikeyi would offer her first-born son to the sages.

Sage Atri's words echoed in her ears. He said, 'We need to transform our thoughts. The time has come for a king or prince with foresight and vision to live among the tribals long enough to understand their problems, befriend them, and treat them as equals. He must also be a great warrior and organizer to lead the local tribesmen in battles against the rakshasas. Bringing an army from his kingdom to this unfamiliar land would not serve the purpose and might further alienate the tribals.'

The king was too old and spent up to face the vagaries of a forest life. Only a young prince could do it. Sage Bharadwaj blessed her that her son would be the Sustainer of the world. Who else but a king could do that? Kaikeyi was thinking about the events of the recent past. 'Dashrath promised my father that our son would succeed him to the throne of Ayodhya. But let that wait. Let my son first go to accomplish the mission of the sages. Living among them, he would emancipate the tribesmen, foragers and hunter-gatherers and bring them into the mainstream Aryan fold. With the help of the aboriginals, he would destroy the evil empire of the rakshasas and unite the Jambudwip into one great nation, an Akhand Bharat.' The forecast of wandering minstrel Narad before her birth must be true. She was ready to play her role in the glorious mission of the sages that would bring an end to the dangerous rakshasa civilization.

Ashwapati sat with his daughter in her palace. His niece Sukriti, or Manthara as they knew her in Ayodhya, was also with them. Kaikeyi looked at her father. He has clearly overgrown in the past few years. His face was more wrinkled than she remembered. His skin was sagging, and his greying facial hair made him much older than his chronological age. Sukriti asked him, 'Uncle, we are worried about your health. You don't take enough care of yourself. I will speak to Yudhajit dada about it.'

'Kriti, there's no need to disturb Jit. I've already overwhelmed him with royal duties. I am merely a king in name, occupying the throne and wearing the crown. All the responsibilities of governance have been entrusted to Jit. Sometimes, I feel I should have let him enjoy a few more years of his own life.'

'Father, how old were you when grandfather expired?' asked Kaikeyi.

'Surupa, you can't compare. Of course, I was much younger than Jit, just in my early twenties, when your grandfather expired. We were not prepared for such a calamity, which struck us like a thunderbolt. We have no control over such things. At that time, I had the support of your mother and strong backing from your uncle Vrihadaksha, a couple of years younger than me. After the death of our father, he stood like a rock by my side and together we came out of the ordeal. I still cannot fathom that Vrihadaksha is no more among us.' Remembering his deceased brother, Ashwapati became emotional.

'But I am still around and should be available to Jit whenever necessary,' added Ashwapati.

'Uncle, you are available not only to Jit dada but to all of us. You are our greatest support. We have faced so many tragedies in the family–the death of my father and the departure of Badi Ma [1], your younger brother and your wife respectively. The two most important people in your life left you midway,' said Manthara. Ashwapati did not reply. Lost in his thoughts, he travelled down the memory lane.

Prince Ashwapati of Kaikeya, from his childhood, was keen to learn everything about horses. What started as a hobby, later on, made his country the largest supplier of the best quality horses in the world. Ashwapati was always eager to learn new things. He learned the language of birds and animals from a sage. The only condition imposed by the teacher was, he would forget this skill if he ever disclosed their conversations to others. Ashwapati married Era, the princess of Yunan. Her friend Yamini married Ashwapati's younger brother, Vrihadaksha. Together, Ashwapati and Era had seven sons and a daughter. His younger brother had only one daughter, Sukriti.

When Sukriti was about two and a half years old, she was afflicted with an extremely rare syndrome that caused her to sweat profusely all the time, regardless of the weather. To save the princess's life, thc Raj Vaidya administered a potion that saved her life but deformed her physically. The treatment damaged her body irreparably. She became a hunchback - her spine bent, shoulders drooped, and neck stiffened. Because of her sluggish movements, people nicknamed her Manthara. Sukriti did not give up in the face of adversities and, disregarding her disabilities, she focused on her mental abilities.

Because of serious subversive activities on the southern and western borders, Ashwapati was mostly away from Rajgriha, the capital of Kaikeya. Queen Era was lonely and felt ignored. She waited for some time, then, in sheer desperation, returned to her parents, leaving a three-year-old Surupa behind. The king was heartbroken and withdrew from the routine work of kingship. Gradually, he handed over the governance to his eldest son and crown prince Yudhajit. Surupa grew up to become a beautiful girl. She had a keen interest in horse riding, archery, and sword fighting. She was an excellent charioteer and battle strategist.

When Kaikeyi was seventeen, her incomparable beauty and virtues became the subject of discussion in all the royal courts of the Jambudwip. Every king and prince wanted to marry her. Some came in person, others sent their emissaries, while the Brahmins and priests represented the rest. The Emperor of Saptsindhu came to the western borders of his kingdom to suppress the insurgent rakshasas. After declaring his anti-insurgency operations highly successful, he was the state guest at Rajgriha. The purpose of his travel to the borders and then being a guest of Ashwapati was his search for a new bride. Like many other kings, he had heard about the young princess and wanted to meet her in person.

The enchanting beauty of Kaikeyi fascinated Dashrath. He asked Vashisth to intervene on his behalf and persuade Ashwapati to give Surupa to him in marriage. The Kaikeya king was initially hesitant because of the age difference between Dashrath and his daughter. He agreed to the marriage only if Dashrath promised that Surupa's son would succeed him on the throne of Ayodhya. Dashrath, in the presence of Vashisth, Vamdev and Yudhajit, willingly accepted the condition.

Surupa had her own concerns. She wanted Dashrath to give up his lascivious ways and stick to his three queens. He wouldn't marry a fourth time, whether present queens could give birth to a son or not. He was also to liberate his sub-wives—the bavatas and *palakalis*— and help them settle down in their new lives. After the marriage, Surupa came to Ayodhya with her cousin Manthara as her maid. Here they addressed Surupa as Queen Kaikeyi, the princess from Kaikeya.

The people of Ayodhya welcomed the new queen with a month-long celebration. Her arrival rekindled their hopes of getting a prince. The prince who would become their next king and bring an end to the uncertainty about the future ruler of Koshala. But something different happened instead: days and weeks merged into the months and years, but Dashrath did not come out of Kaikeyi's palace. No one could meet him. People first accepted it as an aberration and hoped the emperor would be back to governance sooner than later. When the absence prolonged, the citizens became restive and blamed the young queen for keeping their ruler in her captivity.

Incarceration of the emperor finally ended. One day, the king of gods, Indra Sumantu, accompanied by Gidham King Jatayu, came to see Dashrath. Indra came to seek Dashrath's military support against the Asura King, Shambarasur. To end the relict power of Shambarasur, the king of Tamilakkam in the Southern Peninsula, Divodas, had requested his friend Indra's support. The king of gods had approached King Dashrath for his help in forming a grand alliance of like-minded kingdoms. Sumantu apprised Dashrath that King Ashwapati had agreed to join the alliance and would send his army under the command of his valiant son Yudhajit.

Kaikeyi welcomed the development. It came as an enormous relief for the newly wedded princess. She knew from Manthara that the Ayodhyans were despondent because of the disappearance of their king from public life. They held Kaikeyi responsible for keeping him engaged in aesthetic pleasures. She now had the opportunity to impress her husband and the people of Ayodhya by showing her combative abilities who otherwise looked at her only as a young and attractive seductress. To them, she was a young girl without personal merits and an object of pleasure for the ageing emperor.

Kaikeyi would have the time to improve her battle skills while fighting alongside her brother Yudhajit in an actual battle. She insisted on going to the battlefield with the Koshala army, headed by Dashrath himself. Her safety was a concern for Kaushalya and Sumitra. They advised her to desist from the misadventure. Dashrath too was reluctant initially, but he couldn't say no to his beloved queen.

On their way to the Dandaka, first, they went to the ashram of Sage Bharadwaj in Prayagraj. After leaving the holy city, they had a brief stay at Chitrakoot. Kaikeyi, with her husband and brother Yudhajit, visited the ashram of Sage Atri and his wife, Anasuya. After the religious discourses by the great sages during the day, the sages and royalty gathered for an informal chat after supper.

The problem of terrorism in Jambudwip and the war with Asura King Shambarasur came up for discussion. Sage Sutikshana gave a first-hand account of the happenings in the Dandaka Forest because his ashram was deep in the jungle. It was a predominantly tribal terrain ruled by Ravan's cousins Khar and Dushan, and his sister Surpanakha. Sutikshana told them the disgusting stories of their unabated violence. The rakshasas not only lifted their cattle and cows but also abducted men, women and children to eat them.

'The local tribes, whom the Aryans treat as animals, support the rakshasas. Depending on their way of life and costumes, the humans, Yakshas, Gandharvas and gods have assigned them the ridiculous names of the animals and birds. Some tribes worship monkeys, so they dress and take on the appearance of monkeys, including wearing long tails, while others imitate the look of bears and vultures. Thus, one tribe is regarded as the vanaras, the other reechh and the third geedh,' said Agastya.

'Princess, it may sound ridiculous, but most people in the Aryavart believe them to be the real monkeys, bears or vultures who could speak like humans. The fact is, most of them have limited to no exposure to the world. What they find around them in the forest shapes their lifestyle, dressing and eating habits. They are plain, unsophisticated people without education and unpolluted by the vagaries of the modern world,' Sutikshana said, supporting his guru.

This time it was Sage Atri who spoke up, 'There is another problem of cursing and damning our people at the slightest provocation by the seers and Brahmins. Most of the dreaded rakshasas today were humans, Gandharvas or Yakshas, but because of the curse became powerful rakshasas—men and women both. There is an endless list of such cursed rakshasas like Surpanakha, Tataka, Ravan, Kumbhkarna, Kabandha, Khar, Dushan, Trisara and many others.'

'If you, the great seers, acknowledge and understand the problem so well, why don't you take the initiative and resolve it?' asked Kaikeyi.

'Honourable princess, we have discussed the issue extensively with no concrete resolution. Bringing back the fallen to their original fold is the first step, a small beginning.' Atri said in a soothing voice. 'The second and more important step is to embrace the tribals and keep them with us. The rakshasas have weaned away many of them because of the inhuman treatment they received at the hands of the Aryans.

We must take the inhabitants of Dandakaranya and other tribal lands with us. That is the only way to defeat Ravan and his men and prevent their philosophy of terror and violence from spreading.'

'This is not possible for any or all of you to do. Is that what you say?' said Kaikeyi. She looked unconvinced.

'That's right, princess. Had it been possible for us to do, the power of the rakshasas wouldn't have gone this far,' replied Sage Atri.

'Who can do it, then?' asked Kaikeyi

'The God,' replied Atri.

Sage Atri looked at the perplexed faces around him and explained, 'I mean a person with the qualities of God.'

'And you think it is realistically possible?' asked an awestruck Kaikeyi.

'Yes princess, it is possible. If not today, then tomorrow, next year or another millennium. A person belonging to a well-established royal family must offer the foresight and vision of a brave king and a benevolent sage. He must live with the tribals to know them, realize their difficulties, form friendships and respect them as fellow human beings. As a superb organizer and warrior, he must fight the rakshasas with the support of the local tribals,' said Atri.

'We can't tackle the problem of terrorism and the spread of rakshasa culture by sitting in the palaces. Is that what you mean?' asked Kaikeyi.

'That's right, Kaikeyi. Some kind-hearted king or a prince with a humane approach has to take it up as his life's mission. He must reform the existing society and transform it into a new civilization of mutual love, friendship and equality,' said Agastya.

Sutikshana gave his concluding remarks, 'Yes, by doing so, he will become a superhuman, an incarnation of the god or

God Himself. That's what Maharshi meant when he said God would do it. We are looking for such a prince. All of us shall groom him and with our support, he will lay the foundation of one united Bharat, an Akhand Bharat. It will be one cohesive country, geographically and culturally, from the Himalayas in the north to Kanya Kumari in the south.'

Kaikeyi was so deeply drawn into the conversation that she lost the sense of time. The dream of the sages sowed the seed of Akhand Bharat in her youthful imagination. 'She shall be the mother of an illustrious son,' Sage Bharadwaj had prophesied. Why be the mother of an emperor when you could become the mother of the God. If found suitable, her first-born son would help the sages in accomplishing their mission of Akhand Bharat. That was now her life's mission, too.

The grand alliance of the gods led by Indra, Kaikeyan Army under Yudhajit, Koshala Army commanded by Dashrath and the Tamilakkam forces of King Divodas attacked Fort Vaijayanta from four sides. The demon King Shambarasur fought bravely on all fronts. His son, Trighnasur, with his elephant brigade, was up against the Koshala Army. Kaikeyi drove the chariot of Dashrath with meticulous perfection, thwarting the attack by the asuras. In the battle between the youth of Trighnasur and the experienced Dashrath, experience won the first round. But the age of the emperor took its toll by the afternoon. Despite his best efforts, Dashrath was grievously injured in the abdomen, close to his ribcage.

Kaikeyi shifted the king to another chariot and sent him out of the battleground. She took the command of the Koshala Army. From the royal chariot of her husband with a fluttering Koshala flag, she fought so bravely that no one noticed the absence of the emperor. When the asura commander came face to face with Kaikeyi, she killed him by shooting an infallible trident. With the death of Trighnasur, Koshala forces gained a decisive victory. Kaikeyi defeated the asura army, but the asura commander seriously wounded her. It took six months for her to recover fully from her injuries. Dashrath's wounds were deeper and close to his heart and ribcage. It took almost a year for him to recover.

Kaikeyi waited and so did Ayodhya and the emperor. After years of waiting, she remained without a child. After the death-defying injury at Dandaka, he was not as healthy as before. One day, Kaikeyi and Dashrath went to Sage Vashisth. The desperate king said, 'Gurudev, I am confronted with the most unfortunate nightmare of my life. The lineage of Ikshvaku and the Suryavansha will end with me. There is no greater sorrow in the world than remaining childless. What face I will show to my ancestors in heaven! Please guide me on what could be the way forward.'

'O the emperor of Sapta Sindhu, I have told you many times in the past and I repeat the same today: your horoscope gives me the hope that you shall be the father of four sons. The planets and stars don't lie. Don't get desperate and don't lose hope. Have faith in Lord Shrirang-ji.'

'How long Gurudev? My hopes are receding with each passing day,' said Dashrath.

'O the king of the kings, please arrange for performing the Putra Kameshti Yajna. The only person competent to conduct such a sacrifice is Rishya Sringa, the husband of Shanta.'

Dashrath and Kaushalya journeyed to Angdesh, and with great reverence, brought Shanta and her husband to Ayodhya. After successful completion of the Yajna, the yajna-god presented the sacramental rice pudding in a gold bowl to the king. Dashrath gave half of the pudding to Kaushalya. He divided the other half into two.

Dashrath gave half of the pudding to Kaushalya and divided the remaining half into two parts. He gave one part to Sumitra and split the last quarter into two again. One portion went to Kaikeyi, and the other portion went back to Sumitra. Kaushalya gave birth to the eldest son, Ram. Next came Bharat, born to Kaikeyi. Sumitra delivered twins, whom Sage Vashisth named Lakshman and Shatrughna. Watching their children grow, Dashrath and the queens were overjoyed, as if finding their lives filled with greater meaning.

Kaikeyi was a little concerned because her son Bharat was not the eldest of the four princes. She did not know whether her husband would coronate him as heir apparent to the throne. But more important was the mission of the sages. Who would the sages find suitable to lead the operation? If Bharat, she did not foresee any problem. She would make the king agree to send him to the forest. But if it was Ram, how would she prevail upon her husband to send him away. Wouldn't she get the blame for being a stepmother? She would wait for the decision of the seers and then seek guidance from Guru Vashisth.

[1] King Ashwapati's wife and mother of Kaikeyi. An elder aunt of Manthara

Chapter 7

TATAKA

'O the greatest among sages, I am too small to open my mouth before you. Please have mercy on my son. He is only a child. The wise men don't take cognizance of the blunders of children. Scriptures say anger is the root cause of all evils and ruination. An angry person cannot distinguish between right and wrong. There is nothing an angry person might not say or do, even to the point of self-destruction. Kindly don't indulge in anger and forgive my son. Please listen to the cries of a desperate mother.' The princess begged before Sage Agastya with folded palms and teary eyes.

Agastya ignored her supplication. He did not show any mercy on the teenage boy and, taking a little water from his *kamandulu*, pronounced the punishment, 'O son of Sund, you have disturbed my yajna. By distracting me from the fire-sacrifice, you have acted like a rakshasa. I, therefore, curse you to become a rakshasa forthwith.'

The curse of the sage bewildered Tataka with helplessness and grief. After all, Marichi was a young boy of fifteen. In this age, children were full of energy and did many things unintentionally, just for the fun of it. Their idea was not to harm others but to enjoy themselves. She had heard from her father Suketu: 'Forgiveness is a yajna, forgiveness is the highest bliss. It is piety, purity and penance. The universe is sustained through forgiveness and by revenge it gets destroyed.'

She wondered how the great sages and Brahmins could renounce forgiveness and punish people, even children, for their unintentional mistakes. Retribution or 'an eye for an eye' didn't help anyone.

Tataka was returning from the ashram of Sage Agastya, located deep inside the Sundar Van. Her younger son Subahu, who was also with his elder brother Marichi, had run back to his mother. A baffled Subahu told her that Marichi had entered the ashram of Agastya as a tiger. The seers, engaged in the fire-sacrifice, left the proceedings and ran away to save their lives. Marichi removed his costume and laughed at the running sages who were afraid of a fake tiger. Agastya was furious and was about to punish Marichi. Tataka rushed to the ashram and begged the sage for his forgiveness. The sage was too angry to pay attention to a hapless mother's pleas. After Agastya cursed Marichi into becoming a rakshasa, his mother rushed back to inform her husband, Sund.

Sundar Van was a lush green forest with plenty of fresh water available in its lakes, ponds and springs. The forest had an abundance of natural resources, rare plants, and a large variety of vegetation. The trees were laden with flowers and fruits round the year. Lord Indra blessed the place, because here, owing to the collective efforts of many sages, the king of celestials got rid of Vritrasur's dirt and excrement after killing the demon. The serenity of the place and the presence of the sages made carnivorous animals either behave like domesticized animals or leave the forest. Many learned sages with their innumerable disciples had their ashrams in this beautiful forest. The most prominent of these seers was Sage Agastya, one among the Saptarishis. Two small but prosperous independent *janapadas* (republics) of Malad and Karush in the forest's vicinity were founded by Indra.

Suketu, a Yaksha king or a demigod of great valour and purity, lived in the Sundar Van. The Yaksha had no children, so he entered a penance to please Lord Brahma. When the lord appeared before him, Suketu requested the lord for the gift of a girl child. Unlike gods, demons and humans who invariably wanted sons, the Yakshas and Gandharvas mostly preferred female children. A beautiful girl was born and she was named Tataka.

Tataka was an intelligent and virtuous young woman, brimming with boundless energy and possessing the strength of a thousand elephants. In her youth, her impressive physique made her appear much older than her years. Her formidable build, reminiscent of a small hill, made her an unlikely candidate for marriage among the Yaksha princes. Consequently, Suketu arranged for her to marry Sund, an asura chieftain and the son of the mighty demon Jambha. Despite his demonic heritage, Sund was a noble and principled individual. Young, handsome, and courageous, he proved to be a perfect match for Tataka.

Together, Sund and Tataka had two sons whom they raised with the same care and attention given to Yaksha children. The sons inherited their mother's immense supernatural powers and physical strength. Marichi, the elder son, was adventurous and curious, constantly exploring new environments and experimenting with different forms to perfect his shapeshifting abilities. Subahu, the younger, was calm and studious, and held a special place in his mother's heart as her favoured child.

Sund was upset, thinking that the curse was highly disproportionate to the mistake of his son. He went to the Agastya ashram to seek the sage's forgiveness and ask him how the curse could be redeemed. The conversation turned to arguments and then to ugly bickering. The sage, through the power of his austerities, cursed Sund to fall dead. When Tataka and her sons learnt of Sund's death, they, roaring revenge, stormed into the ashram of the sage. On seeing this, the sage cursed Tataka and Subahu to become ugly and cannibal rakshasas. Tataka thereafter became a ferocious demoness. She destroyed the beautiful forest and tormented all the sages in and around Sundar Van to take revenge on Agastya. Thus, the happy family of the Yaksha princess who had hitherto been demigods was downgraded to become the dreaded rakshasas.

The sudden and unexpected development saddened Sage Agastya. On one hand, he and the other sages strived hard to free Jambudwip from the abominable presence of the rakshasas and the elimination of the rakshasa culture that was spreading like wildfire. On the other hand, he cursed a Yaksha woman and her sons to become rakshasas. He closed his eyes and meditated to calm down.

Ravan, who waited for such incidents, summoned Marichi and Subahu to Lanka. After training and indoctrinating, they returned to Sundar Van as the representatives of Emperor Ravan, with many dreaded rakshasas. Like the asuras, the two brothers grudged animosity towards the humans and seers. They slaughtered all the animals and birds in the forest and killed the humans to eat their flesh—raw or roasted. The rakshasas pulled out ancient trees by their roots and flung them at the ashrams of the sages. They desecrated the sacrificial pits by pouring human blood and throwing beef into them. In their relentlessness, the rakshasas constantly harassed the hermits in their prayers and yajnas. The once green and fertile land became barren and hideous. The citizens of Karush and Malad left their countries and settled elsewhere, mostly in the nearby kingdom of Videha. Over a period, the existence of these once prosperous republics was forgotten and became a part of the deserted forest. Because of the dominance of Tataka, the Sundar Van was now known after her—the Tatak Van or the forest of Tataka.

Ram, Bharat, Lakshman, and Shatrughna had just returned from Guru Vashisth's ashram after completing their education. In the royal assembly hall of Ayodhya, King Dashrath was engaged in listening to petitions and requests from his subjects. Meanwhile, a messenger announced the arrival of Sage Vishwamitra. Dashrath set aside the petitions and rushed to greet the revered sage.

Brahmarshi Vishwamitra, once a powerful emperor, had renounced his royal status after a fierce confrontation with Sage Vashisth, choosing instead the path of a seer. With both the authority of the royal credentials and the stature of a Brahmarshi, he commanded great respect.

Dashrath escorted Vishwamitra to his throne and said, 'Today is a momentous day for Ayodhya with your esteemed presence. You must have travelled a great distance. Please, take some rest and refresh yourself.'

'No need. You know I have complete control over my bodily needs through the practice of yoga and austerities. I am above the effects of heat, cold, hunger, fatigue and even decrepitude.'

'Is there anything for me to do? Can I be of any service to you? Please command, I shall obey right away.' asked Dashrath politely.

'O Emperor of Sapta Sindhu, I came all the way to seek a favour from you. I am performing a yagna at Siddhashrama on the next full moon night. But rakshasas are waiting to disturb the holy undertaking. These rakshasas, led by demoness Tataka and her sons, are endowed with immeasurable powers of destruction. The yagna will benefit humanity and will please the gods above.'

'It is my duty as an emperor that we protect the yagna and make sure that it gets completed without disturbance. Please tell me when I send my troops?'

'No need to bother your men. Send Ram with me and he will take care of the safety of my yajna. I know he can.'

'Why Ram when I am at your service? Ram is too young and inexperienced,' said a surprised Dashrath.

'I know what a great warrior you are, Dashrath. But I want Ram to go with me. If you are unwilling, please say so. I'll return empty-handed.'

'O the greatest Brahmarshi, Ram is a child. He is still practising the use of weapons. He can't contend with the mighty demons who possess all kinds of asura powers. I can send my entire army or if you so desire I will myself lead my troops to safeguard the yajna.' The king sounded miserable, and the assembly was tense and silent.

Vishwamitra ignored his lamentations and said, 'Either you send Ram, or I won't have anyone.'

With that, Vishwamitra unceremoniously walked down the passage leading to the exit of the assembly.

Vashisth rushed to the emperor and whispered in his ear. Then, in long strides, he rushed towards a leisurely walking Vishwamitra, closely followed by the king.

Vashisth was not a regular at the court. He blessed the assembly only once in a while or so or on special occasions. Today was no such occasion, but incidentally, he the Rajguru was present. Was it merely a coincidence?

***

While the four princes devoted themselves to studying scriptures, statecraft, and weaponry, Kaikeyi, Bharadwaj, and Vashisth convened in secret meetings to assess their potential. The sages thoroughly scrutinized the merits and abilities of each prince. Vashisth noted, 'Ram and Lakshman both show promise as skilled warriors. Ram's charm and organizational prowess are nearly celestial. Lakshman, though fiercely brave and second only to Ram, has a volatile temperament. Without careful guidance, his anger could be catastrophic. Bharat, on the other hand, exemplifies religiosity and concern for the people's welfare. He is the most capable administrator among the princes and would win the people's hearts as a ruler, rather than simply conquering kingdoms. Shatrughna, while similar to Lakshman, is somewhat milder in nature.'

The sages agreed that Ram was the most suitable candidate to lead the mission of Akhand Bharat, with either Lakshman or Shatrughna—preferably the former—supporting him. However, Dashrath was unlikely to allow Ram to spend such an extended period in the forest, living among and befriending the tribals. For the moment, the focus was on sending the two princes to Siddhashram, the ashram of Sage Vishwamitra, also known as Kaushik. There, they would learn to wield celestial weapons and practice yoga to overcome hunger, sleep, thirst, and fatigue.

Following their training, Vishwamitra would take them to Videha for Ram's marriage to Princess Sita, the daughter of King Siradhwaj. On Vishwamitra's advice, King Siradhwaj organized an open competition for Sita's hand in marriage. The challenge was to lift, bend, and string Pinak, the enormous bow of Lord Shiva. Aside from Lord Shiva himself, his disciple Parashuram, and Vishwamitra, no one else was known to handle the Pinak.

***

Vashisth blocked the way, halting the onward movement of Vishwamitra. He said, 'The king is coming; please don't go. He hadn't said no to you.'

Vishwamitra smiled wryly and said, 'Don't worry, my friend. I came here seeking a favour. It is up to the giver whether to oblige. I have no complaints. There is no reason to prolong my stay. Please let me go.'

'O the greatest among sages, you were once a king and a father too.'

'What has my past got to do with today's request?' asked Vishwamitra.

'It is a humble reminder that the king is an ordinary human being, and you must understand his feelings. Dashrath was childless for a long time and got his children very late in life when he had lost all hopes.'

The king joined them just then and paid deep obeisance to the guest. He said, 'Kindly forgive me for the insolence and return to your seat.'

'For what? You have made a decision and I wouldn't force you into changing it.'

When they were seated once again, Vashisth said, 'O the emperor of Sapta Sindhu, the visit of the Brahmarshi, who is next only to Lord Brahma, must be here with some superior purpose. He knows it but is not revealing. The Almighty is working through him. It is a lifetime opportunity for Ram to go with the sage. Don't stop him, don't block his path to higher learning and superior wisdom. In the end, you will be thankful to the Brahmarshi.'

The mystical words of Vashisth pacified Dashrath. He asked the sage, 'When do you want to leave?'

'Now.'

'Siddhashrama is far away. Let me arrange for chariots, security and the provisions.'

'No need for a chariot and provisions. Don't worry about the prince, I will ease his path,.' said Vishwamitra, comforting the worried king.

'My friend, I suggest Lakshman may also accompany Ram. He is the shadow of Ram and can't live without him. Together, they can achieve the most arduous-looking feats,' said Vashisth.

Travelling on foot with their preceptor, the two princes reached an arid forest. The ponds, lakes and other reservoirs had dried up. All the vegetation had almost disappeared, and green patches were nowhere visible. They found no life except for a few jackals and vultures in the area. Innumerable large and small stumps and broken beams of the trees lay everywhere. The sun-bleached bones of the humans and animals were scattered all over. There was no sign of any recent movement of the men or women in the ghastly forest. Ram asked his guru, 'Gurudev, what is this gruesome place? Why does it look so terrible?'

The sage told them how a beautiful yaksha princess changed into a fierce, ruthless, man-eater demoness. This demoness Tataka possessed the strength of one thousand elephants. Before Vishwamitra could complete the story, they could hear the approaching footsteps of the demoness. Soon Tataka, with a trident in her hands, loomed over them with her red, fire-spitting eyes, brows twitched in fury, and an open cavernous mouth. Holding her trident aloft, she thundered, 'This is my kingdom, the forest of Tataka. No outsider may enter the forest without my permission. I don't allow anyone to pass this way, but your arrival is welcome. It had been long since I enjoyed human flesh. You are sent by God so I don't remain hungry.'

Vishwamitra asked Ram to slay the demoness. But Ram's kshatriya dharma wouldn't allow him to kill a woman however evil she must be. The guru read his disciple's thoughts and said, 'O the descendant of Kukustha, Tataka is a monster and evil incarnate. You must not consider her just like any other woman. Killing a woman of evil intent is not against dharma. Lord Vishnu killed Tribhuvana, the wife of Sage Bhrigu and mother of Shukracharya, to save the gods from the atrocious asuras. She harboured the demons who took refuge in her ashram for the fear of Vishnu. Tribhuvana did not hand over the demons to Vishnu despite his repeated warnings and preferred death to betraying the escapees. Indra vanquished Manthara, the daughter of Virochana and granddaughter of Bhakta Prahlad, a woman who wanted to destroy the world. Indra, after killing Manthara, did not get infamy and earned the gratitude of humanity instead. You will do a great service to humanity by ridding the world of this evil-minded Tataka.'

Ram still appeared unconvinced. If Indra and Vishnu killed women under certain compelling circumstances, how could that be a justification for killing a widowed princess? Vishwamitra was alive to the inner conflicts of the prince. Ram was, after all, a role model or *maryada purushottam* to the world.

Vishwamitra continued, 'Never have mercy on the evil doers whether a man or a woman. The well-being of all the people, irrespective of their orientation, caste, creed, region or personal relations, is the basic duty of a prince. While performing his duties, a king may take certain decisions which are seemingly atrocious and brutal or lenient and merciful. Many times, his acts may be sinful and indictable, but the ultimate aim of such acts must be good for the people. You must, therefore, obey the command of your guru and kill the demoness.'

Ram touched the string of his bow, and a thunderous sound reverberated through the forest, making Tataka deaf. She shot her trident toward Ram and the prince cut it into fragments with a single shaft. She lifted the tree stumps and rocks and hurled them at the guru and his disciples. Ram was still unwilling to slay her. He asked Lakshman to mutate her nose and ears. Lakshman promptly fired three razor-faced shafts and sliced her ears and nose. The demoness was furious. She attacked an unarmed Vishwamitra with her mouth wide open to eat him. To save the life of his guru, Ram now had no choice but to kill her. With a single large iron shaft, he removed the head of the demoness from her body. Tataka fell on the barren land like a hillock stuck down by thunder.

Vishwamitra asked his disciples to go around and spread the news of Tataka's death. Let the people of Karush and Malad return to their homes. Sages like Agastya, who left Sundar Van and went to the Dandaka Forest, may also return if they wished to. To allay the fears of others, that night they stayed in Tatak Forest. It did not look as fearsome now as it did when they first entered. Next morning, Sage Vishwamitra, with Ram, Lakshman and other disciples following, proceeded to Siddhashram, which was on the bank of the holy river Ganga.

Siddhashram was a sacred place where Lord Vishnu undertook tapasya for one hundred yugas and performed countless yajnas. This rigorous meditation empowered him to fulfill his role as the Sustainer of the Universe.

During Vishnu's meditation, Mahabali, the grandson of Prahlad and son of Virochan, conquered both earth and heaven, subjugating them under his rule. The defeated gods, desperate to reclaim their lost realms, turned to Lord Vishnu for assistance.

Vishwamitra Kaushik recounted to Ram and Lakshman the story of Vishnu's intervention. In the guise of Vaman, a dwarf, Vishnu approached Mahabali and asked for three paces of land. With his first step, he measured the distance from earth to the sky; with the second, he covered the heavens. There was no space left for the third step.

Vaman then asked Mahabali where to place his final step. Overwhelmed by Vishnu's divine presence, Mahabali humbly offered his own body as the space for the third step. Vishnu then revealed his original four-armed form and granted Mahabali a boon. The demon requested the kingdom of the netherworld and asked to see Vishnu every morning. Vishnu agreed, promising to become the guardian of Mahabali's palace.

'This is Siddhashram, our destination for now. Here, I will conduct the yajna for the peace and prosperity of humanity. I will begin the ritual under your protection on the night of the full moon,' said Vishwamitra.

Many seers were present in the ashram, waiting for their leader. The preparations for the yajna were already in place. Meanwhile, the rakshasas came to know about the death of their leader Tataka and the performance of the yajna. Marichi and Subahu were furious at Ram and Lakshman because they killed their mother. They waited in the nearby forest, ready to seek revenge, armed with deadly weapons. As the yajna began, they shrieked and howled to distract the sages from pronouncing the mantras perfectly. They poured boiling water and blood and flung offal and excrement at the holy ground. The rakshasas bombarded the yajna mandapam with rocks and sticks and caused mayhem.

The sages were disgusted. Ram and Lakshman looked at Vishwamitra for instructions. The sage nodded his approval and Ram said to the gathered sages, 'Do not feel distraught. Please proceed with the yajna.'

Ram shot up his arrows, creating a canopy to shield the sacrificial arena. Lakshman shot at the rakshasas, killing many of them instantly. Marichi and Subahu came forward and challenged them, citing the name of their mother. Ram, remembering the tragic story of their life, warned them to retreat, but they did not heed. He picked up Manavastra, the least fierce among the celestial arrows, and shot at Marichi. The demon flew in the air several miles and landed on the ground with no physical injury. Ram aimed another shaft at Subahu, but before he could shoot, the demon jumped at him with a mighty sword. Ram sliced the sword into pieces and once again asked Subahu to go away. He instead returned with a trident and attacked Lakshman. Ram, losing no time, eliminated Subahu by separating his head from his body. The rakshasas who had gathered to support their commanders left Siddhashram in fear and panic. When Marichi saw the fate of his brother and desertion of his army, he returned to Lanka with the remaining rakshasas.

Sage Vishwamitra conveyed the message to Sage Bharadwaj, Atri and others about the flight of the rakshasas from their only sanctuary in the North Bharat, the area of the Aryan's dominance. Was it the beginning of the end of the mighty rakshasa empire? Only time would tell.

The sages promptly declared Ram a saviour, the seventh incarnation of Maha Vishnu, who took birth in the human form to eradicate evil from the face of the earth. They spread this message far and wide through the network of their ashrams. Vishwamitra taught Ram the esoteric knowledge of weaponry. He also gave him all the celestial weapons and imparted him with the mantras on how to use them. He told them the secrets of the Yaga and how, through its practice, one could have complete control over physical needs like hunger, thirst, sleep and fatigue. Having accomplished the desire, Vishwamitra asked the princes to accompany him to Mithila. 'King Siradhwaj is performing a great yajna and has requested every sage on earth to participate. The yajna will be followed by a swayamvar for the marriage of his daughter, Sita. All the kings and princes of the world will come to participate in the swayamvar. Let us be a part of the festivities.'

When Vishwamitra, Ram, Lakshman, other disciples and sages arrived near Mithila, they came across a deserted ashram. Ram asked his guru, 'Gurudev, what is this ashram? There is no sign of life. No one appears living here.'

The sage replied, 'It is the hermitage of Sage Gautam. You must have heard about him. Come, let us sit here in this ashram under this tree.' Sitting under an old banyan tree, Sage Vishwamitra told Ram and Lakshman the story of Gautam and his wife Ahalya.

Chapter 8

AHALYA

It is the story of the most beautiful woman in the three worlds, beautiful because Lord Brahma took special care while creating her. Brahma sought to embody the essence of beauty and virtue from across the universe. He drew upon the most stunning celestial features, the most graceful forms, and the most harmonious qualities—to fashion this being. The result of his divine efforts was a woman of unparalleled beauty and grace. Brahma named her Ahalya.

At its core, this is a story of human and divine frailties—the vulnerabilities of a revered sage, a god, and a virtuous woman. It explores the themes of unchecked desire and its catastrophic effects, delving into the domains of love, hatred, seduction, and vengeance.

Ahalya sat in the front row with other rishikas, fully absorbed in the yajna proceedings that were presided over by her husband, Sage Gautam. She sensed an intense gaze from someone among the participants as if a person watched her intently. She couldn't take her eyes away from the puja or turn her head to find out. That would be immodest. She felt a mild quiver on the back of her neck.

After some time, they paused the morning puja and prayers for a short while. Siradhwaj Janak, the King of Videha, and the *yagyaman* (host of the yajna) of the great sacrifice, introduced Ahalya and her husband to Shakra, the king of the gods. Ahalya could read his eyes and knew instantly it was Indra who had been staring at her. Today, for the first time after her marriage, she met him. The weird look in his eyes confounded Ahalya. She knew him well. He was a close friend of her brother Divodas. Gautam too knew him. They had met many times in the yajnas where he was invited to take part, and Indra came to collect his *rashabh* (share in the sacrifices). Janak completed the courtesy of their formal introduction. As the Lord of the gods, Indra was entitled to a share of all the sacrifices.

Gautam, a pious soul, couldn't feel the unease of his young wife. He invited Indra to be their guest at the ashram that was just outside Mithila, the capital city of Videha. Indra, with a charming smile, thanked him and accepted the invite. Ahalya was not too pleased about Indra's presence in their ashram. How Gautam could invite him after knowing everything, wondered Ahalya. Either he seemed overawed by his splendour and aura, or he was just being courteous. She gave a despairing look to her husband. Ahalya must speak to him at the first opportunity. It filled her mind with fleeting bitter-sweet memories of Indra's single-minded pursuit of a young unmarried princess.

The king of celestials, Indra, possessed the finest treasures of the three worlds. His unparalleled riches included the seven-trunked white elephant Airavat, the Kalpavriksha, the wish-fulfilling tree, Kamadhenu, the divine cow and the celestial tree Parijat, among many wonders. He wielded the vajra, an infallible weapon of thunder, and commanded the forces of storms and rain. All the gods, including the sun, moon, Varun, Shani, and Vayu, were under his command. Additionally, he was served by eleven of the most enchanting celestial nymphs, including Rambha, Menaka, Urvashi, and Tilottama.

Indra came to know from his bards and minstrels about a teenage princess on the earth who was more beautiful than all his apsaras put together. He, out of curiosity, came down from Alkapuri, the capital city of the gods, to meet the girl. If she was as gorgeous as they made her out to be, he must have her. He was the Lord of the lords, and everything best must belong to him.

King Mudgal wanted to give Indra a grand reception because he was coming to his kingdom for the first time. He would request him to stay over for a few days. The threat from Shambarasur haunted the father and his young son, Divodas. With Indra on their side, the asuras wouldn't dare attack Vidarbha.

King Mudgal and Queen Nalayani waited outside the palace to receive Indra near the arched gate specially made for the occasion. Their daughter, Ahalya, with the puja thali made of gold, in her long, slender hands, was by their side. They decorated the palace with flowers and colourful banners. Chatursam was spread all over the place for fragrance. Many citizens, men and women, nobles and ministers, stood near the gate with flowers. Two men clambered down from the chariot and entered the palace gate. They were Divodas and Indra. The king and queen paid Indra due obeisance and guided him to the royal assembly. Ahalya showed her respect to the distinguished guest by joining her palms, slightly bowing her head and lowering her doe eyes. The royal couple provided him accommodation in the main palace and not the adjoining guest-palace as was the practice.

The adorable girl holding the overflowing puja plate struck Indra. He couldn't take his eyes off her. Her marine blue silk garments stressed her pinkish-white colour. She looked completely unblemished and pure. When their eyes met, her pink cheeks turned scarlet. Indra felt a sudden rush of blood in his brain, beating the veins of his temples. She was more beautiful than he was told. Her ethereal beauty was beyond description however hard a poet, author, bard or singer tried. Her mother was saying something to Indra, but he was barely listening to her. His unabashed glare made her uncomfortable and Ahalya felt embarrassed.

Ahalya through her lowered eyes, had a good look at Indra. He was an honoured guest and a friend of her brother, a friend who had helped Divodas in defending their country against the attack of Shambarasur. The demon was defeated but not destroyed and could attack again. Indra was a handsome person with above average height, fair-skinned and lion-like shoulders. His features were sharp and attractive. He was as perfect as anyone could be. Was she attracted to him at first sight, Ahalya thought?

The princess of Vidarbha had heard about the victories, power, influence, bravery and wealth of Indra. She had heard about the grandeur of Amaravati and about the beautiful women who surrounded him. How beautiful was his wife Shachi! This all looked so impressive from every angle. Any other girl would have accepted it as a great favour by Indra, but not this girl. She did not have that feeling of crazy, overwhelming attraction for him that a teenage girl would otherwise have for a lover. No doubt he wanted her, but he did not love her. She neither wanted to be with him nor loved him.

Mudgal, Indra, and Divodas sat together to discuss their strategy to vanquish Shambarasur once and for all. They captured most of his forts on the southern peninsula of Jambudwip in the previous battles. The demon king took shelter in his impregnable fort named Vaijayanta at the Dandaka. The king of the gods proposed a joint attack on Fort Vaijayanta. His idea was to take Dashrath, the emperor of Koshala, and Ashwapati, the king of Kaikeya, with them. The joint operation by the armies of the gods, Vidarbha, Koshala and Kaikeya, could break into the impregnable fort and defeat the demon king. Indra would go to Ayodhya to meet Dashrath, and Divodas was to meet Ashwapati.

Following the advice of Guru Vashisth, they sent Ahalya to the ashram of Maharshi Gautam for further studies. His ashram was in the northeast of Jambudwip in the kingdom of Videha. Vashisth told Mudgal that Gautam was one of the greatest among the sages of Jambudwip. He was one of the legendary Seven Sages or the Saptarishis and was credited with having discovered mantras in Sanskrit. He contributed many hymns to the Rig Veda. His ashram was a great place of learning, a sort of university or highest place of excellence, and students from all over the world came here to get admission. Some of his famous disciples included Shandilya, Gargya, Bharadwaj and others.

Ahalya was determined to pursue higher learning, while her mother was eager for her to marry as soon as possible. At sixteen, Ahalya was already sought after by many kings and princes, with Indra being a notable contender and a favourite of Ahalya's mother. So, when the king informed his daughter of her upcoming stay at Sage Gautam's gurukul, she was overjoyed. However, she was not told the whole truth: her stay was primarily for her safety and not for her higher education. Although her brother, Divodas wanted to escort her to Gautam's ashram, Ahalya chose to travel alone with a small security detail to Mithila. After her departure, Divodas turned his attention to preparing for the impending battle.

Gautam's initial reservations about the princess were allayed within a week of her arrival. The sage had made it a practice to accept the students at an early stage for their initiation into a new life. Further, he preferred not to have children from the royal families. It was difficult for them to get adjusted to the atmosphere of the ashram, so used to their cloistered lifestyles. He told his friend Vashisth that he didn't accept older students, but the princess was welcome to the gurukul, live with them and attend the classes of her interest. 'She wouldn't be my student, but I will guide and teach her. We wouldn't have a guru-shishya (teacher-student) relationship as you do.'

The Kuladhipati or the Chancellor Sage Gautam welcomed Ahalya in his gurukul. He informed Ahalya that she was not in the ashram as his pupil. She was under his protection, and he would act as her guardian. 'Then what am I doing here? I came to Mithila to study from you and you say you wouldn't teach me! Do you wish to send me back?'

'That's not the entire truth, princess. You're not just an ordinary student here. You're welcome to attend classes and absorb as much knowledge as you can. Our ashram is a centre of wisdom where learning transcends age, gender, status, and wealth. Knowledge is like an ocean, and it's the capacity of the vessel that determines how much water it can hold. Anyone who seeks knowledge will find it. Feel free to consult me if you have any questions or need clarification.

'I don't understand a thing when you say I am under your protection, Guru-ji. Why do I need to be under your protection as long as I have my father and elder brother?'

'Your kingdom may be attacked by Shambarasur any day, or he has already attacked. The asura king knows about the grand alliance Indra is forming against him. He wants to pre-empt and take advantage of a surprise attack by choosing the time of attack as per his convenience. His strategy is to face them one by one by not giving them a chance to unite and attack.'

'But what am I doing here? My mother is alone in the palace. Why did no one tell me about the asura's attack?'

'They knew you would not agree to come here leaving the queen on her own,' said Gautam in a gentle, reassuring voice. 'The queen is in the palace. She refused to move out. Guru Vashisth had persuaded her to shift to his ashram in case of any danger to the capital and the king's palace.'

Ahalya was sobbing, her soft lotus palms on her pale, bloodless face. Her last few days in the palace flashed before her eyes; why her perseverance for higher education was suddenly agreed to by her father; even mother, who earlier opposed her entry into the ashram, seemed to have fallen in line; Ahalya could proceed without many preparations and any loss of time; why her brother, always so caring, did not insist on accompanying her to Mithila.

Her family was in great danger, and she sat here, far away from them, in the safety of this ashram; that was inexpiable. Gautam, as if reading her mind, said, 'Don't you have confidence in the bravery of your father and brother? Haven't they already done that many times in the past?'

'I know they will defeat the asuras and kill Shambarasur. Divodas has taken a vow to finish him this time. Last time, pitying him, he let him go after overpowering him.'

'Then why are you crying?'

Gautam sat with her almost the whole evening. He told her to make the best use of her time by focusing on her studies and maximizing her learning during her stay in the ashram. He believed her stay would not be too long. By the time Gautam left, Ahalya felt a lot better.

Sitting in her hut alone, she thought of her host. Gautam, the Kuladhipati of the ashram, was a tall, thin, middle-aged man in the prime of his life. He had a broad forehead, dark brown, glinting eyes under thick eyebrows, a sharp nose, and a large mouth with petal-thin lips. His facial hair covered his face with no visible chin and cheeks and a long jet-black beard. He was not handsome like Indra, but had a certain elegance of spiritual power and mental agility that made him attractive. His voice was soft and persuasive, exuding calmness.

Ahalya impressed Gautam and the teachers with her intelligence and noble character. She won over the students, by her gentle smile and down-to-earth behaviour. The students quickly overcame their initial apprehensions about her royal origins and became friendly to her. She was a fast learner and finished her lessons on a day-to-day basis. Her hard work and agility amazed Gautam.

Ahalya didn't know when she began to like Gautam. She always wanted to be in his company and used to find some excuse to remain close to him. With no perceptible sign, she presumed that Gautam too enjoyed being with her. Many times, she would change her path, would rather take a longer one, to bump into him.

Sitting alone in her hut, she found herself smiling for no apparent reason. Her thoughts were consumed by Gautam, replaying his every word and gesture, however small. In conversations with others, she would inadvertently mention his name, revealing her preoccupation. The once-ignored birds in her garden, now observed with fresh eyes, seemed to dance in pairs, reflecting her feelings. She watched a peacock and its peahens with rapt attention, mesmerized by their courtship.

The sky appeared more vividly azure, the flowers seemed to bloom with greater intensity, and the birds sang with an enthusiasm that mirrored her own heart.

This was happening in her mind, but it did not distract her from her studies. The reason was, however, different now. She wanted to impress Gautam with her studies, and each word of appreciation made her work harder. The days were rushing away, and it was a little over a year since her arrival that the news of the death of Shambar and his son, Trighnasur, reached the ashram. The descendants of Puru had won decisively, and they gave the largest share of credit for such a comprehensive victory to Kaikeyi, the warrior queen of Koshala, who not only saved the life of King Dashrath but also won the battle commanding the Koshala Army. Indra also contributed to a great extent. King Mudgal was holding a victory celebration to honour Indra. The messenger told Gautam that shortly Prince Divodas would come to Mithila to take the princess with him. Ahalya had obscure feelings. She was happy that the demons were vanquished once and for all, but she was not yet ready to return to Kampala.

Ahalya travelled back to the palace in the company of her brother. How relieved she was looking at him, alive and smiling. Her throat choked with emotions and tears streaming down her cheeks. Divodas took his sister in a close embrace, wiping her tears. He had so much to tell her about his victory, his exploits, and how his friend Indra had declared him the greatest warrior on the earth. She listened to him in complete silence, occasionally nodding her head. Divodas looked at her wan face and suddenly asked, 'Aren't you happy returning home and meeting mother and father?'

'I am happy about your victory, that everyone is safe, and you got the well-deserved recognition in the entire Jambudwip.

I am happy and waiting to see my mother who lived without us all alone, praying for your safety and victory.' Ahalya paused as if she held back her thoughts and could not decide how far she could reveal. She was so despondent and secretive that Divodas allowed her time to settle her thoughts.

'Then what is the problem? He was surprised at her strange, subdued behaviour, never seen before.

'Because after living in the palace with you, mother and father for some time, I want to return to the ashram to continue my studies. But mother wouldn't allow that,' she said.

What she couldn't tell him was she wanted to return to the ashram as much for her studies as to be with Gautam. She longed to be near him, to learn from him and discuss with him things for hours, sitting under a thatch or beneath a tree with her back against the trunk. She felt incomplete without him.

Gautam was not in the ashram when Ahalya and Divodas left. The prince stayed overnight in the ashram, waiting for the sage. In the morning, his disciples informed the prince that it would take some more time for Gautam to return to the ashram. His deliberate absence overwhelmed Ahalya. Was it his way of showing his love? She was not sure? Was it his disappointment with her? After the messenger from Kampala, Gautam had gone quiet. His gentle and caring behaviour had suddenly turned cold and sometimes intimidating. He ignored her presence and kept away from her. His tender behaviour was now of open indifference, if not contempt, as if she deserted him on purpose.

The sage treated Ahalya like any other student, initially indifferent to her transcendental beauty and imperial upbringing. But he didn't know when she won his heart. After her departure, sitting in his hut alone, he wanted to hear her voice again, to sit with her under a tree and talk to her as they often did. He never felt such a sensation in his life, so strange to a person of such spiritual prominence. Had he fallen in love with her? He knew the answer, but did not acknowledge it.

Gautam was aware of his limitations. Indra was after her, he knew. Ahalya's mother was pushing her husband to agree to Indra's proposal, and her brother sided with the mother. But her father had so far resisted. He was in favour of giving complete freedom to his daughter in selecting her life partner. Gautam, for the first time in his life, was uncertain about himself. He was not as attractive as Indra or other princes and kings vying for Ahalya's attention, but he was better than them in knowledge, mental agility and ingenuity. Why should he presume Ahalya would prefer Indra over him? She was an intelligent girl who respected the inner strength of a person more than his external appearance. He had visited and revisited this argument repeatedly since she had left the ashram.

The moot question was what Ahalya wanted. Whether she loved him, or it was her respect for him as her protector and teacher. She never expressed her love for him. But the same was the case with Gautam. It was only after she had left that he realized how important she became in his life. He felt like leaving everything and going to the Himalayas for tapasya because life without Ahalya wouldn't be worth living. He must consult his friend and the Rajguru of King Mudgal, Sage Vashisth, before taking any decision.

Mudgal was with his guru. Vashisth always gave him sane council in conformity with the social aspects and scriptural righteousness. The king was worried about the haughty pursuit of Indra to marry his daughter. Mudgal knew his daughter's mind but could not oppose the advances of the mighty king of the gods. That too when his wife and son both supported Indra. Mudgal said, 'Gurudev, Ahalya doesn't want to marry Indra. I am also not in favour of this marriage.'

'But why? Indra is the most eligible person to marry your daughter. Don't you think so?'

'No Guru-ji, Indra is not suitable for Ahalya. The humans, celestials and *dasyus* have different social beliefs. They don't think alike. Marriage is the most beautiful relationship between a man and a woman, provided it is a marriage of two souls and two minds. The marriages between the immortals and humans have never succeeded in the past. It will fail again.'

Vashisth nodded in affirmative. Indra was a lecherous, selfish and petulant god but as he was the king of the gods and controlled rain and storms, all feared him.

'With many of his imperfections, I would have agreed to this marriage, but my daughter's decision is my decision. Her happiness is my only concern.'

'Have you decided on another groom for your daughter?'

'No, not yet. I seek your guidance on the matter, Gurudev,' replied the king, his voice unusually soft.

Vashisth declared that Ahalya's marriage would be determined through an open competition. The first person going around the three worlds—heaven, earth and netherworld— would win Ahalya. Indra was the happiest among the contestants. He used his magical powers to complete the challenge. He finally reached Vashisth and demanded the hand of Ahalya. But Vashisth told him that Gautam went around the three worlds before Indra.

Vashisth explained Gautam circumambulated Surabhi while she gave birth to a calf. As per the Vedas, the cow at the time of bearing a calf was equal to the three worlds. Indra was adamant and not ready to accept the words of Vashisth. The matter came up to the king for his decision, who left it to Ahalya. It surprised no one in the family when Ahalya chose Gautam as her husband. They were married shortly and

Ahalya, now a rishika, left the palace for her dream home, the thatched hut of Gautam's ashram. Ahalya proved a perfect wife, and they lived happily.

Indra's ego was damaged badly. He lost against a worthless seer who was no match for his physical prowess, beauty and splendour. How many times did he go to the palace to meet her uninvited? He trained her brother in weaponry and battlecraft and went to war with him. Clearly, for Indra, it was an act of betrayal. The brother and sister both were so selfish. A wounded lion was more dangerous than a hungry one. Indra could never overcome his infatuation for Ahalya. He waited for his chance and sought revenge. He often came near the ashram in a different guise to watch Ahalya from a distance. But fearing the anger of Gautam and rebuke from Ahalya, he never entered the ashram gate.

After the yajna, Gautam and Ahalya returned to their ashram. Ahalya told her husband about her apprehension and why she was not comfortable with Indra in their ashram. Gautam assured her that there was nothing to worry, and he would keep a watch on the king of gods. Ahalya couldn't explain her innermost feeling of an imminent premonition to her husband. The next day, Indra arrived. He had left his staff in the palace of Siradhwaj and came alone in his chariot. Gautam had made arrangements for his stay in a large hut next to his own.

The exemplary behaviour of Indra allayed within a couple of days Ahalya's fears. He followed the trying daily schedule meant for the students, starting early in the morning and continuing until late evening. He helped Gautam in the farm and cowshed. Most of his time was spent with Gautam and he hardly looked at Ahalya. She was now a married woman and a rishika. But she was a young and extremely good-looking woman and being ignored by someone who was so much after her before the marriage disturbed her. It always felt good to be validated, wanted, and appreciated. Ahalya sought Indra's attention by taking care of his daily needs personally. Gradually, he warmed up to her friendly gestures, and they got along well, many times talking about Kampala and her family. Occasionally, Gautam also joined them in their conversations.

While in the ashram, Indra watched the habits of the sage and noticed that Gautam used to leave his ashram daily at dawn and was away for a couple of hours for his bath and prayers at the river. Indra never got over his infatuation and to teach a lesson to Ahalya and Gautam got her by subterfuge. Assuming the form of Gautam, he entered Ahalya's hut after her husband left. She felt someone entering her bed. Was Gautam back, she thought, almost sleepy? But what made him return to bed? The figure moved close, almost brushing her head to toes, and pulled her even closer, holding her waist. His hands massaged her bare back, sliding up from her waist. But the touch was so different, so unknown. No, that was not Gautam; she froze, staring at the man in her bed realizing instantly that he was not Gautam.

Ahalya was fully awake now, her eyes wide and alert. She turned to see that the figure beside her was not Gautam, but Indra in disguise. Her disdain for the intruder surged within her. 'Don't be afraid, Ahalya,' Indra said with a smirk. 'No one will ever find out about our affair. After our time together, I'll return swiftly as Gautam. I know you crave affection too, don't you?'

Ahalya shook with rage. 'How dare you come in? Aren't you afraid of the curse of a chaste woman and—'

Before Ahalya could complete the sentence, Indra's powerful hand pressed against her mouth and his tall and athletic body pinned her under him. He tore apart her clothes, ignoring her vehement protestations. Her hands pushed him away without success, her fingernails clawed on his bare shoulders. That was the moment Gautam entered the hut. While on his way to the river, he intuitively felt that something was wrong. Indra wanted to escape, thrashing the sage away, but Gautam stood upright on his way. He cursed Indra to get castrated by losing his testicles forthwith.

'Your body has sinned. You cannot take part in the sacrifices as my wife anymore. I know you are not at fault, but your body has certainly become impious. I am abandoning you and leaving the ashram with my disciples. When a righteous person born to eliminate evils will come this way and accept you back in society, that will be your redemption.'

Vishwamitra completed the story here. Lakshaman, always eager to listen to the stories, asked, 'What happened after that Gurudev? Where is Ahalya now?'

'Lakshman, you must address her with respect. She is like a mother to us,' reprimanded Ram.

'Ram is right. Rishika Ahalya is an illustrious and chaste lady. She was a princess and could have married a king and lived in a palace, but she chose the life of a rishika instead. The story had stayed still for the past twenty-five years. Ram, it's time to put an end to the ordeal of Ahalya.'

Vishwamitra and the two princes entered the ashram. The sage pushed the door of the hut and it opened. Ahalya, who was meditating, opened her eyes. Recognizing Vishwamitra, she went into hiding, unwilling to show her face. He was the first human she had seen in the last twenty-five years.

'Brahmarshi, why have you come to this forsaken place? No one ever came this way after Gautam left.'

'Please come out, Ahalya, and see who is here to seek your blessings,' said Vishwamitra.

'You know I am a sinner. How can I bless anyone?'

'You are pure and unblemished. You don't have to hide from the world.'

She came forward hesitatingly, her face glowing from her long ascetic devotion. She saw Ram and Lakshman standing with the sage, who introduced them as the sons of King Dashrath of Ayodhya. The guru then directed the princes to pay her their obeisance. They bowed to her and touched her feet in complete veneration, the act that restored her social status. Ram thereafter became the redeemer of the guilty and sinner.

Chapter 9

SITA

There were celebrations all around in Mithila. Rain had arrived in the parched lands. Now the people of Videha in Mithila would be able to cultivate food grains and live happily. King Janak was the happiest person in the world. His beloved kingdom of Mithila was facing severe drought, and the king had approached Sage Ashtavakra for a solution to the problem. The wise sage had advised the desperate king to plough the land with a golden plough with his own hands and the solution would be automatically presented to him by the Supreme Lord. While using the plough on a field, King Janak discovered a baby girl wrapped in a silken cloth, kicking her little legs joyously in a basket. The girl had a lovely smile on her face and was so beautiful that Janak could not help hugging her close to his chest. He looked around to see whether any person would come forward to own her. But after waiting for a few minutes, he decided that this sweet little child was a gift from God and he took her to his Queen Sunaina. The royal couple, who were childless till then, considered this child to be the daughter of

Goddess Earth (Bhumi Devi) as he had found her while tilling the land and named her Sita. The moment of the appearance of infant Sita coincided with the moment rains poured over Mithila. Janak and Sunaina were overjoyed as were their subjects, and they decided to adopt the child and bring her up as their daughter. Thus, Sita became Janaki, the daughter of Janak. She was also known as Mythili and Vaidehi, the princess of Mithila and Videha, the regions ruled by King Janak.

Sita is considered as an incarnation of Goddess Mahalakshmi and her advent on earth is said to be because she wanted to join Lord Vishnu's avatar Ram and help him in his fight against evil and provide justice on earth.

King Janak was known for his wisdom and broad-mindedness in those times. His penchant for providing quality education for everyone regardless of caste or gender made him one of the most respected kings. Within a short while, after Sita was adopted, Maharani Sunaina gave birth to a daughter called Urmila. King Janak's brother, Kushadwaja, and his wife Chandrabhaga, also had two daughters Mandavi and Shrutikirti. The three younger sisters were in awe of Sita and loved her more than their lives. All four girls were educated in all forms of arts and even weaponry and warfare. They grew up to be beautiful and talented young women. There has been an ancient Shiva Dhanush in King Janak's possession since the times of his predecessors. It was by accident that Janak happened to see Sita lift the table on which the Shiva Dhanush was placed for worship. And he was stunned! The powerful Shiva Dahnaush, which could not be lifted by many strong men together, was nonchalantly being moved by his young daughter all by herself in her search for a ball that had fallen there while playing with her sister Urmila.

King Janak thought to himself, 'Sita is not an ordinary young woman. She is divine. And with her divine qualities, it becomes my responsibility as her parent to give her in marriage to a man equally divine and powerful.'

He made a decision then and there. He would give Sita in marriage to a man who could lift the Shiva Dhanush, which she had lifted so effortlessly. When Sita's swayamvar was announced, he sent invitations to all the powerful kings and princes in the vicinity. The precondition for winning the beautiful Princess Janaki's hand was the ability to lift the sacred Shiva Dhanush.

The first time Sita saw Ram is beautifully described in the Kamba Ramayan, and it was not during, but before the swayamvar event. It was love at first sight for both of them. Sita fervently prayed at the Mata Gauri temple to make Sri Ram her husband, before she proceeded to the palace for the swayamvar. Her wish was echoed by all her three sisters, who felt that the handsome and calm Sri Ram was the best possible choice for Sita's varmala.

As expected, there were many kings and princes who were enraptured by her beauty and wanted to try lifting the Shiva Dhanush. But each of them failed. Ram and Lakshman were at the swayamvar as protégés of Vishwamitra. Stories of their valour against the dreadful demoness Tataka and the divine redemption of Ahalya had preceded their arrival. When King Janak expressed his disappointment at not finding even one capable person who could lift the Shiva Dhanush, Lakshman sprang up to say that such a statement could not be made where his brother Sri Ram was present. It was at Vishwamitra's bidding that Sri Ram got up, prostrated before his guru and the Shiva Dhanush, and lifted it with ease. While he was stringing the bow, it broke with a thunderous sound. Sita was overjoyed.

Her sisters and her parents were also happy and relieved. They accompanied her as she walked towards Sri Ram to garland him with the *varmala*.

Meanwhile, the loud sound of the breaking of the Shiva Dhanush disturbed the meditation of Sage Parashuram. His anger was visible as he walked firmly into the palace.

'Stop,' he shouted. Seeing the sacred Dhanush broken into two, he could not control his fury.

'Who broke this?'

Sri Ram smiled and said, 'I did, revered sage.'

'Parashuram angrily turned to look at Ram, but his anger melted as he could envision Mahavishnu in Sri Ram's face. He realized that Sri Ram was the next avatar of Mahavishnu and was getting married to Sita, who was the incarnation of Goddess Mahalakshmi. He blessed them both and went away peacefully, much to the relief of King Janak and Sage Vishwamitra.

King Dashrath, his queens, and Bharath and Shatrughna were then informed and invited to Mithila by King Janak. Vishwamitra was contemplating the forthcoming marriage of Sri Ram and Sita when it suddenly occurred to him that Sita's three sisters could be married to Ram's three brothers. The sage suggested this and it was mutually decided by the kings of both the countries, that Sita's three sisters would be given in marriage to Ram's three brothers. Bharat was to marry Mandavi, Urmila to Lakshman and Shrutikirti to Shatrughna.

The marriage of all the four couples took place in the same hall at the same auspicious moment. The four couples sought blessings from their parents. King Janak and his brother Kushadhwaja, along with their queens Sunaina and Chandrabhaga, tearfully bid adieu to their beloved daughters, as they accompanied their respective husbands to Ayodhya.

The kingdom of Ayodhya was enraptured by the arrival of the new brides. People expressed their joy in various ways. But no one was prepared for what was going to ensue later. Everyone who has read or heard of the Ramayana knows about the sequence and far-reaching effects of these events. The departure of Bharat and Shatrughna to the kingdom of Kaikeya, the announcement of Ram's coronation, Manthara's poisoning of Kaikeyi's mind and Kaikeyi demanding her pending two boons from King Dashrath, one being Bharat's coronation and the other being Ram's exile for fourteen years from Ayodhya. Ram prepared to leave for the forest to respect his father's words. Though Ram tried to stop her, Sita was adamant about accompanying Ram saying that she wanted to perform her wifely duties. Lakshman, who could never be separated from Ram, decided to go with them and guard them against any harm. Urmila, though she wanted to accompany her husband, was requested by Lakshman to remain behind and she sadly agreed. King Dashrath could not bear the separation from his beloved son and collapsed thereafter. Bharat and Shatrughna were called urgently to perform their father's funeral rites.

Meanwhile, the exiled trio of Ram, Sita and Lakshman had crossed the Ganga river on a boat rowed by Guha, a close tribal friend and devotee of Sri Ram. They reached the Bharadwaja Ashram at Prayagraj, where they sought the blessings and advice of Sage Bharadwaja before they left for the Dandakaranya forest to spend their exile. They reached Chitrakoot, a picturesque spot, where Ram and Sita sat mesmerized by the ecological beauty of the place. A mountain with its peak almost seeming to touch the sky made it more attractive with the chirping sound of birds of every kind, this was exactly where the divine couple decided to spend their exile. As per their wish, Lakshman built a sturdy hut at Chitrakoot. Ram and Sita are said to have stayed happily for a major part of their exile at Chitrakoot. The famous Ram-Bharat Milap also took place at Chitrakoot.

After finishing King Dashrath's funeral rites, Bharat and Shatrughna, along with their mothers and their wives, decided to search for Ram and bring him back to Ayodhya. Almost everyone capable of walking in Ayodhya accompanied them, such was everyone's love for Ram. But when they found him, Ram refused to return to Ayodhya for fourteen years. Bharat came back with his brother's sacred *paduka*s and placed them on the throne. He also decided to lead an ascetic's life and lived in a hermit's hut with Mandavi at Nandigram on the outskirts of Ayodhya. Shatrughna and Shrutikirti helped Bharat in the administration of the kingdom in the absence of Ram.

Chitrakoot was also the place where Ram and Sita met Sage Atri and his chaste spouse Anusuya and sought their blessings. Anusuya is said to have explained the importance of *satitva* (chastity and total devotion to one's husband) to Sita. Anusuya then offered Sita some surprisingly magnificent and divine gifts, apparel that would never fade or become dirty, a garland of flowers that would never wither, jewels, a scented cosmetic and a divine body cream that would keep her body ever-youthful. Sita accepted the gifts with humility and love.

After visiting and seeking the blessings of many hermits and sages in the Chitrakoot region, Ram, Sita and Lakshman made their way deeper into the Dandakaranya forests. They reached Panchavati, the land of five Banyan trees, on the banks of the river Godavari. They were peacefully living here, when once, Surpanakha, the sister of Ravan, happened to lay her eyes on Ram and fell in love with him. She changed her appearance to that of a beautiful young woman and tried to lure Ram. He refused to be attracted by her beauty. She then tried to lure Lakshman, who was even more nonchalant and impervious to her charms. Surpanakha realized that Sita was the main cause of their refusal. She was extremely jealous and tried to harm her. This is when Ram signalled Lakshman to give her a suitable punishment and Lakshman cut off her nose. Seeing Surpanaka in such a pitiable state, the mighty demons Khara and Dushana summoned their huge army to fight against Ram and Lakshman. But the brothers were adept at killing demons and vanquished them and their armies. In pain and bleeding, Surpanakha went to Lanka and complained to her brother Ravan about the incident. Ravan was justifiably angry. But what Surpanakha said next changed the course of events to follow.

'Brother, I saw Sita. She is the most beautiful woman in the world,' she exclaimed. 'But one has to be careful, as her husband and his brother vanquished the mighty armies of Khara and Dushana. So, you can imagine their power and strength.'

Hearing about the matchless beauty of Sita, Ravan wanted to see her. But Surpanaka's words in praise of Ram's strength made him think twice.

He decided to use the services of Marich, his uncle, to kidnap Sita.

Marich had first-hand experience with the power and strength of Ram and did not want to face him. However, when Ravan threatened him, he decided that death at the hands of pious Ram was preferable to death at the hands of evil Ravan. Marich took the appearance of a beautiful golden deer and walked in front of the hut where Sita lived.

The golden deer was so attractive that Sita wanted to have it. She pleaded with Ram to get it for her. Since she had never expressed a wish for anything before, Ram agreed but cautioned Lakshman to not leave Sita under any circumstances. The deer led him away to a far distance and when Ram killed the deer with an arrow, the deer, who was, in reality, Marich, screamed in Ram's voice, 'Lakshman, Sita, save me! Lakshman, save me!'

Sita was perturbed. She asked Lakshman to go and save his brother. But Lakshman in deference to his brother's orders refused.

'Nothing can happen to Ram Bhaiyya, Mata,' he said. 'He is the lord of the three worlds.' But Sita was not convinced. Ram's voice imploring for help from both of them kept ringing in her ears.

'Lakshman, please go and help your brother, I beg of you!'

'Mata, Bhaiyya has ordered me to not leave you alone. Please be convinced that no harm will befall Ram Bhaiyya.'

Sita got frustrated and angry. She started blaming Lakshman for not helping Ram as he had evil intentions towards her and his brother. This hurt Lakshman. Still, he insisted that he had never disobeyed his brother till then. Sita's next words pierced his heart as she insinuated that he was in connivance with Bharat waiting for Ram to die so they could usurp the kingdom. Lakshman closed his ears. He could not bear to hear any further. With no choice left, unwillingly, he left the hut but not before he had drawn a circle around the hut with a darba grass reciting some mantras.

'Mata, I am leaving to help my brother as per your wish. Please don't leave the hut for any reason. I have drawn this circle round the hut which will protect you as long as you remain insidc the hut.'

He then left for the forest. This circle or *rekha* drawn by Lakshman for the protection of Mata Sita became famous as 'Lakshman Rekha'.

Ravan was waiting for this opportunity when both the brothers were not there with Sita. He disguised himself as a Brahmin and arrived at her doorstep to ask for alms. Sita, the daughter of Janak and Sunaina, had been brought up to respect Brahmins and offer *bhiksha* (offerings). When Ravan approached as a Brahmin, her first thought was to respectfully offer him food. Ravan wanted to follow her into the hut, but the Lakshman Rekha spewed up flames as soon as he set his feet or hands on it. He understood that he would have to trick Sita to come out of the hut. When Sita returned with food, she remembered Lakshman's words and asked Ravan to take it from outside the Lakshman Rekha.

Ravan pretended to be furious.

'Do you think I am a beggar that I have to accept food from you from a distance? Won't you offer me water and a proper *aasan* (seating mat)to sit and have my food in peace?' he asked.

Sita was in a dilemma, but her sense of reverence to Brahmins won over her anxiety to not cross the Lakshman Rekha. As soon as she crossed it, Ravan turned into his original self and took her away in his magical flying vehicle to Lanka.

Sita's cry for help was heard by an aged bird, Jatayu, who was a good friend of King Dashrath. Jatayu tried to protect Sita, by first talking to Ravan about his sense of righteousness. How could Ravan justify carrying away another man's lawfully wedded wife against her wishes? But Ravan was in no mood to hear Jatayu's wise words and asked him to leave his path. The bird then fought with all his strength to make it difficult for Ravan to move ahead. The demon king lost his temper and chopped off his wings. The huge bird fell to the ground and was left to die by Ravan who proceeded on his journey. Sita could not bear to see Jatayu's slaughter. Yet, she requested the dying bird to inform her husband about her abduction. She then turned towards Ravan.

'You thief!' she screamed, her eyes red with anger and grief and her frail body cowering away from Ravan. 'Is this your show of courage? Do you think people will laud your action of waiting for my husband to be away and then kidnapping me like a petty thief? The mighty king of Lanka fought a valiant old bird and killed him just because he dared to try and defend me?"

Just then, Ravan's flying vehicle passed above the Rishyamook mountain.

Sita, who was anxiously looking for someone to pass on information to her beloved husband, saw a group of monkeys atop the mountain. She cried again for help and tearing a piece of her garment, she wrapped her jewels and threw them to the monkeys.

Meanwhile, Ram and Lakshman returned to the hut to find it empty. They understood that something had gone horribly wrong in their absence. They started searching for Sita. On their way, they came across the dying Jatayu. Jatayu had held on to life just to inform Ram about Sita's abduction by Ravan. Ram performed funeral rites for the great bird. They then met the old devotee Shabari who directed them to the Rishyamook mountain, where Hanuman and Sugreev lived with a few of their friends. They were relieved to see the jewels of Sita wrapped in a piece of her garment as it meant she was still safe.

Ravan landed in Lanka with Sita in tow. But despite his pleadings and orders, Sita refused to enter his palace. So, she was kept in captivity at Ashok Vatika with lots of dangerous *rakshasis* standing on guard. Three women helped Sita retain some normalcy in her captivity: Trijata, the daughter of Vibhishan, who stood by her throughout her captivity and was her constant companion; Sarama who gave her solace and saved her from committing suicide; and Kala, Sarama's daughter, who informed her about the determination of Ravan to make her his wife.

Ram and Lakshman had requested Sugreev and Hanuman's help for searching Sita. When the group of monkeys led by Angad moved southwards, they reached the sea. Sampati, the brother of Jatayu, who had laid down his life to defend Sita against Ravan, informed them that Sita was held captive by Ravan in Lanka which was on the other side of the ocean. It was left to wise old Jambavan to remind Hanuman about his powers and his ability to cross the ocean. Hanuman reached Lanka by flying over the ocean and proceeded to search for Sita. He looked through the palaces of Ravan but did not find her. He finally came to Ashok Vatika where Sita was sitting under an Ashoka tree and holding a blade of *durva* (a type of grass used in religious occasions) in front to protect herself from Ravan, during his advances towards her. Her purity and single-minded devotion to Ram did not allow Ravan to even come near her as the grass would light up in flames. Her weeping face made Hanuman draw in his breath. She was so scared of Ravan's treachery that she would not believe anyone. How could Hanuman approach her and convince her that he was an emissary of her beloved husband? He looked at Ram's ring in his hand and devised a plan. He started softly chanting Ram's name and reciting the story of Ram right from birth up to the time Ram went to catch the golden deer. Sita was enchanted with the sound of Ram's name and looked around to see the sound's source. When her glance fell on Hanuman, perched atop the tree, she was stunned. Hanuman immediately took the opportunity to slowly come down to her. The recent events had made Sita wary of any person. She suspected that this could be a trick by Ravan. But Hanuman, with his usual guile and patience, praised Ram, and when he showed her the ring sent as identification by Ram, she was convinced that he was a messenger sent by her beloved husband. Seeing the ring brought tears to her eyes. She blessed Hanuman and asked him about the welfare of Ram and his dear brother. Hanuman assured her that they would come to Lanka to fight and retrieve her from the clutches of cruel Ravan. He told her about his first meeting with Ram and Lakshman. He told her about the ensuing friendship between Sugreev and Ram, Ram's vanquishing of Vali and the subsequent coronation of Sugreev. Sita sat listening to the recounting of Hanuman's search for her and his flight over the ocean into Lanka with rapt attention. When Hanuman suggested that he carry her away from Lanka and return her to her beloved Ram, Sita vehemently refused.

She said, 'Hanuman, my child, I know about your strength. But since I have been abducted and kept as a prisoner in Lanka for months, I want my husband, Ram, to come, fight the battle, defeat Ravan and take me back with honour.' Hanuman admired her love and belief in her husband's prowess. He asked Sita for something to show Ram as proof of him seeing her. Sita handed over her chudamani (jewel decorating the hair) and said, 'My Lord will recognize this as he had placed it in my hair. Also, tell him about the way he had punished the mischievous Kakasur, when he had had the temerity to attack me while Ram was resting on my lap. This is known only to my Ram and me.'

Then she told Hanuman to ask her husband to come speedily to rescue her from this painful captivity. Sita also blessed Hanuman that he would not feel the searing heat of fire or the sharpness of the cold.

Hanuman then decided to have a look at the Lankan palace and army for strategic reasons. He jumped into the neighbouring forest garden which had ripe and sweet fruits. His erstwhile hunger made him devour the fruits and he managed to destroy some of the trees in the process thereby attracting the attention of the Lankan army to himself. Though the guards and the army could not catch him, Indrajit, the son of Ravan, sent the Brahmastra against him. Hanuman allowed himself to be tied up and accompanied Indrajit docilely to the palace of Ravan. Seeing the havoc caused by the monkey, Ravan wanted to kill him but was stopped by Vibhishan.

'Let us hear what he has to say!' he exclaimed.

'I am Hanuman, a messenger from Sri Ram, whose wife you have unlawfully kidnapped,' said Hanuman boldly. 'My Lord is very powerful and has killed a whole lot of demons as you may already be aware. It is in your best interest that you hand over Sita Mata to him in a dignified way. Otherwise, my Lord will prove to be the cause of your death.'

Ravan was furious at hearing this from a mere monkey. Though Vibhishan restricted him from killing Hanuman, saying that it was not correct to harm a messenger, Ravan wanted to teach Hanuman a lesson. He asked his men to set fire to Hanuman's tail. They began to wrap the tail with cloth dipped in oil. But Hanuman was no ordinary monkey. The length of his tail continuously increased till all the cloth and oil in Lanka had been exhausted. They then lit the tip of the tail with fire. Hanuman flew up in the sky and swished his burning tail all over Lanka, thus almost burning up the entire Lanka. Because of Sita's boon, the fire did not have any effect on his skin. He dipped his burning tail in the ocean and flew back to Lord Ram.

Sita was sitting silently, contemplating what could have happened to Hanuman, when Trijata entered, exclaiming in excitement, 'The monkey has set Lanka on fire with his burning tail.' She proceeded to give an account of Hanuman's escapade and his return from Lanka. Sita felt reassured. Her Lord would now know her whereabouts, and she was certain that he would come to release her from Ravan's captivity.

Hanuman had succeeded in his mission. On hearing of Sita's safety, Ram, Lakshman and Sugreev led the Vanar Sena to the seashore. They built the bridge of stones with the help of the divine engineers, Nal and Neel. Nal and Neel had earlier received a boon that any stone thrown by them in water would not sink.

News of the construction of the bridge and Ram's arrival reached Sita through Sarama and Trijata. Hope kindled in Sita's heart. She prayed for his successful entry into Lanka.

In the palace of Ravan, there was an urgent discussion on the new development. Vibhishan, the righteous young brother of Ravan reiterated that Sita should be sent back to Ram. But Ravan was furious and banished Vibhishan from the palace. Vibhishan sought refuge at Ram's feet and he was accepted graciously by Ram.

The monkey army led by Ram and Lakshman was now ready to invade Lanka. The great battle began and one by one, the various generals and valiant sons of Ravan were killed. Kumbhakarna was awakened from his sleep. He expressed his opinion that Sita Mata should be sent back to Ram as Ravan had not won her after direct combat with her husband. He had stolen her away in his absence. But Ravan refused to be counselled. Kumbhakarna entered the battlefield and after some valiant efforts lost his life to Ram's arrow.

All the news of the battle was being delivered to Sita by Trijata. But one day Ravan entered thc Ashok Vatika with the slain heads of Ram and Lakshman. Sita fainted. When she recovered, she asked Trijata to prepare a funeral pyre for her. But Trijata reassured her that the slain heads were just illusions created by Ravan to confuse Sita. Later, when Indrajit struck Ram and Lakshman with his Nagaasthra, Sita was taken on a survey of the battlefield by Trijata under instructions from

Ravan. When she saw Ram and Lakshman lying unconscious, bound by the Nag Pash in its deathly grip, she was devastated. She was aware that the Nag Pash or serpent arrow was endowed with great magical powers. But Trijata once again assured her of their well-being after speaking to Vibhishan.

Sita also came to know of Indrajit's death from Trijata. Finally, the battle between Ram and Ravan took place which ended with the death of Ravan. With the permission of Ram and Vibhishan, the newly crowned king of Lanka, Hanuman went to Ashok Vatika to convey the news of Ram's victory to Sita. Her eyes were filled with tears of joy. When Hanuman saw the rakshasis who had been harassing Sita during her captivity, he expressed a desire to kill them. Sita's compassion is beautifully expressed in the words she speaks to Hanuman:

'No, my son. No one is blameless in this world. You are a noble soul. You must be compassionate towards sinners. And these poor women were not actually at fault. They were only obeying their king's orders. Their wicked king has been punished.'

She sent word through Hanuman that she was waiting to see her beloved husband. Hanuman delivered the message, but Ram's brow darkened. His attitude seemed to have suddenly changed. No one could read his mind when he asked that Sita be brought bedecked in fine clothes and jewels. Sita wanted to come to Ram as she was, but in deference to his wishes, she arrived as he wanted. The words next uttered by Ram were beyond comprehension.

'I have defeated Ravan and I have retrieved you. My duty as a Kshatriya has been fulfilled. But it does not give me joy as you are covered in the shadow of doubt. As a true Kshatriya, how can I accept you and live with you anymore, as you have spent so many months in the captivity of another man.'

Sita was stunned. Lakshman, Hanuman and Vibhishan stared at Ram in astonishment.

Her eyes emitting fire, Sita finally said, 'How could you even utter these words? Is it my fault that Ravan forcefully abducted me? I am pure and unsullied and you know it. Yet, since you have raised a doubt about my chastity, I will prove my innocence in the only way I can.'

She turned to Lakshman, who was looking disturbed and sad at his brother's words, and said, 'Create a pyre with wood faggots.'

Lakshman collected some wooden faggots and set them afire. Sita circumambulated the pyre, prostrated before her husband and looked up to the sky while saying, 'Oh gods and goddesses! O great sages! I, Janakanandini, Sita, offer you my namaskar. Oh, Agnidev (God of fire)! You are aware of my purity. So please accept me as your own.' She then jumped into the burning pyre.

From the fire appeared all the gods and Agnidev brought Sita out unblemished and unhurt. He offered her to Sri Ram who accepted her with joy. He then said, 'Think not, my dear, that I doubted your purity for a moment. It was only for the sake of our subjects, who may doubt that Ram had wavered from his Kshatriya dharma and given way to his desires and accepted his wife who had been in the dwelling of another man. I did not want that aspersion of doubt to be cast on you.'

The divine couple, accompanied by Lakshman, Hanuman and all their monkey friends, returned to Ayodhya via the Pushpaka Vimana. Bharat was overjoyed to see his beloved brother again and happily handed over the reins of the kingdom to Ram. The entire family was united again and the coronation of Ram was performed with great splendour.

It is said that Sita stayed happily with her husband and family in Ayodhya for some years. She was pregnant and everyone in the kingdom was happy. But one washer-man happened to tell his wife that he could not accept a woman who had lived outside his dwelling for even one day. He mentioned that he was not like King Ram, who had accepted his wife after so many months of separation. Ram overheard this conversation and that made him perturbed. Seeing her husband in an anxious state, Sita wanted to know the cause. It is not clear whether Ram took the decision to send Sita on exile once again to the forest or it was Sita's own decision to go away from Ayodhya to prove the greatness of her husband. Lakshman was ordered to drive a pregnant Sita to the forest and leave her. He had to obey the order of his brother although he didn't want this to happen. Fortunately, she was abandoned in the forest close to the Valmiki Maharshi Ashram. Sage Valmiki recognized her and kept her safely in his ashram with lady attendants to take care of her needs. Sita delivered her twins at this ashram and they were named Luv and Kush by Sage Valmiki. Luv and Kush grew up under the tutelage of Sage Valmiki and were adept at handling weapons as well as being well-trained in arts and singing. They learnt the verses of the Ramayana composed by Valmiki and are said to have mastered it musically.

Meanwhile, at Ayodhya, Ram was asked to perform the Ashwamedh Yajna. However, there arose a dilemma among the sages as Ram refused to remarry. He was on an ekapatni vrat in his avatar as Sri Ram. For the yajna to be performed, the wife of the king needed to be present. Ram ordered a golden replica of Sita to be made and sat beside the replica to perform the yajna. The horse, let loose after the yajna, was stopped by Luv and Kush. They fought victoriously against the mighty army of Ayodhya, led first by Shatrughna, then by Bharat, then by Lakshman and finally by Ram. Hanuman had been bound by the twins. It was the sight of the bound Hanuman that made Sita cry out in anguish when she was told about the adventurous capers of her sons. Valmiki stopped the fight and when they returned to the Ashram, Sita revealed their identity to them for the first time. The boys were saddened and wanted to meet their father. They were instructed by Valmiki to go to Ayodhya and sing the Ramayana on the streets. They sang and how! The people of Ayodhya were charmed by the beautiful verses sung by the two innocent boys. They were led to the palace where they continued singing the Ramayan in front of their father, his brothers and all the family members. Everyone was mesmerized by the beauty of the song and the melody of their voices. The queen mothers could not control their tears. The boys were followed by Valmiki, who brought Vaidehi along with him hoping to hand over the three of them to their rightful owner, Sri Ram.

He announced in front of everyone that the twins were the offsprings of Ram and Sita. Valmiki's words were respected as he never spoke anything but the truth. The queen mothers looked at them with love and affection. Bharat, Lakshman and Shatrughna were not surprised by this announcement. They had suspected it as the boys had defeated them in battle, and no one in the world except Ram could defeat them. Ram lovingly embraced his sons.

Valmiki then asked Sita to step forward. 'Dear Ram,' he said, 'Sita has been in my ashram since the time she was abandoned in the forest. Your children were born there and I have given them all the knowledge and education I could impart. Sita is blemishless. Please accept her.'

All the subjects of Ayodhya roared in appreciation. But there was again one voice of dissent. This angered Sita and she implored Mother Earth to take her in her arms. 'I am tired of proving my innocence time after time. If I have been faithful to my husband, let mother earth take me in her fold,' she declared.

Everyone knows about the *agnipareeksha* that I underwent to prove my chastity before returning to Ayodhya. I have done my duty by bringing up and entrusting my children to their illustrious father. They will be taken care of properly by him. I am tired of living here, where women are always viewed with suspicion. Please open your arms for receiving me, dear Mother Earth. Take me and let me rest peacefully in your lap.'

Sita's words stunned the entire palace into silence. And suddenly with a sound akin to thunder, there appeared a crack on the earth. The crack widened and Mother Earth came out in her carriage. She took Sita lovingly in her arms and placed her on her lap. The crack closed before anybody could react and Sita had left for her heavenly abode.

Chapter 10

URMILA

A few months after Sita was discovered by King Janak while tilling the land with a golden plough and adopted by the royal couple, Queen Sunaina became pregnant. Sita had brought rain and happiness to the people of Videha in Mithila and even the good news of the queen's pregnancy was attributed to the good fortune brought to the kingdom by Sita. King Janak held his little daughter in his arms as a faint cry of a child was heard from the closed room. In a few minutes, a woman emerged with drops of perspiration shining on her forehead as she held out the crying baby to the father.

'*Badhai ho Maharaj*! (Congratulations, my Lord!) Mithila has been blessed with another little Mahalakshmi!' exclaimed the woman.

The king smiled, set little Sita down, and accepted the baby girl in his arms. Sunaina had delivered an adorable baby girl. Sita tugged at her father's arms as she wanted to see the baby.

'Sit down dear,' said Janak with a tender smile.

Sita obeyed. Her father placed the baby on her lap carefully. And what a surprise! As soon as the baby was placed in Sita's lap she stopped crying. Her eyes opened and stared at the beautiful face of her elder sister. A smile curved around Sita's lips. She loved the baby. The bondage of affection between the sisters had begun in those few seconds and continued to grow stronger through the years.

The baby was named Urmila by her parents, and right from the beginning, Sita was protective of her little sister, who just adored her in return. Urmila grew up in the shadow of her divine sister. King Janak and Queen Sunaina always gave prominence to Sita and her wishes. Though Urmila was the only biological offspring of King Janak, it was Sita who was called Janaki (daughter of Janak), Vaidehi (Princess of Videha) or Mythili (Princess of Mithila). But never for a moment did it bother or even arouse a slight feeling of envy in Urmila's mind. She was completely devoted to Sita and loved her too much to allow such petty thoughts to enter her mind. She was happy to be basking in the reflected glory of her beloved sister.

King Janak was called a Raj Rishi because he believed in spreading peace and imparting knowledge to everyone, regardless of caste or gender. Thus, Sita and Urmila, along with their cousins, Mandavi and Shrutikirti, were privy to the best of education in the Vedas, warfare and all forms of arts. They loved playing in the lush green gardens of the palace and discovering new hideouts. It was during one of these excursions, that Sita and Urmila came across the mighty Shiva Dhanush placed on a huge table. The Dhanush had been in King Janak's possession for generations. Since it was slightly tilted because of their hurried clash with the table, Sita quickly lifted the bow and adjusted its position. King Janak exclaimed incredulously at this feat as no ordinary man could ever lift this powerful Shiva Dhanush. 'Being a little girl, Sita has lifted the divine bow. How is it even possible? Sita, my dear daughter, is endowed with special powers and has the blessings of Lord Shiva.' Urmila, his other daughter, who was present there agreed wholeheartedly.

Time passed. The four cousins grew up to be beautiful and talented women. King Janak arranged for a swayamvar for Sita and the condition was that only a man who could lift the sacred Dhanush would be a suitable bridegroom for her. Kings and princes had arrived in Mithila from various regions to vie for the hands of the beautiful Mythili. Ram and Lakshman had been protecting the yajna of Sage Vishwamitra and the fearful Tadaka had been vanquished. They accompanied the Sage to Mithila and were plucking flowers for the Sage's morning puja, when the sisters, Sita and Urmila came out from the Gauri Mata Temple. Sita's eyes were locked with Ram's, whereas Urmila drew in a breath of admiration for the handsome Lakshman. In seconds, Sita had fallen in love with Ram. Urmila's attraction for Lakshman did not go unnoticed by her sister as soon as she collected her thoughts. She smiled to herself as her gaze shifted to the younger prince. He seemed to be equally mesmerized by Urmila's beauty. The sisters returned to the palace, both in their own world of dreams.

The palace was abuzz with visitors. All the four cousins were waiting for the moment of reckoning when Sita's swayamvar would start. King Janak announced the condition once again and one by one the kings and princes present there tried to lift the Shiva Dhanush and failed miserably. Urmila's eyes roved around the entire durbar to see if she could spot Lakshman. Her eyes caught Sita too searching anxiously and saw it settle on a separate seat offered to Vishwamitra. And there they were. The handsome young Ram and Lakshman were seated respectfully beside their Guru. It was the turn of the mighty Ravan to lift the Dhanush. Being a devout Shiva bhakt, everyone thought he would lift it easily, but he too failed in his attempt and walked away angrily. The kings and princes present at the swayamvar started murmuring that King Janak had tricked them into looking like fools. The sad king got up and exclaimed, 'Is there no one in this entire land who is brave and strong enough to fulfil the condition of lifting the Shiva Dhanush and marrying my daughter?'

Urmila suddenly caught her breath as Lakshman rose and said angrily, 'O king, how can you say that there is no one capable when my elder brother, Dashrathnandan Shri Ramachandra of the Suryavanshi clan is present here?'

Urmila's eyes opened wide in admiration for the young prince. She saw Shri Ram calming down his brother. Sage Vishwamitra then rose and asked Ram to lift the bow and string it. Shri Ram respectfully prostrated before his guru, circumambulated the mighty Shiva Dhanush and prayed to Lord Shiva before lifting the bow easily. While stringing the bow, it broke into two. Lakshman's face was a huge smile. You could call it a smile of achievement, contentment, or an expression of 'I told you so'. Urmila could not help noting this telling smile on Lakshman's face. She looked happily at her sister who was praying sincerely to Goddess Gauri. On finding that the bow had been lifted and broken by Ram, a delighted smile appeared on Sita's lips. Prompted by her parents, she coyly walked forward, accompanied by her beloved Urmila, Mandavi and Shrutikirti, to garland Shri Ram.

King Dashrath, Bharat and Shatrughna were then informed and invited by King Janak. Later, to the great delight of Urmila and Sita, who were finding it very difficult to think of the ensuing separation, it was mutually decided by the kings that the four sisters would be given in marriage to the four brothers. Bharat was to marry Mandavi. Urmila's heart skipped a beat in joy as her marriage to Lakshman was announced. Shatrughna would get Shrutikirti as his wife.

The marriages were conducted and the four girls tearfully took leave of their parents, King Janak, Queen Sunaina, King Kushadhwaja and Queen Chandrabhaga. They then accompanied their respective husbands to Ayodhya.

Love filled the air. The city of Ayodhya celebrated the arrival of four royal couples with diyas, songs and dances. There were murmurs and sharp gasps of admiration as the royal carriages carrying the couples rolled in. Ayodhya seemed to have come alive with the advent of the newlywed princes.

Months passed by. There was an invitation from the kingdom of Kaikeya for Bharat from his grandfather. King Dashrath and Kaikeyi happily permitted him to visit his grandfather. Shatrughna, who followed Bharat like a shadow since childhood, also wanted to accompany him. The two young men left. Within a few days, King Dashrath felt that the time had come to crown Ram as the king of Ayodhya. He discussed with his ministers and they were elated by the decision. He then mentioned it to his wives, who were equally happy about Ram being crowned as the next king. But Manthara's incessant poisoning of Kaikeyi's mind against the king's decision and requesting her to ask for the boons which had been granted much earlier for saving the life of Dashrath during a battle resulted in chaos. Kaikeyi insisted that Bharat should be crowned the king and Ram should be exiled from Ayodhya for fourteen years. Dashrath was devastated by this demand. When Ram came to know about the boons demanded by Queen Kaikeyi, he comforted his father and almost immediately got ready to leave. Sita too decided to follow her husband in exile. The next to follow Ram was Lakshman. And knowing that they could not stay away from each other right from childhood, Sumitra encouraged her son to take care of his brother and sister-in-law. When Urmila heard about her husband accompanying Ram and Sita, she appeared on the scene hastily.

'Please allow me to accompany you,' she requested. But Lakshman adamantly refused to take her along.

'My job for these fourteen years will be to guard my brother and sister-in-law from any harm. I cannot afford to get distracted from my duty. Your presence will distract me as I will have to worry about your welfare too,' he stated. 'You remain here in the palace and take care of our parents. That is also part of your duty. I also want you to promise that after I leave, you will not shed tears.'

Her heart broke into pieces. But could she show it to anyone, least of all to her beloved husband? She rushed back into her room and gave vent to her tears. Knowing that her husband would come to take leave of her any moment, she took control of her emotions.

It was not that Urmila did not understand Lakshman's point of view. He loved his brother more than anyone in the world. Urmila could relate to that and admired him for it. She knew that he had voluntarily taken on the mantle of being his brother's guardian. He wanted no distractions from performing this duty to the best of his ability. But everything said and done, Urmila could not bear to be separated from Lakshman. And fourteen years was a long long time.

But Urmila was strong-willed and courageous. She made her decision. She would help her beloved husband in the way she could. But doubts about her ability to handle the responsibility of the aged king and queen rose in her mind.

'How could she do it in the absence of her sister, her husband and the divine Ram?'

She ran to Sita and embraced her. Sita could sense that her sister was facing a dilemma. She comforted her little sister and asked her what was troubling her. Urmila blurted out her whole conversation with Lakshman. Sita knew what a big sacrifice was being expected of her sister. She said, 'Urmila, don't worry. I will grant you a boon to help you carry out your duties.' She caught her sister's hands and continued, 'You will have the ability to do two things at any given point in time. This will help you to perform your duty towards our parents, our land and our subjects.'

Urmila was comforted by her sister's boon. She regained her confidence. Her only thought now was to remove any memories of herself from Lakshman's mind.

'How do I achieve that?' she wondered. It came to her mind that Lakshman would not remember her if she made him hate her. She washed her face, decked herself in her finest garments and jewellery and waited for Lakshman to see her.

Lakshman was amazed. He had been debating in his mind about what he would say to console her for his impending absence from her life for the period of exile. Fourteen years was a long time and especially for a newly married young girl full of life and rosy dreams. But to his surprise, his young wife was looking her best as she waited for him to take leave of her. He was furious. 'Is she emotionless? Or is it that the palace comforts attracted her more than me?' said Lakshman to himself.

'We are leaving for the forest now. Yet you are still dressed in your royal clothes and jewellery. How can you? What is the difference between you and Mata Kaikeyi?!' he ranted. Urmila just remained motionless. The pain searing her heart at being compared to the person responsible for this episode was unbearable.

But she had made a conscious decision. This was the only way she could inculcate hatred for her in his mind. That hatred would help him not to get distracted by her memories and perform his duties well.

Urmila stopped him. 'You may proceed. I promise you that I will not shed tears after you leave. But let me tell you, I need something from you too.'

Lakshman was furious. 'What do you want now?!'

'I want your word that you will not think of me for even one moment when you are in exile. I don't want thoughts or memories of me to distract you from performing your self-imposed duty of guarding your brother and my sister from any harm,' she said scornfully.

Lakshman was taken aback. He said to himself, 'Would any woman ask her husband to put her out completely from his thoughts? What sort of a woman was his wife?'

He just could not fathom her thoughts. He quickly turned around and went away to join Ram and Sita on their journey. Urmila stared at the two most important people in her life, her beloved sister, Sita, and her love and life's companion, Lakshman, departing from her life. Can anyone even imagine how hard it would have been for young Urmila to watch their departure without shedding a single tear?

In a few minutes came the news of King Dashrath's collapse. She rushed to the room where the three Queens were weeping close to the lifeless body of King Dashrath. Kaushalya clung to Urmila like a small child searching for support. Her innate strength came to the fore. She did not shed tears in deference to her husband's request. In the absence of all four sons, she understood the gravity of the situation and took it upon herself to handle it. Vashisht arranged to inform Bharat and Shatrughna to return immediately. Till they arrived and performed the last rites for their father, it was young Urmila who handled every problem that arose in Ayodhya. Even the ablest of ministers looked to her for guidance in performing their duties.

Bharat returned and on learning everything there arose an inexplicable hatred for his mother Kaikeyi. He performed the last rites for his father with a heavy heart. And almost at once, he decided to search for Ram, Sita and Lakshman and bring them back to Ayodhya respectfully. Everyone, including the Queens, accompanied Bharat. But Urmila stayed back. She knew that Ram would keep his word and not return to Ayodhya for fourteen years. She knew that if she accompanied Bharat, Lakshman would be reminded of her and get distracted from his duty. Though it was a tempting thought to see her beloved husband, even for a few minutes, she compelled herself to decide against it. As she had foreseen, Bharat returned only with Ram's *padukas*, which he placed on the throne and ruled Ayodhya in the name of Ram, while living like a hermit in an ashram at Nandigram.

There are folk versions where it is stated that when Janak and Sunaina heard that Urmila was left behind while her husband proceeded to the forest with Ram and Sita, they came to Ayodhya to take her back to her maternal home for some time to ease the solitude resulting from her husband's absence. But Urmila is said to have refused as she had been instructed by her husband to take care of the ageing Queens.

Meanwhile, in the forest, Lakshman constructed a hut with a thatched roof and made a comfortable bed of leaves. While Sri Ram and Sita were resting for the night, Lakshman remained awake. He wanted to stand guard so that no harm befell them at any point.

During the night he had a mysterious visitor. Goddess Nidra appeared before him and asked him to rest awhile.

'Mother, please excuse me,' said Lakshman. 'I have vowed not to sleep for the fourteen years of my exile as I have to make sure that no harm befalls either Sri Ram or Sita Mata.'

Nidra was impressed. What love! And what affection Lakshman professed towards his brother and sister-in-law! But can the law of nature be overlooked?

She said, 'Dear Lakshman, I understand and admire your devotion and duty towards your brother. But, you do know that the law of nature cannot be ignored. I can allow you to remain awake for fourteen years, provided someone else takes over your sleep during that time.'

Lakshman thought for a moment. He thought about his wife Urmila for the first time since coming to the forest. He thought about the problems that she would be facing at the palace alone. 'Mother, please approach my wife Urmila. I am sure she will oblige,' he told Goddess Nidra.

Nidra at once approached Urmila at the palace. She explained to her that her husband Lakshman had taken a vow to remain awake for fourteen years, which would not be possible unless another person took on his share of sleep.

Without a moment of hesitation, Urmila replied, 'Mother, I am ready to accept my husband's share of sleep for the next fourteen years. But can you please give him the strength to do his duty without any hurdles and also remove any strain or fatigue that may occur because of his lack of sleep?'

Goddess Nidra was astounded by the love and understanding between this couple and their devotion to duty. 'What a great sacrifice this young girl is taking on!' she thought. She readily agreed to bless Lakshman. Urmila promptly fell asleep and slept for fourteen years. Urmila's sleep had far-reaching effects on the results of the war between Sri Ram and Ravan. One of the mighty and almost invincible warriors in the Lankan army was Ravan's son, Meghnad, also called Indrajit. He had received a boon that he could be killed only by a man who had not slept for fourteen years. Lakshman could only stay awake for the entire exile span because of his wife. And during the battle, it was Lakshman who killed Indrajit and contributed to winning the war for his brother.

There is an interesting story of Hanuman being shot down by Bharat while carrying the Sanjeevani to revive Lakshman. Hanuman meets Bharat and shares that a battle is being fought to recover Sita from Ravan who had abducted her. Lakshman was lying unconscious on the lap of Sri Ram and he needed to reach Lanka before sunrise to revive him. Bharat apologized and asked him to continue his journey. Hanuman's eyes fell on Urmila. Urmila called him in with a smile.

'I have recognized you, Marutinandan,' she said. 'And I also know that you are carrying the Sanjeevani leaves to revive my unconscious husband.'

'I can't understand the significance of your smile Mata,' said Hanuman curiously.

'Hanuman-ji, nothing can happen to my husband when he is lying on the lap of the Paramatma. They are just performing a *lila*. The sun cannot rise till you reach the battlefield. I am confident you will be able to revive my husband and make Sri Ram happy. Also, this entire incident is a result of Lakshman disrespecting the 'jhoota ber' offered by Mata Shabari with so much love. The sanjeevani leaves on the mountain you are carrying are nothing but the ber transformed into medicine. That is Lakshman's retribution.'

Hanuman was amazed at her composure, confidence, devotion to her husband and her belief in the divinity of

Sri Ram. Another interesting episode about Urmila and Lakshman: when Ram and Sita return to Ayodhya from exile, the coronation or *pattabhishekam* was arranged for Sri Ram and Sita Mata. Suddenly Lakshman started laughing. All the people in the hall were wondering whether it was because of something they had done. When asked for an explanation for his laughter, Lakshman said, 'Look there! Urmila has awakened after fourteen years of sleep. Now, according to the pact, Nidra Devi wants me to sleep at this moment of my beloved brother's coronation, for which I have been waiting all my life.' But probably being Sheshnag's avatar, he did see the coronation along with Urmila.

When Sri Ram, Sita and Lakshman returned to Ayodhya after their exile was completed, the tension between Urmila and Lakshman was visible to Sita. She had seen the happy reunion among the brothers. But her thoughts wandered as to why Lakshman, who was seeing his beloved wife after fourteen years, was acting aloof. Later, when the opportunity presented itself, Sita pulled her sister aside and asked her what was troubling them. Urmila broke down for the first time in fourteen years and narrated the way she had spewed hatred for herself in Lakshman's mind so that he would not be distracted from his duty. Sita realized the extent of sacrifice that her little sister had made and the anguish she had suffered. She could not bear it. She explained everything to Lakshman and said, 'Even hundreds of Sitas cannot compare with the sacrifice that my little sister did for you.' Lakshman finally realized the love Urmila had for him and apologized to her, regretting his harsh words.

Valmiki Ramayan and Tulsidas's Ramacharitamanas describe Urmila's character in a few lines as Lakshman's wife. There is hardly anything further written about her in these two versions. Some of the above-mentioned stories do not appear in the original Valmiki Ramayan. Even Kamba Ramayanam does not have much information about her. It is more from regional folk tales and song traditions handed down from generation to generation that we know about the character of Urmila, her supreme sacrifice and her love for her husband. It is also said Urmila managed to take care of the Queen Mothers and the palace administration in deference to her husband's wishes, because of Sita Devi's boon of being capable of doing two things at a time.

When Sita was sent to the forest by Sri Ram for the second time, Urmila was stunned. She was furious that her beloved sister was being sent away when she was pregnant, just because some washer-man was creating a ruckus with his wife. And she did not hesitate to confront both Ram and her husband. Lakshman was already in grief while performing this task, as he knew about the purity of Sita. When Urmila confronted him, he went to Ram and said, 'Abandoning my respected Sita Mata in the forest, that too when she was pregnant, was the hardest duty I had to perform for you. In this avatar, I have been born as a younger brother and I have to do as you order me to. But not anymore! In the next avatar, I will be born as the elder brother and will not take instructions from you like this.'

Later, Urmila, who was also pregnant at the time, gave birth to two sons named Angada and Chitraketu.

Chapter 11

MANDAVI & SHRUTIKIRTI

There was joy and celebration everywhere in Sankasya, where King Kushadhwaja and his wife Chandrabhaga had become proud parents of a beautiful baby girl. They called her Mandavi. King Kushadhwaja was the younger brother of King Janak of Videha and ruled over Sankasya.

Mandavi was a lovely child, intelligent and fond of learning. In a few years, the king was blessed with another daughter named Shrutikirti. Mandavi and Shrutikirti were soulmates. They loved being together. As per King Janak's principle of providing quality education to all, irrespective of gender, the two sisters joined their cousins Sita and Urmila in acquiring knowledge in all forms of art from the best of gurus. The four girls were inseparable. They loved each other's company and most importantly, the younger three loved, respected and looked up to their elder sister, Sita, as a role model.

Coincidentally, when they grew up to marriageable age, their marriages were fixed with the four princes of Ayodhya. There are mentions in folk tales that Mandavi had an unquenchable thirst for knowledge and Shrutikirti was not ready for marriage so early in life. (She was the youngest among the sisters.) But, the allure of being together for a lifetime with their siblings made them agree to the wedding proposal.

Their happiness was not long lived though. In the absence of Bharat and Shatrughna, when King Dashrath planned the coronation of Ram, due to the evil mind game played by Manthara on Kaikeyi, Ram was exiled for fourteen years. Their beloved Sita accompanied Ram and Lakshman to the forest. Dashrath collapsed. Bharat and Shatrughna were summoned back to Ayodhya. Their return was preceded by the demise of their father.

The brothers had no idea of what had transpired in their absence. They were informed by Sumantra about the sorrowful events that took place before his father's demise. Bharat was totally taken aback.

'I am ashamed to call you my mother,' he exclaimed. 'I have lost all respect for you. I hate you.'

Kaikeyi was stunned. She had not expected such a reaction from her beloved son.

Bharat ignored her and turned to Mata Kaushalya for solace. He wept uncontrollably. Mandavi had been watching the whole scene and could not bear the sorrow of her beloved husband.

'My innocent husband did not even know that Kaikeyi Ma had planned such a thing!' she thought sadly.

Her mind wandered towards her dearest Sita. 'Where would she be? Would she be able to bear the rigours of the life of an ascetic after living the cosy life of a princess?'

She glanced at Urmila. The poor girl was all alone but had put on a brave countenance.

'At least Sita is with her husband,' she consoled herself. 'Look at Urmila. How will she bear the separation of fourteen years from Lakshman?'

Her heart wept for Urmila, who had been forced to spend fourteen years without her husband through no fault of her own. She clasped Urmila's hand and pressed it tightly. Urmila glanced at her. She pressed Mandavi's hand in turn to show her that she understood. Shrutikirti was looking at both. She seemed to be more relaxed.

'Why not?' thought Mandavi. 'It was not Shruta's husband's mother who had banished Ram to the forest.'

However, Shrutikirti did feel sorry for Mandavi and Urmila. She wanted to console them, comfort them and convince them that they could depend on her at all times. But being the youngest, she was not sure about their reaction.

The funeral rites of King Dashrath were completed.

But while Bharat's anger was directed at Mata Kaikeyi, Shatrughna's eyes fell on Manthara. He was even prepared to kill the hunchback maid for putting evil thoughts in Mata Kaikeyi's mind, which resulted in his brother Ram's exile. Knowing her husband well, Shrutikirti was watching her husband and when she saw him drawing his sword to kill Manthara, she stopped him. She also called out to Bharat, who immediately came running and stopped Shatrughna before the deed could be committed. Shrutikirti and Bharat made him understand that his beloved brother, Ram, would not approve of this violence against Manthara.

Then, Bharat came out to address the people. He was accompanied by Mandavi, Shatrughna, Shrutikirti and Urmila.

'Let me first tell you all that I am not your King,' he announced. 'I never will be. My brother Sri Ram is the only one who has the right to rule over Ayodhya. I am going to the forest to search for him and request him to come back. Anyone who wishes to join me in this, is welcome.'

The crowd let out a huge sigh of relief. Their Prince Bharat, at least, was pure in his thoughts and intentions. A huge procession started from Ayodhya in search of their beloved Sri Ram. The Queen Mothers also followed Bharat and Shatrughna in a carriage. Mandavi and Shrutikirti joined their husbands. Urmila was the only one who remained behind in the palace.

The procession reached Chitrakoot. Lakshman saw Bharat followed by a huge number of people and mistook it to be an attack on Ram.

'Bharat is coming with a huge army to attack you. Shall I stop him before he approaches our hut?' he flared.

Ram, as calm as ever, said, 'Lakshman, control yourself! Bharat cannot attack me. He is too loving and respectful for that. Let us go and greet him and find out what important message he has to convey.'

Ram, accompanied by Sita and Lakshman, came out of the hut. No sooner had Bharat set his eyes on Sri Ram, he ran and fell at his feet, crying for forgiveness. His brother lifted him and embraced him.

He said tenderly, 'Bharat, my dear brother, you have done nothing wrong. So, what is there to forgive? Please calm down and tell me if everything is fine?'

'No. Nothing is fine Ram Bhaiyya. Ayodhya has lost its King. Our father passed away in his longing for you,' grieved Bharat.

Ram tottered for a moment. Lakshman held on to him.

Shatrughna joined in and embraced first Ram and then Lakshman, his twin brother, saying 'Our father is no more.' His eyes were full of unshed tears.

All the four brothers were silent in grief for a few minutes. Mandavi and Shrutikirti were looking on, their sorrow written on their faces. They got down and embraced their sister Sita.

She patted them consolingly and wiped the tears, which were rolling unchecked.

Then Ram suddenly asked, 'Where are our mothers?'

'They are here with us,' said Bharat. He led Ram and Lakshman to the carriage where the three Queens were seated. Ram brought them lovingly to the hut and made them sit in comfort. He took blessings from each of them. When he prostrated before Mata Kaikeyi, Bharat looked away in shame. Ram noticed it. He also noticed the tears in Mata Kaikeyi's eyes. He took Bharat aside and admonished him for treating his mother so badly.

He and his brothers performed Shraddh rites for their deceased father.

After that, Bharat proceeded to make his request. 'Please return to Ayodhya. Everyone wants you to come back Ram Bhaiyya. You are the only person who has the right to rule our country. Please, please,' he entreated.

'I cannot go back on my father's word, Bharat, and you all know that,' replied Ram firmly. 'I assure you that I will return to Ayodhya, the day the fourteen years of my exile period ends. Till then you and Shatrughna have to take on this duty.'

'I don't want to rule Ayodhya,' said Bharat plaintively.

'You will have to Bharat,' Ram was firm. 'Shatrughna will help you with the administration.'

Seeing that his pleas were falling on deaf ears, and realizing that Ram would not waver from his stance, Bharat said, 'Then, at least give me your *Padukas*. It will not be me, but your *Padukas* which will rule Ayodhya till you return.'

Ram removed his padukas and presented them to Bharat, who ceremoniously carried them on his head while starting on his return journey. Sri Ram, Sita and Lakshman emotionally took leave of their mothers after seeking their blessings.

On reaching Ayodhya, Bharat went to the palace, changed his clothes from princely attire to simple ascetic wear, and went to Mandavi to apprise her of his decision. Mandavi was waiting for him.

'Mandavi, I seek your help,' he said. 'There is a forest just outside Ayodhya at Nandigram. I am going to build a hut like the one at Chitrakoot where my brother is staying. And from now till my brother comes back, I will be staying there.'

'Please let me accompany you,' said Mandavi immediately. But Bharat was insistent that she would have to take care of the mothers and the palace affairs.

'Don't worry Nath,' said Mandavi. 'I will divide my time equally amongst all of you and you will have no complaints in this regard.' She too changed her attire and exclaimed that she would remain like an ascetic whether at the palace or at Nandigram, till her husband remains one.

Shrutikirti, the youngest of the sisters, had been a silent observer throughout the events. She saw her husband lost in thought and wondered what was going on in his mind. Shatrughna was in a dilemma. He wanted to follow Bharat to Nandigram and live the life of an ascetic. But what would happen to Ayodhya in the absence of all four brothers?

He mentioned this aloud. Shrutikirti at once caught his hand and said, 'Nath, may I express my thoughts?'

Shatrughna nodded.

'I feel that you should assist Bharat Bhaiyya, by taking over the physical administration of the kingdom.'

'But Shruta,' he remarked. 'I have always been carefree and never involved myself too much in the affairs of the Kingdom. My brothers were always there and they were capable enough.'

'Bharat Bhaiyya has relocated to Nandigram. He has placed Ram Bhaiyya's Padukas on the throne and vowed to rule

Ayodhya through them. But he needs assistance, doesn't he, especially as he will not be physically present here?'

'You are right Shruta. Maybe that is what I should do. Though it is a great responsibility, with my brother's guidance and leadership, I should be able to take care of the affairs of the kingdom.'

Throughout the fourteen years of Sri Ram's exile, Shatrughna acted as an efficient caretaker. Shrutikirti, the carefree, fun-loving young girl turned responsible overnight. She gave her inputs as and when they were required to Shatrughna, helping him whenever he was confused. In addition, Shrutikirti, along with Mandavi and Urmila, took care of the palace administration. The sisters looked after the Queen Mothers well.

The exile was not meant only for Sri Ram, Sita and Lakshman. Staying in and around Ayodhya, Bharat and Shatrughna were equally in exile as they led the lives of celibate ascetics, with no princely comforts. Urmila took over the sleep of Lakshman and sacrificed the entire fourteen years of her life in solitude. Mandavi and Shrutikirti were also denied the happiness of married life.

Finally, when it was time for Sri Ram to return, happiness returned to Ayodhya and its subjects. The four couples were finally reunited.

Bharat and Mandavi had two sons Taksha and Pushkala after a few years and happily lived under the guidance of Sri Ram in Ayodhya.

There is a wonderful story in the oral folk tradition of Sri Ram's desire to give something to his brothers and their wives. He expressed this wish to his mother Kaushalya. She at once arranged for all of them to be present before Ram. Ram tenderly asked each one of them what boon they wanted from him. Everyone asked for Ram's continued blessing and love, except Shrutikirti. She had tears in her eyes. She said, 'Ram Bhaiyya, I want the bark clothes that you wore in the forest while in exile.' Ram was surprised and asked her for the reason for such a strange request.

Shrutikirti said, 'Young princes happily accept the crown and kingdom from their fathers. But you were happy to accept exile from your father at the peak of your youth. Therefore, even the clothes that you wore during the exile period are worthy of sincere worship. Can you please give me your bark attire?'

Ram was touched. He happily gave her his exile clothes, which she cherished and worshipped till the end.

A few years after Sri Ram's coronation, there came a complaint from Sages and holy men, that a demon called Lavanasur was creating havoc and terror in the world. He ruled in Mathura. Lavanasur was the son of Madhu, a pious demon king, and Kumbhini, the sister of Ravan. He had in his possession, the divine Trishul of Lord Shiva, which proved to be his protection.

Sri Ram agreed to vanquish the powerful Lavansur. But, when Shatrughna offered to fight the demon, Sri Ram gave him divine weapons and blessed him on his journey to Mathura. He also gave him instructions regarding the power of the divine Trishul. He asked Shatrughna to kill Lavanasur when he was not in his palace. Shatrughna waited for the opportunity. When Lavanasur was returning from a hunt in the forest, he invited him for a fight. Lavanasur could not but accept the challenge. Since he was outside the palace and not under the protection of the divine Trishul, Shatrughna succeeded in killing Lavanasur with a Vishnu ban given to him by Sri Ram. Sri Ram at once crowned Shatrughna as the king of Mathura. Shrutikirti joined her husband in Mathura with her sons Subahu and Shatrughati and lived there happily for a long time.

Chapter 12

MANTHARA

Mithila, the capital of Videha, was celebrating. The celebrations began after Ram lifted the Shiva Dhanush and finally was eligible to marry Sita. The festivities lasting a few months ended with the departure of King Dashrath with the four brides, his two sons Ram and Lakshman, and the wedding party. Sage Vashisth asked King Ashwapati to take his grandchild Bharat, and Shatrughna, with them to Kaikeya to train them in jungle warfare. Ashwapati and his sons came to Mithila to attend the marriage of his grandchildren at the invitation of Dashrath, his son-in-law. No one opposed the foresight of Vashisth. It wasn't long ago when Vashisth had prevailed on Dashrath and ensured that Ram and Lakshman went with Sage Vishwamitra to protect his yajna. The result was for everyone to see. Except for Vishwamitra, everyone was astonished at the abrupt decision of Sage Vashisth.

The development initially astonished Kaikeyi. She welcomed Mandavi, her newly wedded daughter-in-law, with warmth. However, in Bharat's absence, Kaikeyi postponed many post-marriage customs and rituals. She learned from her husband that their guru, Sage Vashisth, had decided to send Bharat to Kaikeya. To gain more insight, Kaikeyi visited the sage, where she met her guru's adversary-turned-ally, Sage Vishwamitra. The sages convened for a long discussion, and Kaikeyi was pleased with Vishwamitra's efforts to enhance the reputations of Ram and Lakshman.

Vishwamitra had successfully portrayed Ram as an incarnation of Mahavishnu, following the defeat of Tataka, the redemption of Ahalya, and the breaking of Shiva's Dhanush, Pinaka. Additionally, Parashuram, the son of Sage Bhrigu and Vishwamitra's guru-brother, also affirmed Ram's divine status as an incarnation of Lord Vishnu. They declared that Lakshman was the incarnation of Shesh Nag. After their training at Siddhashram, Ram and Lakshman were now prepared for the next phase of the Mission Akhand Bharat.

At this juncture, Kaikeyi's role became crucial. To perform her role perfectly, however, Manthara, her handmaid, needed to be removed from the equation to prevent her from causing disruptions.

Manthara, or Kooni as they addressed her, wanted to visit Kashi for the holy darshan of Lord Vishveshwara for the longest time. On her way, she intended to take a dip at the Triveni Sangam in Prayagraj . Kooni also wanted to stay in the ashram of Sage Bharadwaj for a few days. Kaikeyi held her back because of the preoccupation with the marriage ceremonies of the princes. Now that's over, Manthara could go for a fortnight. The period of her absence and the exact day of her return to Ayodhya must be decided meticulously. The stakes were too high for the seers. Kaikeyi and the sages were not sure what stand Kooni would take and whether their plan to exile Ram and make Bharat the interim king would get support from her.

Maharshi Bharadwaj in Prayagraj would be told to keep her there as long as necessary and send her to reach Ayodhya one day before the coronation ceremony.

Manthara, the hunchback, was the elder cousin of Kaikeyi, the only daughter of her father's younger brother, Vrihadaksha. When Sukriti, as she was then known, was a child of three years, she was inflicted with the rarest of rare diseases. This malady made her sweat profusely all the time, irrespective of the weather. The ailment was incurable and, within a short time; the girl became decrepit and reached the terminal stage. In a desperate attempt, the Raj Vaidya administered her a potion, a kind of moderate poison that would save her life but might deform her physically.

The lifesaving treatment damaged Sukriti's body irreparably. Her spine bent, shoulders drooped and neck stiffened. But that was not all. Because of her weak immunity, she was inflicted with severe chicken pox. That resulted in her face becoming dark and pimpled with the crossed right eye. Because of the *tridosh* or triple-frailty, her movements were slow and hobbling. Hence, people nicknamed her Manthara, the slower one. She was, behind her back, addressing the Kubadi or Kooni. She was so ugly that no man, a royal or a commoner, would ever agree to take her as the bride. Unable to withstand the agonizing condition of his daughter, Vrihadaksha fell seriously ill. He did not last too long despite all the efforts of his elder brother.

The loss of her father and the condition of her dumb-struck mother devastated Sukriti. When Sukriti grew up, she overcame her physical limitations by falling back on her mental abilities. She focused on her studies: learning polity, philosophy, diplomacy and the scriptures. But she was fascinated by history—the history of Jambudwip, the history of the devas, daityas and the rakshasas and of the great wars fought among them. With her commitment and hard work, she excelled in her studies. She was ahead of her cousins, older than her, in studies. Her uncle and mother were proud of her accomplishments.

After Kaikeyi's marriage to Dashrath, Sukriti accompanied her cousin disguised as a handmade princess. But she was in Ayodhya with a purpose. She was an unofficial representative of King Ashwapati, her uncle. She went to Ayodhya to facilitate the implementation of Dashrath's pre-marriage commitment, that the son of Kaikeyi would follow him to the throne of Koshala. Vashisth and Kul Purohit Vamdev witnessed this undertaking by the king. Sukriti lived as the head of the maids in Kaikeyi's palace and had full access to the queen. Except for the servants who came from Kaikeya, no one knew the truth behind the enormous powers wielded by this hunchback. They were just envious of her.

Due to his advancing age, King Dashrath requested Sage Vashisth, his guru, to determine an auspicious moment for the coronation of Ram as the crown prince of Koshala. Having already married off his children, the king was eager to proceed without delay. One day, Dashrath visited Vashisth's ashram and respectfully asked, 'Gurudev, I seek your blessings to retire from my royal duties. I have served as king to the best of my abilities. While my faculties are still intact, I wish to abdicate the throne and devote my remaining years to prayer and meditation. Please find the earliest suitable date for anointing Ram as the king of Kosala.'

Vashisth agreed and assured Dashrath that he would consult with Vamdev, the family priest, and other seers to determine the most auspicious time for the ceremony.

Only Vashisth and Vamdev were aware of Dashrath's urgency. The king, a skilled astrologer himself, had discovered that three powerful malefic planets had aligned in the eighth house of his horoscope, surrounding his birth star. This alignment, known as Markesh Dasha, signalled impending death or deathlike suffering. Dashrath wanted to ensure Ram's coronation before this period fully took effect, to prevent any claim by Kaikeyi for Bharat to take the throne.

Additionally, Dashrath was cautious about keeping the coronation date confidential. He feared that Kaikeyi's father, Ashwapati, might oppose Ram's ascension and demand the fulfilment of his pre-marriage commitments. The king was also concerned that if Ram learned of his father's pre-marriage promise to Kaikeyi's father, he might refuse the crown, complicating the transition of power.

Bharat's presence in Ayodhya would spoil the plan of Vashisth, Kaikeyi, and the seers. That was why Vashisth sent Bharat and Shatrughna to Rajgriha directly from Mithila. Bharat wouldn't allow Ram to go to the forest. If following the command of his father or stepmother, Ram left Ayodhya, Bharat wouldn't have stayed there either. He was certain to accompany his elder brother to where he went. The throne couldn't remain vacant for fourteen years. The presence of Bharat, an excellent administrator, was therefore required in Ayodhya in the absence of Ram.

Vashisth prepared a plan to ensure that Ram went to the forest when Bharat was not in Ayodhya. The king and Vashisth kept the date of coronation secret and revealed only three days in advance. Kooni was not around who might send a message to Rajgriha. But she would arrive one day before the ceremony. Her response and reaction were a matter of speculation. They did not take Ram into confidence as yet. While in the Siddhashram, Vishwamitra indoctrinated him about the need to fight the rakshasas. But they did not reveal the details of the

Mission Akhand Bharat to him. Sage Atri would speak to him at length when Ram reached Chitrakoot. Meanwhile, Ram's glory as a great warrior and redeemer of the fallen spread all over the Jambudwip through the network of the ashrams.

After a well-spent fortnight on the pilgrimage of Kashi and Prayagraj, an enormous surprise waited for Kooni in Ayodhya. She reached the Sarayu bank in the late afternoon and was taken aback by the unprecedented festivities that engulfed the city. No such event was planned till a fortnight ago when she left for the holy voyage. She observed that the roads of Ayodhya were cleaner and brighter today, and *chatursam*, a paste of sandalwood, saffron, camphor and musk spread a wonderful fragrance. Either side of the road was beautifully adorned with golden arches, banana plants, mango twigs and countless red, white, pink and yellow lotus garlands. Manthara felt exhausted and her back ached tediously. She was forced to abandon her chariot on the Sarayu bank as roads leading to the royal estate were packed with singing, dancing, and rushing-out people.

While Manthara walked, she could see that people had decorated the main gate of their houses with sandalwood paste and garlands of the widest variety of fresh flowers. The grand palace-like houses on both sides of the Rajpath were adorned with the holy and auspicious *bandanvar* or the door-hangings made of mango and Ashoka leaves in gold and silver strings. Beautifully crafted and geometrically perfect rangolis with auspicious religious symbols were made on every doorstep competing with its neighbour in beauty, finesse, and artistry. Every housetop had a royal flag fluttering high in the fading sunlight of a spring evening. The flags and banners of a large variety and hues covered the sky.

Kaikeyi prepared for her evening meeting with her husband. She received a message from the Dashrath's maid, Champa, that the king would visit her late in the evening. It was a long-standing practice that Champa informed the concerned queen beforehand about the king's visit to her palace. When Manthara entered the imperial chamber of the queen, she became furious to look at a perfectly made-up and well-dressed Kaikeyi. On her way to the palace, Kooni went toward Shrirang-ji temple when she saw Sarangi, the handmaid of Queen Kaushalya, distributing alms to the needy. From Sarangi she knew about the coronation of Ram the next morning. The drudgery of her whole life came to nothing. The emperor went back from his commitment. Even more shocking was the involvement of Vashisth. He was a witness to the king's commitment and a custodian of the trust her uncle placed in him.

She signalled other maids to leave the chamber and confronted her younger sister, 'What is going on here? Have you gone crazy?'

'What happened didi, why are you so upset?' asked Kaikeyi.

'Where have you been? Were you in Ayodhya or, like me, you had also been away?' asked Manthara quietly.

Kaikeyi curiously looked at a distraught Manthara. She waited, her face composed and unsmiling. She knew her cousin had not finished.

'Aren't you aware of the happenings around you? Haven't the maids told you anything? You appear all dressed up and ready to take part in the celebrations.' Manthara was visibly agitated. She gasped, her face scarlet with rage, eyes bulging out and saliva dripping from the corners of her mouth.

'Didi, I am not dressing up to participate in any celebration. I don't know if there is one. I am preparing, as I always do, for the visit of my husband. Champa informed the emperor would visit late in the evening.'

'So, at last, he could spare some time for you.'

Manthara told Kaikeyi about the coronation ceremony. She said, 'The king is cheating our family. He is coronating Ram tomorrow as the crown prince of Koshala. Shortly, Dashrath shall retire to the forest.'

Kaikeyi pretended shock and disbelief. She said, 'No didi, I don't believe you. It's not possible. The world knows the emperor for his righteousness. He has, in the past, always been unwavering in his commitments. He can never do injustice to his wife.'

'Nothing would change whether you believe it or not. They have already decided. A few hours from now, the king will crown Ram as the new ruler.'

'We must not allow that to happen and find some way to stop this. Whatever possible we must do,' said the queen, her voice drained of life.

'Our only hope is Vashisth. Follower of the truth and wisdom, he is above all worldly aspirations and is a true hermit. He is universally respected, and the king must agree to what he has to say. Vashisth-ji is not only the Kul-Guru but also one of the two witnesses to the king's commitment. I am sure he wouldn't let us down,' said Manthara with some effort.

They decided that Manthara, however tired she must be, would approach Vashisth on the queen's behalf and seek justice for her.

A little later, Manthara returned with a dejected face. Sage Vashisth refused to meet her. He was busy in the preparations for the next day's puja. Vamdev was also with Vashisth. He would be available only after the coronation ceremony. The information didn't surprise Kaikeyi. Things moved smoothly as they planned.

The sisters now worked on a contingency plan. Manthara said, 'Do you remember two boons that the king said he would grant you when you saved his life during the battle of Vaijayanta? Isn't this the right time to ask for them?'

'I have lost faith in my husband. He has deceived us once he would do it again,' said Kaikeyi in a low and exasperated voice.

'No, it will not happen,' came the emphatic reply. 'The king made the promise at Rajgriha within closed doors and known only to a few people. He granted the boons in the open court in the presence of his courtiers and the subjects. Even if he wished, his illustrious family history wouldn't allow him. He is a prisoner of this exalted legacy. The legacy that would never let him descend so low,' said Manthara.

'What is in your mind didi? What should I demand from the emperor?'

'I must warn you, it will not be easy. The king would consent to grant you two boons as soon as you remind him. But he will never agree when you tell him the actual boons.'

'Why don't you talk straight, didi? What do you suggest?'

Manthara deliberately held back the strategy. Kaikeyi, in consultation with Vashisth, had decided the two boons well in advance. She, however, waited for Manthara to open up. At last, Manthara said, 'You must make the king rescind tomorrow's ceremony and coronate Bharat as the crown prince. That is the first boon.'

Kaikeyi expected this. What else Kooni could propose? 'That is a difficult proposition, but certainly possible. Are we seeking the second boon today itself or will wait for a suitable opportunity in the future?'

Manthara did not respond to the question. Instead, she said, 'Before asking the boons, you ensure the king is under the oath, the oath of Prince Ram. Ram's oath would ensure that he doesn't retract this time. Under the oath, he must give you whatever you seek.'

'Oath of Ram! Isn't that going too far, didi?' Kaikeyi stammered. Her love for Ram and Sita was well known.

Ignoring Kaikeyi's response, Manthara said, 'That was about the first boon. We are getting the second boon today itself. As the second boon, we are seeking fourteen-years banishment for Ram. He must live the life of a hermit, dressed in coarse clothing and deer skin without treasury or security personnel. He will carry only his personal weapons.'

'What Bharat's coronation has got to do with the banishment of Ram? That is unnecessary, and I don't agree with it.' Kaikeyi protested vehemently. She was surprised listening to her didi. Was it merely a coincidence, or the sages approached her also? Both the boons she suggested were the same as decided by the sages Atri and Vashisth.

'Let me explain why Ram must be exiled before Bharat's coronation. Ram's immense popularity and emotional bond with the people of Ayodhya make his presence a significant concern. If Bharat were to become king despite Ram's popularity, would he truly be able to rule with full authority? There would likely be two competing power centres in the kingdom: Ram and Bharat. My concern is that this could lead to severe conflict, potentially even a civil war or a military coup supporting Ram as king. In such a scenario, both the king and Bharat could end up imprisoned or exiled from Koshala. To mitigate such risks, it is crucial to ensure that Ram remains away from Ayodhya.

'I can't imagine Ayodhya without Ram and Sita. I wouldn't agree with you under any circumstances. Ram is maryada purushottam. He will never support the traitors who revolted against King Bharat. I know him well. He loves Bharat and loves me, too. His love for all the mothers is equal and dignified. That includes the bavatas and *palakalis*.'

'Power changes even the best of the souls. The history is replete with such instances. You know how King Nahush, after becoming Indra, made the Saptrishis carry his palanquin and kicked them.'

'Ram is unlike any person ever born on earth, didi. He wouldn't leave the path of righteousness even after becoming the emperor of the universe.' Her voice was less assertive now and had lost its edge. She couldn't ignore the underlying truth about what her sister just said.

Manthara observed uncertainty on her sister's face. Manthara used this situation and said, 'Have you thought about your and Bharat's future with Ram as the emperor and Kaushalya as the queen-mother? Lakshman, being close to Ram, will rule the kingdom in his name. No problem for Sumitra as Lakshman will take care of his mother.'

'Didi, what is on your mind?'

'Believe me, I am not intimidating you. If Ram gets coronated, you will see Bharat either getting banished from Ayodhya or languishing in the prison.'

'That's not possible as long as his father is around.'

'You are mistaken, my sister. The king, under the burden of his guilt, will keep Bharat away. With a little foresight, you will realize the king is already doing that. Wary of an altercation, the king would never trust you nor Bharat with any significant responsibilities.'

Kaikeyi replied, 'You are overlooking one important point. Ram's love for Bharat and Bharat's respect for his elder brother is deep-rooted. Didi, you may be right about the king to some extent, but Ram could never do that. I have full faith in his comity.'

'Agreed. But tell me, has Ram come to seek your blessings? I know he hasn't. I don't blame him. It must be a conspiracy by Sumitra and the king. Ram may not be aware of their machinations. And try to understand, this is the situation when the king is still around and in control. What happens after his departure? I can foresee you and Bharat as slaves; you drudging for Kaushalya and Bharat toiling for Ram.'

Kaikeyi was alert now. Bharat languishing in prison, even as a thought, was fearsome for her. A chill ran down her spine. Manthara continued, 'You must have heard the stories of Kadru and Vinita, Devyani and Sharmistha, Suniti and Surichi, and hundreds of others like them. A *matey sautan* made of clay is more pernicious than your worst enemy. Kadru made her elder sister Vinita her slave, and so did Devyani. She made Sharmistha, her closest friend, her maid. So why do you expect Kaushalya to behave differently? You are neither her sister nor a close friend.'

'I am not too sure about Sumitra didi, but Kaushalya didi has always been good to me. There is no instance when she went against me.'

'I agree with you. Kaushalya is good-natured and kind-hearted, but Sumitra is sharp and cunning. Remember, she comes from Kashi, the land of pundits. She has Kaushalya under her thumb and will make her do as she wants. If this continues, you will have a place in Ayodhya only as their slave.'

'I will take my life before becoming a slave to my sautans,' said a visibly shaken Kaikeyi.

'Then, you have no place in the palace of Ayodhya.'

At the advice of Manthara, Kaikeyi entered the *kopa-griha*, a chamber of anger and dissent in the palace's rear. She replaced her fine clothes and jewellery with one-piece coarse clothing. Dashrath found her there, sprawled on the floor in the semi-darkened room, her hair dishevelled, and makeup withered. The king was sorry to look at his favourite queen clad in indifferent clothes in the forsaken surroundings. He stooped down and said, 'I am sorry, my dear, for the delay. I wanted to bring the news of Ram's coronation to you personally. I know you are happy with the decision.'

'I am not deaf or blind not to see the surrounding happenings,' said Kaikeyi.

For an ageing king, it was difficult to bend so low and speak. He said, 'Princess, why don't you come out? We may sit comfortably and discuss.'

'You may have all the comforts you want. I am comfortable on the floor with rags.'

'Why do you speak like this? The entire country is rejoicing, let us be a part of the celebrations.'

'At this stage, I will rejoice a bowl of poison. Please ask someone to get it.'

After much persuasion, Kaikeyi said, 'You offered me two boons of my choice long ago. Do you remember?'

'How can I forget it? Today I live because of your valour. You may ask for anything, anytime.'

'Will you swear by Ram?' asked Kaikeyi.

The emperor was not comfortable with Ram's oath. He said, 'Tell me what do you want?'

Kaikeyi once again reminded him of the promised boons, the glory of the clan of Ikshvaku, their origin from the sun god and the oath of Ram. After taking a deep breath, she said, 'Crown Bharat as the new king and exile Ram for fourteen years to Dandaka Forest.'

It took some time for Dashrath to sink in what he had heard. When he understood the import of her words, he walked a few paces away and muttered, 'Do you know what are you telling me?'

'Send a messenger to fetch Bharat. Please coronate him on his return. But don't hold back Ram. Let him go away with the first rays of sun.'

Dashrath made all efforts to convince Kaikeyi, but she didn't agree. The emperor sent for Vashisth to speak to her. But he declined to get drawn into the private matters of the husband and wife. Dashrath offered a compromise. He said, prostrating before Kaikeyi 'Let Bharat get crowned, but let Ram remain in Ayodhya. You know Ram, he wouldn't harm anyone. I beg you. I will not survive without Ram. Have mercy on me.'

Ram was ready to go. Lakshman, without seeking his permission, or anyone else, was ready to accompany him. Sita also decided to go with her husband. She did not heed the request of Dashrath or Kaushalya. Ram's mother was crestfallen. She had pitched all her hope on Ram becoming the emperor. She would either go with Ram or drown herself in the Sarayu river. Ram pacified her. He said, 'Mother, your place is by the side of your husband. You know he is facing the most difficult phase of his life. He needs you more than ever. I will return after completing the exile period. Fourteen years would pass like fourteen days. Don't you remember how my last stay with Sage Vishwamitra brought countless blessings for me and the family? This could be a better opportunity.'

Manthara left the palace unannounced. Her chariot and the personal driver were on the bank of Sarayu river, waiting for the crowds to clear. She walked down, unnoticed among the crowds, and asked her driver to leave immediately. She feared violent retaliation from Lakshman and the people of Ayodhya. Before her role surfaced, she would cross the borders of Koshala.

The departure of Ram and Sita devastated Kaikeyi. She was worried about the fast-deteriorating health of her husband. Her mission was so great that any cost paid for its success was not too much.

Dashrath asked Sumantra, the prime minister, to take Ram, Sita and Lakshman in his chariot for three days and bring them back after a holy dip in the Ganga. Ram refused to return and Sumantra came back with the empty chariot. They crossed the holy waters at Shringverpur. Sita worshipped the river goddess Ganga who appeared in person to bless her.

Chapter 13

GANGA

'Mother, you gave salvation to our ancestors, the sons of Sagar (an ancestor of Ram). You give life to the millions of people by nourishing thousands of acres of land. You transform and cleanse the living, dying, and dead of all their accumulated sins with a sip of your holy water. By dissolving the last remains, one gets salvation without effort. I beg you, the beloved of Lord Mahadev, the daughter of Himwant, the mountain and Maina, the well-being of my husband and brother-in-law during our exile and safe return to Ayodhya after fourteen years of exile. I, accompanied by my husband and Lakshman, promise to worship you again on my return journey.' Sita, struck with deep sorrow, made an emotional appeal to Mother Ganga. She took a holy bath in her cool and sparkling waters. She had yet to overcome the trauma of their banishment amid the preparations for the coronation of her husband.

Obeying the command of his stepmother, Ram, Sita and Lakshman left Ayodhya in their austere garb, riding the chariot driven by Sumantra. On the first night, they stayed on the banks of the Tamasa River. Travelling through the day, by the next evening they crossed the borders of Koshala and reached the friendly country of Sringberpur. Guha, the Nishad king, welcomed them. After an overnight stay under a susumpa tree, Ram requested Sumantra to return the next morning. They crossed the Ganga on a boat and then walked on foot to Prayagraj. After taking a bath at the Triveni Sangam, Sita worshipped the salvation-giving goddess.

The family in which the Mother Goddess Kutila incarnated comprised her mother Maina, father Himwant, her one hundred brothers and two sisters Ragini and Parvati. The three sisters were beautiful and virtuous. They were ardent devotees of Lord Shiva and passionately desirous of having a son from him. So, they undertook penance to get Shiva as their husband and bear a son from him. A determined Kutila, later known as Ganga, vowed that by her indefinite tapasya she would make Shiva agree to marry her and bestow her with his son. But Brahma thought otherwise and asked her to give up the idea of marrying Shiva as he prepared Parvati to marry him. Kutila disagreed with Brahma and continued her tapasya. Unhappy over the refusal, Brahma cursed her to become all water and she, in her rage, flooded the Brahma Lok. The Creator then took Kutila to the heavens and turned her into the overflowing celestial waters and named her Ganga. The boon from Brahma satisfied her elder sister Sandhya. She would become the mother of Shiva's child. Sandhya went to the sky and merged with the constellation of Kritikas, the Pleiades, on the advice of Brahma.

Brahma did not find an imprudent Ganga suitable to carry Shiva's seed, whereas Ganga insisted she was more suitable than her younger sister Parvati. Ganga was desirous of Shiva from the heart and determined to hold him within her aqueous body. She was as beautiful as the rays of the moon and as gifted as Parvati. Shiva was to face an unending rivalry between the two sisters concerning him. Kutila, after becoming the holy water in the heavens, did not give up her austerities. Pleased with her tapasya, Shiva promised her to fulfil her desire to become the mother of his son.

Parvati's youth and beauty failed in making Shiva fecundate her. She was instrumental only to the extent of arousing him. He controlled his seed through his yoga power and, at the request of the gods, spurt it into the mouth of Agni. Agni carried the seed within him and, when commanded by Brahma, deposited it into Ganga. Ganga was pleased at the fulfilment of her lifelong desire of carrying the seed of Shiva. She carried it within her body but couldn't bear it for too long. While Ganga carried the seed within her, it transformed into a bright and healthy embryo. She deposited the embryo in the forest of reeds on her bank. On the bank of the Ganga, the embryo transformed into a beautiful child. After some time, six Kritikas came for the holy bath and saw the divine child. They picked him up and became his foster mothers. They named the child Kartikeya. The six holy women wanted to feed the child. So, the infant transformed himself into a child with six faces. That is why the son of Shiva is also known as Shadanan, or the God with six faces.

All three daughters of Maina and Himalaya were thus instrumental in the nativity of Shiva's son. Parvati had stirred Shiva, but he deprived her of receiving his seed. Ganga had carried the embryo and transformed it into a child. Ragini, merged with Kritikas, nursed the newly born child.

Ganga was not happy just as the mother of Shiva's son. She wanted Shiva to bow down before her through her austerities. She was mad about him and wanted to be with him always, more than Parvati or anyone else. Ganga, therefore, once again undertook tapasya to get Shiva. After long and arduous tapas, Shiva, pleased with her dedication, agreed to keep her with him, but she must wait for an appropriate time.

The great Suryavanshi Emperor Sagar of Ayodhya was a benevolent ruler with distinction. He had sixty thousand sons from his younger Queen Sumati, the daughter of Sage Kashyap. The princes were obedient sons and fearsome warriors. From his elder Queen Keshini, the princess of Vidarbha, he had only one son named Asamanj. Asamanj was the eldest among the princes. But he was a wicked person who took no interest in the state affairs. He did not respect the saints and elders and tormented his subjects for no reason. The only son of Asamanj was Anshuman. Sagar deprived his eldest son of the imperial inheritance and instead nominated his grandson Anshuman as successor to the throne of Ayodhya. Anshuman was a noble-hearted prince and a favourite of his grandfather, uncles and the subjects.

Sagar performed all the yajnas, big and small, many times over and finally at the helm of his glory, planned the most difficult and potent sacrifice—the Ashwamedh Yajna. As a part of this yajna, a resplendent horse, fully caparisoned and decorated splendidly, was set free to roam around. It trotted at will without caring for the borders of the other kingdoms. A large army followed the horse. Any country that allowed the horse to pass through its territory accepted the over-lordship of the horse's owner. If anyone tried to stop or hold up the consecrated horse, it was taken as a sign of a battle invitation. The army accompanying the horse then attacked the country where the horse was stopped. If the horse's owner won, they set the horse free again, and the horse continued marching.

All the rulers of the countries through which the horse passed became the vassals of the king and they accepted him as their liege-lord. The emperor invited all such rulers to the great Horse Sacrifice, and they came with gifts and fealty depending on their stature. The king was thereafter addressed as Chakravarti Samrat or the Emperor of the Earth. Such emperors were respected as much as Lord Indra and were certain to get a place in heaven with the gods. As they were invincible by any king on earth, they might very well challenge Indra and extend their empire to the heavens. Indra and the gods were always apprehensive and when a king performed such yajna anywhere on earth, they tried to sabotage it.

That happened with Sagar's horse as well. After going around the earth, sixty thousand victorious sons of Sagar with the horse in the lead returned to Ayodhya. The yajna began with thousands of learned Brahmins. All far and near relatives and friendly and subjugated kings were also present. But before they could complete the yajna, the sacrificial horse miraculously disappeared from the yajna premises. Indra, envious of the success of the sacrifice, abducted the horse and disappeared with it. To keep it out of sight, he kept the horse in the ashram of Lord Kapil in the netherworld . Sage Kapil was a great saint and a partial incarnation of Lord Vishnu. The Lord, living in complete seclusion, was deep in his meditation when Indra brought the horse to his ashram. Sagar asked his sons to search for the horse everywhere, but they failed to find it. They now became sure that the horse was in the underground world.

The Brahmins conducting the yajna cautioned the king against abandoning the sacrifice midway, as doing so would be a grave sin and provoke the Yajna God's anger. Following their father's guidance, Sagar's sixty thousand sons began to dig into the earth. Each prince dug an area of one yojana, resulting in three-fourths of the earth's surface being turned into deep, wide pits. Eventually, they reached the underground ashram of Sage Kapil and found the horse tied to a tree trunk behind the sage's ashram.

The deep excavation of the earth fatigued the young sons of Sagar. Intoxicated by their recent exploits, they kicked the meditating saint. They tormented him by calling him a thief and a coward. Not knowing the truth and about the mischief played by Indra, they assumed the seer stole the horse. Lord Kapil was furious at the disruption of his tapas midway. He opened his bloodshot eyes and with his angry glare reduced the ruthless princes into cinders. Some soldiers following the youngsters, who reached a little later, escaped the fury of the seer. They returned to Ayodhya and told Sagar about the fate of his sons. Sagar had taken *diksha* for performing the yajna so he couldn't leave the pavilion. He sent Anshuman to get the horse back after apologizing to the sage. Anshuman went to the ashram, and after worshipping the saint, sought his forgiveness. He beseeched him to help his grandfather to complete the yajna and tell him how his uncles could attain salvation.

Anshuman brought the horse back to Ayodhya, and Sagar completed the Ashwamedha Yajna with the intricate rituals and sacrifices prescribed by the scriptures. Following the ceremonial sacrifice of the horse, Emperor Sagar and Queen Keshini took a symbolic bath in the Sarayu River, marking the successful completion of the yajna. In celebration, the emperor generously distributed vast amounts of money, cows, clothing, and gold and silver among the Brahmins, the poor, and the needy.

Despite the grand festivities, Sagar was deeply mournful over the loss of his sons. Shortly after the yajna, he abdicated the throne and retired to the Himalayas with his queens, leaving the kingdom to his grandson. Anshuman, grieving the loss of his uncles, remembered the words of Lord Kapil, who had said that only the holy waters of the Ganga could bring salvation. However, the Ganga resided in heaven and would never agree to descend to earth.

On his deathbed, Anshuman confided his lifelong sorrow to his son, Dilip. He implored Dilip to dedicate his life to bringing the sacred river to earth. Dilip, a renowned and benevolent emperor of the Suryavansha, known for his extensive generosity, struggled with the daunting challenge. Despite his noble intentions, he too found himself unable to summon the courage necessary to accomplish this formidable task.

Dedication and persistence made the seemingly impossible possible. While his great-grandfather, grandfather, and father each found reasons to avoid the daunting task of bringing the river-goddess Ganga to Earth, Bhagirath accepted it as a challenge. Growing up, he was haunted by the fate of his sixty thousand ancestors and made it his life's mission to secure their salvation. As a young prince, he was deeply pained by the fact that the spirits of his forefathers were stranded, their mortal remains awaiting after-death rituals. Despite no heir to take care of the kingdom during his absence, Bhagirath remained undeterred.

He entrusted the governance to his ministers and set out for Gokarna Tirth. There, he engaged in intense penance, standing on one foot to appease Lord Brahma. He first lived on dry leaves, then subsisted on water, followed by sunlight, and finally endured on nearly nothing. Moved by his devotion, the Creator appeared and offered to grant his wish. Bhagirath requested, 'The remains of my forefathers lie scattered underground. Please help me in bringing the salvation-bestowing goddess, Ganga, to Earth. Additionally, please bless me so that the lineage of Ikshvaku will always have a male successor.'

Brahma replied, 'I may request Goddess Ganga to descend to earth. But if she came down, the earth wouldn't be able to withstand her flooding and may go to the netherworld. Nothing can ever bear the force of her descent. I don't find anyone except the three-eyed Lord Mahadev capable of holding her up from the direct impact. You must please the Great Lord and request him to accept her on his head.'

Bhagirath began another tapasya, this time focusing on Shiva. For one year, he stood on the tip of his single toe. When the Lord appeared he said, 'O Lord of the lords, the souls of my ancestors are hanging midway without gaining salvation. Mother Ganga is agreeable to come to earth to facilitate their entry into the heavens. Kindly hold her on your head.'

Shiva remembered his promise to Ganga that she would find a permanent place with him. He replied Bhagirath, 'Let the daughter of Himalaya and Maina come down. I will make sure that not a single drop of her water is wasted.'

Bhagirath prayed Ganga for another year. At the end of one year, Ganga began her descent from heaven in a thunderous deluge. Shiva stood atop the Himalayas, looking towards the sky, his feet firmly on the ground, arms akimbo. When the flooding stream was about to hit and pulverize the earth, he took the impact on his head and the flooding deluge disappeared within his matted locks. Shiva took her turbulence on his forehead like a garland of pearls. Ganga, who wanted to press Shiva down to the netherworld by her raging whirlpools, could not find an outlet from the stocks of his meshed hair. Not even a drop came out of Shiva's hair. It seemed as if it was the end of Ganga.

Bhagirath was troubled but not disheartened. Despite three enduring tapasyas, his prayers had yielded no results. His forefathers remained stranded, awaiting their final journey.

Undeterred, Bhagirath began another round of penance, this time to appease Lord Shiva, the Gangadhar. His relentless dedication and perseverance became legendary, making his name synonymous with tireless effort. Shiva, having tested Bhagirath's resolve, finally allowed the divine Ganga to flow from his hair.

Bhagirath guided the sacred river from the Himalayas to Patal Lok, the netherworlds, passing through Ganga Sagar. Along the way, many rivers and streams joined the Ganga in reverence, transforming the small stream into a mighty river. The first to greet her was the Alaknanda at Devprayag, followed by the Yamuna at Prayagraj. The Triveni Sangam in Prayagraj, where the Ganga, Yamuna, and the mythical Saraswati meet, became a significant pilgrimage site.

Thanks to Bhagirath's unwavering efforts, his ancestors attained salvation. His toil benefited humanity in both worldly and spiritual realms. The vast pits dug by Sagar's sixty thousand sons were filled with the waters of Bhagirathi, as the Ganga came to be known, and transformed into seven huge oceans.

Brahma did not find an impetuous Ganga capable of carrying the seed of Shiva. But she was determined to hold the seed of Shiva within her body. The fierce and proud Ganga was intensely desirous of Shiva. She wanted to crush him with her violent turbulence so that the pieces of his bones mixed with her water-body like mall conch shells. She would then sweep him to the netherworld, away from Parvati, away from Nandi and the ganas, and keep him only for herself. But Shiva had the power to hold her on his head. He caught and entrapped a descending Ganga in his locks. He always carried her on his head like an ornament close to the crescent moon. When he danced in ecstasy, she glided in the matted skeins of his hair, scintillating like a mermaid with the waves of his hair spreading through the cosmos.

Ganga fulfilled her mission of purifying the ancestors of Bhagirath and facilitated their ascend to heaven. Since then, her work never ceased. She gave salvation to the dying and joy to the living. People called her 'Mokshada' or the one who releases people from the cycle of life and death. She is also called 'Bhogada' or the giver of happiness to the living. Parvati was envious of her presence, but Ganga didn't pay heed to her younger sister's jealousy. Her desire to become the mother of Shiva fulfilled her desire. She gave birth to a boy and, living in his matted hair, she forever remained close to him.

The holy river flows thrice: in heaven, on earth and in the netherworld. She is Mandakini in heaven, Ganga on earth, and Bhogawati in the netherworld.

Ganga appeared before Sita in all her radiant glory, her beauty as cool and soothing as the rays of a full moon. Mounted on a crocodile, she wore a shimmering white crown. In one hand, she held a *kalash* (water pot), a water lily, and a rosary, while her other hand was raised in the abhay-mudra, a gesture of protection. With folded hands, she bowed to Sita and said, 'O Vaidehi, beloved of Ram, who is not aware of your power and influence? With just a glance, you can create and dissolve entire cosmos. I am grateful for your request, as it elevates my own dignity and significance of my boons. To demonstrate the truth of my words, I will grant you your wish. I shall wait here, ready to welcome you upon your return with Ram and Lakshman.'

Sita was delighted listening to the gratifying words of Mother Ganga. She bowed to her once again and the river goddess disappeared in clear rhythmic waves of the majestically flowing stream. Ram, Sita and Lakshman went to the hermitage of Sage Bharadwaj, a little distance upstream on the banks of Ganga. On the advice of Bharadwaj, the three proceeded to

Chitrakoot, meeting Sage Valmiki on their way, and crossing the dark blue waters of the river Yamuna, the sister of Yama.

Dashrath couldn't cope with Ram's exile. He left for the heavenly abode thinking of the curse of Shravan Kumar's blind parents. Bharat performed his last rites after his return from Kaikeya. He, as they expected, refused to accept the throne. He decided to go to Chitrakoot and convince his elder brother to return to Ayodhya and accept the kingship. Kaikeyi supported the idea and persuaded Bharat to take her along. After initial hesitation in view of her culpability, she could convince him. She would tell Ram that the boons received by her stood withdrawn and he must abandon his banishment forthwith. She was confident that it wouldn't happen, and Ram would never return without completion of the exile term.

Kaikeyi's primary concern was the safety of Ram, Sita and Lakshman. She wanted to meet Rishi Atri and request him to arrange an impregnable security cordon for Ram and others with the help of his disciples, local tribal heads, and King Jatayu of Gidham. Kabandh and Viradh, the local commanders of Ravan near Chitrakoot, must know about Ram's presence and the purpose of his fourteen-year stay in the Dandaka. The rakshasas might try to attack Ram and harm Sita. She was also eager to update herself regarding preparations for the ensuing fight with the rakshasas. She must know how much time sages would require to complete the arrangements for the last assault.

Kaushalya and Sumitra were eager to accompany Bharat to Chitrakoot, as were Guru Vashisth and Mother Arundhati. Many prominent citizens of Ayodhya also expressed a strong desire to join, believing that their collective prayers might persuade Ram to return. For Ram's coronation as crown prince, holy water from various rivers and other sacred items had been gathered. Bharat took these materials with him, along with half of the Kosala Army. After Ram's coronation in Chitrakoot, he was expected to return as an emperor, in accordance with imperial protocol, with the army in tow.

Upon reaching Prayagraj, Bharat took a ritual bath in the sacred Triveni and worshipped Mother Ganga. With his palms outstretched, he pleaded, 'O Goddess of Salvation and Giver of Life, I beseech you, even though our Kshatriya tradition forbids begging. Please grant me the boon to bring my brother back from the forest.'

As tears rolled down Bharat's face, the river goddess remained silent, flowing gently towards her destination, where Bharat's ancestors had once been reduced to ashes. With renewed resolve, Bharat folded his palms once more and continued his journey to Chitrakoot.

As Kaikeyi expected, Ram did not agree to return to Ayodhya. Ram's father-in-law, King Janak, also arrived with Vishwamitra, Satanand, Jabali, Gautam and other great sages. None of them asked Ram to abandon his banishment prematurely. Siradhwaj took Bharat aside and told him in confidence about the forecast of Saint Yagnavalk. They left it to the superior wisdom of Ram to decide whether to return or continue staying in the forest.

Kaikeyi and Bharat went to the ashram of Sage Atri and Mother Anasuya. Atri told Ram that he was in the Dandaka to complete the task assigned by gods and sages. He would return to Ayodhya after killing the rakshasas and destroying evil from the face of the earth. Ram, as a Chakravarti Samrat, would rule the earth indefinitely. He told Bharat that his mother was helping Ram to achieve what he was born to do: annihilation of the evildoers and to re-establish dharma.

Chapter 14

ANASUYA

Bharat could not comprehend the full context of what King Siradhwaj told him. When the world humiliated and insulted his mother, he addressed her as a goddess. It was even more surprising because Kaikeyi sent his daughter Sita and son-in-law Ram to the forest and deprived them of the opulence of their palace in Ayodhya. The king of Videha, finding Bharat circumspect, advised him to meet Sage Atri and his wife Anasuya, along with his mother. The sage had their hermitage a little distance away on the banks of Mandakini to the south of Chitrakoot.

Chitrakoot is on the southern side of the Aryavart, bordering the Vindhyachal escarpment. It was part of the inhospitable forest area of the Dandakaranya, which extended from Chitrakoot towards southern peninsular Jambudwip. The thousands of square miles of the Dandakaranya was inhabited mainly by the tribals, foragers and hunter-gatherers. Of late, the rakshasas had strengthened their presence on the entire forest area of the Dandakaranya. Chitrakoot as part of the Dandaka was the northern border of the rakshasa empire. Ravan's cousins Khar, Dushan and Trisara, and his younger sister Shurpanakha, ruled the area with half a million soldiers camped there. However, to avoid daily skirmishes with each other, they accepted the area of Chitrakoot on both sides of Mandakini as a common territory of the Aryans and the rakshasas. Neither the rakshasas nor the Aryans tried to engage each other. The local commander of this region was Viradh, supported by a headless rakshasa Kabandh. Viradh was nicknamed the 'Terror of Dandaka'.

That was the place Ram, with his wife and brother, made his home in the first phase of their exile. Chitrakoot was a lush green beautiful forest because of the mild weather and abundance of water with three rivers—Payasvini, Gupt-Godavari and Mandakini—meandering through its low mountainous terrain. The forest was full of a large variety of fruits and flowers. The presence of many saints and holy men added serenity to its existence. With thousands of natural caves and fountains all over the hills, it was genuinely the most suitable place for tapasya.

Once, because of a long and deadly dry spell of ten years, Chitrakoot suffered a severe famine. The famine had a catastrophic impact on the people, animals and vegetation. There was a widespread shortage of food, which resulted in malnutrition and starvation. A large number of people died of the pandemic caused by hunger and malnutrition. The place was almost deserted as thousands migrated for their survival to the Gangetic plains, leaving their cattle unattended. The animals and birds started dying without water and food. Once a dense green forest, Chitrakoot turned into a desert with no green plants and trees in sight that provided fodder to the animals. The havoc wrought by the long dry spell distressed Mother Anasuya. She, with her husband Sage Atri, stayed in Chitrakoot in the face of this calamity when others left in large numbers.

Anasuya was the daughter of Sage Kardam and Devahuti, a princess born of Chakravarti Samrat Manu and Shatarupa. Kardam and Devahuti had nine daughters and one son. Sage Kapil, the youngest among the siblings, was a partial incarnation of Lord Vishnu.

The nine beautiful and virtuous sisters were married to nine renowned sages. Anasuya was married to Sage Atri, one of the seven great sages known as the Saptarishis.

The loss of innocent lives and the slow, agonizing deaths they suffered deeply distressed Anasuya. Using the power of her chastity, she stormed the heavens and compelled Brahma to grant her a wish. To address the persistent issues of drought and famine, she brought down the river Mandakini, an incarnation of Mother Ganga, from heaven.

The appearance of Mandakini transformed the region's topography forever. Chitrakoot, once barren, became fertile and lush, abundant with a diverse array of fruits and flowers. Soon, it became a favoured destination for sages and sannyasis.

Bharat knew about Mother Anasuya and Sage Atri. He, while studying the scriptures at the ashram of Guru Vashisth, came across many hymns in Rigveda composed by the great seer. Vashisth was an admirer of Atri and Anasuya. Bharat heard the story from his Guru-mother Arundhati, about how the three great gods who tried to test the power of Anasuya's chastity became her sons.

The wandering minstrel Narad once went to the Kailash. Goddess Parvati, after welcoming him, asked about the happenings around the three worlds. The Goddess asked, 'Is there a woman in the triple world who loves her husband more than I do? Is someone more chaste than I and takes more care of her husband? Of course, I am the most beautiful in the universe that goes without saying.'

Narad smiled mischievously. He said, 'Narayan, Narayan. Mother, you love Mahadev and take care of him like a dutiful wife would do. You are, beyond doubt, chaste and faithful to him. There are women on earth who are humans but greater than the goddesses because of their unflinching devotion to their husbands.'

'Tell me the name of at least one such woman. Let me know who is she?' asked an envious and anxious Parvati.

'She is Anasuya, wife of Sage Atri.'

'Why should I believe you? How Anasuya's devotion can equal mine? The entire universe worships me as the most devoted wife of Lord Mahadev.'

Narad told her the story of Anasuya and how she, through the power of chastity and devotion to her husband, walked into heaven. She forced Brahma to send Mandakini to earth. The presence of the river was necessary to protect and preserve the life of the humans, animals and the vegetation. 'She is as beautiful, if not more, as you are. Mother Anasuya owns the divine ornaments gifted to her by her mother Princess Devahuti, the daughter of Emperor Manu. She has a magical herbal potion that makes face and body angelic and ageless.'

Parvati was upset. How these lesser beings, weak and mean mortals, could compete with the celestials? Narad could see the expressions of disbelief on her face. He asked, 'Who do you meditate upon and whose name you utter while praying?'

'My Guru Vamdev gave me Ram Mantra and that is the name I repeat while praying.'

Narad smiled politely and said, 'Anasuya doesn't know any guru or a mantra. She worships her husband and utters his name while praying. She knows no other man in her life.'

The time was up for Narad. He picked up his beena and left Kailash. His brother Daksha cursed him he couldn't remain in one place for over twenty-four minutes.

Narad entered the Kshir Sagar where Lord Vishnu and Goddess Lakshmi lived. Lakshmi asked him, 'It has been long since you last visited us, Narad. What is happening in the Trailokya?'

Narad told her the story of Anasuya and how she helped the inhabitants of Chitrakoot by bringing down the Mandakini. Lakshmi was surprised to hear about Mahasati Anasuya. She was envious of the rishika but couldn't stop Narad from speaking his mind. Vishnu was also in agreement with Narad. This was unacceptable to Lakshmi, who couldn't withstand the praise of another woman by her husband in her presence. Narad said, 'Anasuya is extremely virtuous and most devoted woman to her husband in the entire universe. Her husband is well known for his good deeds and knowledge. Believe me, mother, she is not the only one. There are women who are equally chaste and virtuous. Damayanti, Savitri, and Arundhati, just to name a few.'

Lighting a blaze of jealousy in the hearts of Parvati and Lakshmi, Narad moved on, singing the holy name of Narayan. From Kshir Sagar, his next destination was the Brahma Lok. After paying obeisance to his father, Brahma, he went to Brahmani. This time, without being asked, he told her about his visit to the Kailash and Kshir Sagar. He repeated his conversation with Parvati and Lakshmi and how they became envious of Anasuya. Brahmani asked her husband, 'Is it true that with no tapasya or boon from any god, she could march into heaven and return to earth with the Mandakini?'

Brahma reaffirmed, 'Yes, that is true. She, through the power of her chastity, which is superior to any tapasya undertaken by an individual in the universe, came to heaven.

Anasuya requested me to send down Mandakini with her.'

The goddesses were envious of Anasuya. She was superior to them in more than one aspect. That's what Narad said. Their husband's approval of what that wanderer boasted about the woman heightened their agony. The three goddesses met secretly without the knowledge of their husbands. They must compromise the modesty of Anasuya. The goddesses asked their husbands to molest her, but they refused. They wouldn't do any such thing. The curse of a chaste woman was infallible. Vishnu, reminding Lakshmi, said, 'Have you forgotten what happened when I physically abused virtuous Brinda? She cursed me into becoming a black rock. I don't want to face a similar situation now.'

The three great gods gave in when their wives threatened. They would return to their parents if their husbands did nothing to undermine the virtue of Anasuya. They may or may not violate her, but must do something that raises questions about her chastity. The trinity too wanted to test the power of a sati and also, if what Narad told about her was true, teach a lesson to their headstrong wives. Together they went to Chitrakoot near the ashram of Anasuya.

Brahma, Mahesh and Vishnu did not miss the generous use of religious symbols in front of the cottage that was neatly plastered with a thin layer of cow dung. Anasuya marked the place with the auspicious signs of thunderbolt, goad, lotus flowers and conch shells. The green trees of mango, peepal, plantains, ashoka, pakad, pannaga and kovidar surrounded the beautiful hermitage. For any hermitage, three trees of mango, pakad or white fig and peepal were mandatory. Peepal was recommended for meditation, pakad for performing yajna and sitting under a mango tree one remembered god. The trees were laden with fruits and flowers. They could see a row of tulsi plants running through the length of the courtyard planted by the house lady who regularly watered and worshipped them. The birds chirped and cool wind whispered in the leaves. The slow and rhythmic music of the Mandakini waves flowing nearby pleased the ears.

Shiva, Vishnu and Brahma waited in the nearby forest and when Atri left the hermitage, approached Anasuya, who was engaged in her household chores. The gods took the form of naked yogis and called the lady of the house, requesting alms. Anasuya came out with a basket of fruits and roots, enough for three people. But the sages refused to accept the food. One sage said, 'We are *digambar* (unclothed) hermits, followers of Lord Mahadev and accept food only from a house lady who serves us without clothes. If you serve us food unclothed, we will accept it, otherwise, we will go back hungry from your doorstep.'

It was against the dharma of a homemaker to send back anyone hungry from her doorstep, more so if he happened to be a hermit. Anasuya was in a dilemma. Atri was not in the ashram for advice. The dictate of the yogis was bizarre. She had given alms frequently to the unclothed yogis, but they never made it conditional. How could she go before the yogis without clothes? Such a demand from a woman was certainly inappropriate.

When Anasuya closed her eyes, she saw the yogis' actual form through her mystical powers. She also knew the purpose of their visit. The rishika, after understanding the whole matter, decided to reply to them in their language. She took some water, with which she washed the feet of her husband, in her right hand, invoked her husband's name for support and sprinkled the water on the yogis. The three medicants immediately turned into infants of six months. She made them lie on a bed and breastfed them as a mother would feed her children. When Atri returned, he saw the children in the cradles. Knowing the truth through his divine vision, he did not ask his wife about the children. He instead said, 'Anasuya, the gods have come to our ashram to seek a mother's love they were deprived of. Please take care of your sons.'

The gods enjoyed their new life. They were self-born eternal gods without parents. They did not know what the love of a mother was like. Anasuya treated them like her own sons. For the first time, they knew that a mother's love was incomparable. The gods relished the newfound love of a mother. They forgot everything else. Anasuya, who did not have children of her own, poured out her heart on them.

Brahmani, Gauri and Shri waited anxiously for the return of their husbands. They expected them to return within no time after breaking the austerities of Anasuya. When there was nothing heard about them for a long time, they summoned Narad to find out the whereabouts of their husbands. Narad advised them to go to the Anasuya Ashram and look out for them. The three goddesses went to Chitrakoot and tried to locate them surreptitiously, but they were to find nowhere. Panic-stricken, they went to meet Anasuya.

'Welcome daughters-in-law. For the first time, you have come to the home of your mother-in-law. I must, therefore, welcome you like newlywed brides coming to the house of their in-laws,' said Anasuya.

This unexpected welcome took aback the goddesses. Anasuya had nothing against them. Her name rightly denoted 'free from envy and anger'. The goddesses, forgetting their resentment, bowed to her feet, and she blessed them with the eternal blessing and ever-lasting life of their husbands. They enquired Anasuya about their husbands. She took the goddesses inside her thatched cottage, where the three infants lay squealing with delight and laughing out innocently in their respective cradles.

'Who are these children?' asked Parvati.

'They are your husbands. I have, through my austerities, transformed them to their present state. As the chaste and devoted wives, please find out who among the three is your husband. If you could identify correctly, the entire world and I will accept you as the most devoted wife in the universe. Like any mother, I can very well differentiate among my children, though they may look identical to you. You may rightfully take your husband with you once you identify him. I will let you know whether you are right once you take your chance,' said Anasuya.

The goddesses went around the cradles looking for some identification mark, but there were none. They looked identical in all aspects. They were shamefaced and humiliated. After trying for some time and discussing among themselves, they surrendered before the Mahasati. They sought her forgiveness and requested her to return their husbands. Anasuya said to Lakshmi, 'The baby in the centre is Vishnu, your husband. You should have recognized him by his beautiful smile and demeanour.'

Then she looked towards Parvati. 'Don't you recognize that baby on the left? Observe the rhythmic movements of his hands and feet as if he is performing the Tandava. He is Mahadev, your husband.'

Finally, she addressed Brahmani, 'The baby on the right is so cool and serenity is imprinted all over his face. He is not as agile and playful as the other two. He is Brahma, your husband.'

The revelation embarrassed and humbled the three goddesses. How could they miss such telltale signs of their husbands? It was so simple, but they failed miserably. Their devotion to their husbands was tested and they couldn't prove themselves. They once again requested Anasuya to return them their husbands.

Sati Anasuya brought the gods back to their original form. They bowed before her in obeisance and expressed their desire to remain in the ashram with their mother. In desperation, their wives started sobbing. They requested them to return to their abodes. The Trinity, however, said, 'As the sons of Mother Anasuya, we are bound by her command. Without her permission, we can't go anywhere.'

Parvati held the feet of Anasuya, and the mother lifted her up in a close embrace. The gods then asked Anasuya to seek the desired boon. 'I don't have to seek anything from others as I have Atri with me. But if you are so keen to get rid of me as your mother, give me three sons like yourselves.'

Vishnu said, 'Mother, I shall be born with the attributes of the three of us. My name as your son will be Dattatreya.'

Shiva said he would take birth as Durvasa, one of his nineteen avatars. Brahma blessed her with the most beautiful son Chandra.

With that, the three gods with their consorts left for their respective homes praising the character of the chaste woman.

That was the story Bharat heard from his guru in the ashram. Today, he had an opportunity to meet her and seek her blessings. He will also know why Sage Bharadwaj asked him to see Sage Atri. Bharat and Kaikeyi travelled to the Anasuya Ashram in a small two-wheeled chariot. Anasuya and Atri welcomed them at the gate and took them inside. Kaikeyi had met the mother before. She embraced the widowed queen and Kaikeyi for the first time burst into uncontrollable tears and wept bitterly with her head on the mother's shoulders.

They sat in a small cottage where Atri told Bharat about the mission of the sages. He said, 'I, Sages Agastya, Bharadwaj,

Sutikshana and Vashisth have joined hands and took the responsibility of protection, preservation and expansion of the Vedic culture. We are working towards the unification of Jambudwip into a single political entity. Bharat, your mother is the sixth most important person in our endeavour towards this noble mission. Besides, Vishwamitra has also been assigned an important role.'

'But the leader and chief executor of this mission is none of us,' Atri said somewhat mysteriously. 'We planned it before you four were born and the execution began when Ram and Lakshman went to secure the yagna of Vishwamitra in the Tataka Van. It was an exercise, an initial training as a part of the preparations for this mission.'

'Am I right in assuming that Dada is the chief executor of this mission?'

Looking at his wife and Kaikeyi, Atri said, 'Yes he is.'

'How about Sita and Lakshman?' asked Kaikeyi.

'We haven't got Lakshman on board as yet. Sita has some idea but is not keen on knowing the details. She would faithfully follow Ram in any enterprise. We have left it to Ram to involve them whenever he feels necessary.'

'But guru-ji, why the mother didn't share it with my father? He would have agreed to send Ram to the forest for the greatest ever cause of humanity. Mother would have escaped all the humiliation and ignominy and we could have saved father's life.'

'Bharat, your honourable late fathcr would never agree to such a request. He wouldn't risk the life of his sons, at least of Ram's, by permitting them to get involved in the operations against the rakshasas. He never thought beyond Koshala,' said Kaikeyi.

Atri supported her and said, 'We tried to get him involved through Vashisth, but he did not agree to get into it. Your mother knows, as she was a witness to it, how difficult it was for us to convince the emperor to permit Ram to accompany Brahmarshi Vishwamitra to the Tatak forest. He has lost any appetite for a battle after his life-threatening injuries in the Battle of Vaijayanta. Then we took this idea over to your braveheart and visionary mother.' Atri took a deep breath. After a brief pause, he said, 'And thanks to the great sacrifice by your mother, the dream of a great united Bharat is closer now than it had ever been in the past.'

Ram with Sita and Lakshman left the picturesque woods of Chitrakoot at the advice of Sage Atri after taking permission from the hermits. The trio had stayed here for over twelve years waiting for the message from the sages. They stayed at the Anasuya Ashram for three days. Sage Atri briefed Ram about the future course of action and the sage's expectations of him. Sita lived with Anasuya as if she was living with Kaushalya.

Atri said, 'From Chitrakoot, now you are shifting to Panchavati, the most horrendous place in the Dandaka Forest. On the left bank of the Godavari River, it is close to Janasthan, the capital of Khar and Dushan, the stepbrothers of Ravan. On your way to Panchavati, you will face some challenges from Viradh and Kabandh, the commanders of the advance guard of the rakshasa army. Sage Sutikshana, the disciple of Maharshi Agastya, will take you to his guru where you will collect the celestial weapons and other weapons of mass destruction and learn their operations.'

Ram and Lakshman listened attentively. Atri continued the narrative. He said, 'The weapons received from Agastya will help you destroy the entire rakshasa army at Janasthan. When you move on, Rishika Shabari will guide you further to Kishkindha, where Sugriv will be waiting with his army of the monkey tribes.'

Atri also advised Ram how he must eliminate Vali, the elder brother of Sugriv, who was on friendly terms with Ravan. Sugriv, as the new king of the monkeys, would help Ram reach Lanka. The discussion went on for three days till each point was deliberated and satisfied.

Sita became so attached to Anasuya that she did not leave her for a minute. They were like a long-lost mother and daughter. Anasuya said to Sita about the virtues of a chaste woman, 'Thinking about another man or woman always leads to grave misunderstanding between a husband and wife. It ultimately results in a breakup. Respect for each other's sentiments is the foundation of a relationship. Be honest with each other; commitment and trust between the two must never fade.'

She gave Sita celestial ornaments that made a woman look more divine and better than the Apsaras. She also gave her ointments and body lotion that kept the skin always fresh and young. Anasuya insisted that Sita, well prepared with makeup and ornaments, went to Ram and surprised him with her beauty. Sita initially hesitated, but when Anasuya insisted, she agreed. Ram was awestruck, looking at his wife. But recovering immediately, he said, 'I am in exile and must live like a celibate. You have vowed to follow me with mind, words, and actions. You must neither use the ointments nor wear jewellery till the end of our banishment.'

Sita agreed. Anasuya asked her to take the ornaments with her. Ram consented to the offer. The next morning, they left for Panchavati and Lakshman constructed a cottage on the banks of Godavari with bamboo sticks, wooden logs and dry grass. One day, while they still lived in Panchavati, Demoness Surpanakha came to their ashram.

Chapter 15

SURPANAKHA

A teenage girl carelessly wandered in the forest on the outskirts of Trikuta Hills near the seashore. The sea was not directly visible to her because of the dense foliage. But she felt the humid saline wind blowing across her fragile frame and dotting her dense black hair all over her face. She heard the rhythmic sound of arriving and departing sea waves. The sound of the sea always calmed her. The girl was lost in her deep thoughts. Her claim to outstanding beauty was certainly questionable, but from her costumes, swagger and self-esteem, in every inch, she looked a princess. At her age, all the girls looked beautiful, or at least they thought so. This girl was no exception.

Oblivious to a young man who followed her from a distance, she enjoyed herself moving around, plucking flowers, tucking them in her hair and quickly abandoning them. A little later, her internal security sensor, or the sixth sense, warned her of another person's presence.

She whirled around abruptly on her heels and found herself facing a handsome, athletically built young man. He was lean and tall, with broad shoulders and long arms. His dark black hair almost touched his shoulders. A long, dense moustache extended to his ears, and his dark complexion hinted that he was not of Aryan descent. Yet, he wasn't an asura either. The girl stared directly into his glistening, mocking black eyes and demanded, 'Who are you? How dare you come up behind me? Don't you value your life? Do you even know who I am?'

'You are roaming all alone in the forest in the company of trees and plants and birds and squirrels. This means you have no friends in the palace and you get bored there. Aren't you on good terms with your Bhabhi Mandodari, who must be of your age?' replied the young man.

It surprised the girl that this man knew her family. He came closer and stood in front of her, too close to her comfort.

She asked, 'You haven't told me about yourself. Are you a friend of my brothers or a guest of Lanka?'

'Princess, I am none of the two. Actually, I am the enemy,' replied the young man with a mischievous smile.

'You are what?!'

'I am Viddutjivha. You must have heard my name. I am the enemy of your brother Ravan.' The young man studied mixed expressions on her face and enjoyed her discomfort.

'How could you reach here? You may get caught any moment by the patrolling guards.'

'Why do you worry about my life? I am your brother's most powerful foe.'

The girl lowered her eyes, avoiding his direct glance.

'I heard about your exceptional beauty from my friends. I couldn't hold myself back and came all the way to meet you.'

'Are you out of your mind? Go away before the soldiers of Lanka sever your head from your body.'

'Fine, I will go. But before leaving, may I tell you that you have the largest and most beautiful eyes I have ever seen? Is that why your name is Meenakshi, the dame with the beautiful eyes?'

The appreciation had the intended effect. Any young man had, for the first time, openly admired her beauty. No one would dare speak to her like that for the fear of her mighty brothers Ravan and Kumbhakarna. She looked at the young man from head to toe with curiosity. The woman within her was melting like butter softening before the sunlight. Viddutjivha did not move from his place. He stood tall and imposing before her, looking straight into her eyes. She, too, did not want him to move away. She felt the urge to touch him but restrained herself.

'I will wait for you tomorrow at the same time. But not here. It's too risky. We shall meet near the base of Mainak Mountain, a little distance from here,' said the young man.

Meenakshi couldn't say no. She rather welcomed it with a fit of mock anger. Before she uttered a word, the man disappeared as quickly as he appeared without waiting for an answer. The girl stood looking around for one more glance at her lover. She wasn't too excited about meeting him again. Was she worried about his safety or the impossibility of this relationship to reach a happy ending? Her brothers would never agree to her marriage to their sworn enemy. She thought about the next day's meeting. She must meet him just once and tell him never to come again. The sister of Ravan had nothing to do with his enemies.

Unknowingly, Meenakshi arrived at the designated place earlier than decided. The spot was beautiful, enveloped by lush green trees and vibrant flowering plants. She had adorned herself for the occasion, wearing light jewellery, deep red-blue silken robes, and a heavily embroidered, bejewelled corset. Her hair was styled in a bun, adorned with a lavish white jasmine gajra. Hidden from the footpath, she sat on a white sphatik stone, watching the bumblebees buzz from one flower to another, swiftly sucking their nectar. They seemed proud and victorious, conquering one bloom after another. Was this the fate of a flower? After draining its nectar and leaving it to wither, the bee had no further interest in it. Her thoughts drifted to Viddutjivha. Was he another bumblebee? Meenakshi was so lost in her reverie that she didn't notice when her lover approached and stood just behind her.

'O fish-eyed beauty, why do you tempt the bumblebees with a bunch of flowers in your long, silky hair? Isn't your beautiful face already enough to attract them?' Viddutjivha asked.

'I am not impressed by your words, which you probably have used hundreds of times before to attract other girls. You are no better than these bumblebees who move away after ruthlessly withering a flower,' said Meenakshi, looking unflinchingly straight at Viddutjivha.

'Don't you agree, Meena? While it's the bee's delight to gather nectar from the flowers, isn't it also the flower's joy to offer its sweetness to the bee? For both, the bumblebee and the flower, giving and receiving are natural needs, and both derive equal pleasure from this relationship,' Viddutjivha said soberly, addressing the girl by her shortened name for the first time.

'Why do I believe you? I don't even know you?' said Meenakshi with the faint contemptuous question mark.

They talked for hours. Viddutjivha told her he was the leader of the Kalkeyas, a powerful tribal community who remained invincible by any asura, mortal or gods. Ravan, after overthrowing Kuber, his stepbrother, from Lanka, tried to conquer this neighbouring country on the western seashore.

The rakshasa's army retreated after huge casualties because of fierce opposition from the Kalkeyas. It became an eyesore to Ravan who had the entire southern peninsula and some parts of the north and west Bharat under his control. After a few meetings, Meenakshi and Viddutjivha became close to each other. Viddutjivha asked Meenakshi to marry her, but she wouldn't agree. Ravan would never accept this marriage, and both would face Chandrahas, the dreaded sword of the rakshasa king.

Meenakshi went to the palace of Vibhishan, the youngest of her three brothers. She told her Bhabhi Sarama, Vibhishan's wife, that she loved Viddutjivha and wanted to marry him. Sarama advised her to speak to Kumbhakarna. He was the only person who could speak to Ravan on equal footing without undue fear or hesitation. Kumbha was the noblest of the three brothers. Inside his gigantic frame, he had a heart of pure gold. He was kind and reasonable, like his father Sage Vishrava, but a fierce fighter like his elder brother Ravan and maternal grandfather Sumali. Most people believed him to be a more powerful warrior than Ravan. But Kumbha was a simple and pious person, unlike his elder brother who was diplomatic, shrewd, lascivious, and power-hungry.

Kumbhakarna went to Ravan and told him about the wish of their sister. He reminded Ravan and their mother Kekashi that the rakshasa culture allowed their girls to choose their husbands, abandon them at will and remarry as many times as they wanted. Ravan was furious. He would slay them before allowing his sister to marry his enemy. Kumbha reasoned with him, 'How can you make an exception to the practice followed by the rakshasas? You advocated such a practice all your life. We have always claimed that we rakshasas were better than the Aryans because we gave equal rights to our womenfolk.

Second, will it be easy for you to kill Viddutjivha? We have already made half a dozen attempts to defeat him but every time we returned licking our wounds.'

Malyavant said, 'Dashanan, the Kalkeya king is a powerful man commanding a powerful army. It is better to have such person as an ally than an enemy.'

'It is a *pratilom* marriage, a superior Brahmin girl marrying an inferior tribal man. Such marriage is not permitted.'

'Brother, since when did we start following the social codes of the Aryans?' asked Kumbhakarna scornfully. Ravan had no reply, so he retreated.

'I don't believe this scoundrel. He has trapped our innocent sister in his game of love. He, through our sister, wants to capture the throne of Lanka.' Ravan protested.

Ravan knew how stubborn his sister could be. She was the youngest and only girl child in the family and hence the favourite of her mother and brothers. Her brother Kumbhakarna and sister-in-law Mandodari, Ravan's wife, loved her like their kid. She was a close confidante and a friend of his youngest Bhabhi, Sarama. Kekashi, since childhood, accepted all the demands of her daughter. Today, again, she would favour her.

With Kumbha, Malyavant and Kekashi favouring her, Ravan, after lots of persuasion, agreed to the marriage, but only on the condition that Viddutjivha and Meenakshi would live in Lanka. The Kalkeyas' chief must accept him as his sovereign and his army of bandits must become a part of the Lankan Army. He would, thus, neutralize the mightiest clan in the peninsular Bharat with no bloodshed. Once they surrendered their weapons and joined the rakshasas, Ravan would gradually relegate them to insignificant positions. But what about their king? Would his presence in Lanka create an independent power centre? Eventually, Dashanan must get rid of him.

Meenakshi and Viddutjivha were married in a grand ceremony. Meenakshi had never been happier. Viddutjivha earned his respect and place in the royal court by his humble behaviour and quick wit. He was now an esteemed member of the ruling family. Only Ravan still held him in contempt. He believed that one day he would rebel and raise a banner of revolt by splitting his commanders. Kekashi, though agreed to her daughter's wish, was not comfortable with her son-in-law. He, being a non-rakshasa, would pollute her lineage. The mother and son hatched a plan to get rid of Viddutjivha. Within three months, Meenakshi was pregnant. The couple was happy at this development, believing that their child would strengthen their bond with the emperor and the queen-mother. The couple, however, did not share the good news with their family members.

One evening, Kekashi invited her daughter and the son-in-law to her palace for a feast. Meenakshi, who was otherwise fond of beverages, refused to take any pretending to be unwell. As a pregnant woman, she must avoid alcohol. They offered Viddutjivha repeated servings of the best drink. After dinner, they walked back to their palace, a short distance away. On the way, he complained of headache and retching. By the time they reached their place, Viddutjivha started vomiting uncontrollably and fainted. Meenakshi rushed a messenger to Raj Vaidya, royal physician, Sukhen. By the time he arrived, her husband was dead. Sukhena examined the corpse and adjudged it as death by administration of the snake poison. The news of the death of Viddutjivha by poisoning spread like wildfire in Lanka. The Kalkeya warriors united and revolted. But the Lankan troops ruthlessly massacred them.

The pronouncement of Sukhen wrenched her heart. Meenakshi couldn't believe her ears and what lay before her as if she were in a trance. No, he couldn't die. He was so strong, so brave, and so powerful. Kumbha was first to arrive with his wife Vajrajwala, closely followed by Vibhishan and Sarama. Mandodari and Meghanad, mother and son, came next. Ravan and Kekashi were the last to arrive among the close relatives. Meenakshi lifted her head and looked at her brothers. The grim but unperturbed face of Ravan, which screamed of guilt, confirmed her suspicion. Her mother could not conceal her sense of accomplishment.

'Aren't you ashamed of your treachery? You couldn't face him on the battlefield, so you killed him deceitfully by poisoning. You are a coward!' Meenakshi screamed, staring at Ravan.

'If you dare to listen, please listen Meena. Mother and I did kill the traitor. He was silently planning a coup and trying to usurp my throne. I have put many of his co-conspirators in dark dungeons where they will never see the light of the day,' replied Ravan. without meeting the glare of his sister's eyes.

'I don't believe a single word you just said. You never agreed to our marriage and waited for an opportunity to get rid of him.'

Kekashi interrupted, 'He was a traitor, Meenu. Before usurping the throne, he usurped you from us. We knew you wouldn't believe it, so we did not confide in you. I did not want a barbarous child from that dreadful tribesman to contaminate our pure rakshasa blood.'

'Sorry mother, you can't stop that. I am ready to give birth to Viddutjivha's child.'

Meenakshi left Lanka fearing that her mother would force her to end her pregnancy or administer her some drug to terminate the yet-to-be-born infant. She would cherish the memory of her husband, the only man she ever knew and loved. She went to Janasthan, where she lived with her cousins Khar and Dushan. Meenakshi gave birth to a son and named him Samba. She wanted him to be a pious soul and a great warrior like her brother Kumbhakarna. She raised him as a Kalkeya prince so that he could avenge the death of his father. Meenakshi sent him over to Lanka to live and train with Kumbha. When still a child, Kumbhakarna advised Samba to undergo tapasya and seek the desired boon from Brahma, as he himself and his two brothers did. Samba meditated in the dense thickets of Dandaka, sitting peacefully under a tree.

One day, Lakshman, while clearing foliage, unintentionally killed the boy with a stroke of his sword. When Lakshman, looking blood on his sword, searched through the bushes, he found a young sage lying in a pool of blood. After the death of her husband in the most brutal manner, the death of her son, the sole support of the young widow, came as an unendurable calamity. She had already severed relations with her mother and eldest brother. Vibhishan was lost in his world of austerities. Only the righteous Kumbha cared about her, but he slept most of the time under the lavish dose of drugs Ravan so eagerly administered.

The princess turned into a monster. She stopped caring for her clothes, hair, or nails. Her nails grew long and hard. Beautiful Meenakshi was thereafter nicknamed horrendous Surpanakha or the sharp-clawed. She wandered into the Dandaka, thinking about how she could avenge the death of her husband and son. She suspected foul play and wondered whether her elder brother and mother were involved in the death of Samba. As was customary among the rakshasas, Kekashi wanted her daughter to marry again, but she refused.

Khar and Dushan couldn't figure out who slew Samba. They searched every village and habitat for the culprit, but with no result. Finally, they zeroed in on the two princes and a beautiful girl accompanying them. They must be involved in the killing. They lived in their ashram in the Panchavati on the Godavari River's bank with the enchanting surroundings. Surpanakha wanted to kill them immediately without further investigation, but Khar and Dushan consulted Marichi. He had known them since his Tataka forest days.

'Don't even dream of confronting the princes. In Siddhashram they killed my mother Tataka, brother Subahu and other rakshasas with little effort. They are much more powerful now after getting the celestial weapons from Sage Agastya,' said Marichi.

'Don't underestimate the power of the rakshasas. Dushan, Trisara and I can destroy the largest army in the world. We are as powerful as Ravan and Meghanad, if not more. A great army of five hundred thousand fierce warriors is here to support us. Let us kill the brothers and gift the young woman to our king,.' replied Khar.

'As the commanders of Janasthan, you must contact the emperor before taking an imprudent and hasty decision. Don't forget Ram killed fierce rakshasa warriors, Viradh and Kabandh, with a single arrow. Ravan knows them and met them in Mithila during Sita's swayamvar. Ravan couldn't even move the Shiva Dhanush, which was strung and broken by Ram effortlessly. Inform the emperor about Ram, Lakshman and Sita near Janasthan. Tell him you suspected the princes of the murder of Samba.' Marichi reasoned out with them.

Marichi told them that most people in the Aryavart believed Ram to be an incarnation of Lord Mahavishnu born to destroy Ravan and mitigate the fear of the rakshasas from the hearts of men and gods. He came to Dandaka with a purpose: to establish peace, righteousness, and justice in the world.

Surpanakha was suddenly interested in the two princes. She would achieve through them what she could not achieve because of the untimely death of her son. Would the murder of his sister's innocent son be an ample reason for Ravan's provocation to the extent of fighting the young princes? Or she must top it up with something more bizarre, more damaging to the highly inflated ego of Ravan. Her son was not around anymore to avenge the death of his father. Whether the two princes could defeat Ravan and overthrow his demonic empire, she wondered. If what Marichi said was true, she would meet them and assess whether she could bet on them.

Ravan wanted to marry Sita. He travelled to Mithila, putting aside the displeasure of queen consort Mandodari, to take part in the swayamvar. Ravan failed to fulfil the condition of stringing the Shiva Dhanush. People ridiculed and humiliated Ravan, who returned to Lanka as a defeated man. Same Sita was now at his doorstep. A lascivious Ravan who could molest Rambha and Vedvati against their fiery resistance would not miss this chance to revenge his humiliation in the swayamvar. Could Sita be that allurement to bring Ravan into confrontation with Ram? Surpanakha thought. Surpanakha would go to any length to avenge the death of her love. She would ruin those who ruined her life, whether it was her family, her race or her country. She might get killed or maimed but it didn't matter.

Ram and Lakshman were mortals. Could they challenge the might of Ravan, who was blessed by Lord Brahma and Shiva? He was the greatest devotee of Mahadev who blessed him with the thousands of heads and nectar hidden within his body at an undisclosed place. His boon from Brahma made him invincible. No one could defeat or kill him; not the gods, demi-gods, demons, Nagas Yakshas and others. But the list did not include humans because he considered them lesser mortals, weak and avaricious. Was that the reason Mahavishnu took birth as a human? She must take her chance.

One evening, Surpanakha, taking the form of a beautiful damsel, approached Ram's cottage. Lakshman, ever vigilant in his watch over Ram and Sita, heard the soft jingling of ornaments approaching them. In the woods, he spotted a woman of extraordinary beauty—her body sculpted to perfection, with sparkling teeth, rosebud lips, and fishlike eyes. Even the austere Lakshman found himself momentarily transfixed by her otherworldly charm. He did not stop her as she made her way to the gate of the hut. When she approached Ram, half shyly with lowered eyes and a radiant smile, he welcomed her, saying, 'You are welcome, O perfect one. May God bless you. Please tell me who you are, where you come from, and what I can do for you?'

'I am the daughter of Sage Vishrava, the son of great Maharshi Pulastya. I am half-sister of Kuber, the wealthiest man in the three worlds.'

Ram, concealing his misgivings, asked politely, 'You mean, you are Emperor Ravan's sister Meenakshi?'

'Yes, unfortunately, I am. But I left Lanka because I abhor the ways of my brother Ravan and other relatives. I despise their sinful ways and cruelties and respect people with virtues and righteousness. After giving up the rakshasa ways of life, I earned this beauty through long and arduous tapasya.'

'That's wonderful. I am happy for you. Please tell me the purpose of your visit. It will please me to help you if the request is proper,' said Ram with his everlasting, serene smile.

'It's not proper for a girl of higher breeding to convey her feelings to a man. But I have no one to speak for me and in extreme desperation, I must speak to you. My beauty and womanhood need the sustenance of a handsome man like you.'

Ram felt pity for the woman standing before him. He didn't like to be harsh with her. 'I am a Kshatriya, and you are the daughter of a Brahmin. The scriptures do not permit such marriages.'

'But my mother is an asura and for a girl from this class, marriage with all classes is permitted.'

'I am a human and you are a rakshasa hence I cannot marry you.'

Undaunted, Meenakshi kept pleading with Ram, while looking at Sita with threatening glances and knit brows. Sita's godly appearance stunned her. What she had heard about her profound beauty was no exaggeration. Ram, knowing about the death of her husband and the son, felt kindly towards her.

'Princess, I am already married. This is my wife, Sita. I have taken a vow of monogamy. Why don't you approach my younger brother Lakshman?'

Surpanakha went to Lakshman who sent her back to Ram, saying that he was a motley servant of Ram and undeserving for a girl of such beauty and prominence. She by now realized that Ram and Lakshman were gentle souls and wouldn't harm her, whatever she said. So, she left the Panchavati Ashram and returned to her cave. She must change her strategy to provoke them. To take revenge for the murder of her husband, she was ready to get hurt or face death.

The next morning, hidden in the woods, she saw Ram come out of the hut and go towards the river for his morning chores. A little later, Sita emerged to gather flowers. Sensing an opportunity, Surpanakha pounced on Sita like an animal and brought her down on the ground. She noticed an alert Lakshman guarding Sita from a distance. He would certainly punish her for harming his sister-in-law. Lakshman pulled her up by grabbing her hair and kicked her in the abdomen. While

Surpanakha fell to the ground, he pulled out his sword and chopped off her ears, nose, and breasts.

'I am sparing your life because you are a woman. Otherwise, anyone touching my Sita Mata would have gone to the abode of Yama.'

Surpanakha rushed to Khar, Dushan and Trisara. They attacked Ram with an enormous army of the rakshasas. Ram sent Sita and Lakshman to safe hiding and killed the rakshasas alone using the divyastras given by Sage Agastya. Surpanakha was now one step closer to her life's aim. She knocked at the door of Ravan. More than about her humiliation and elimination of the rakshasas at Dandaka, she spoke at length about the beauty of Sita. She described her elegance in minute details. She conjured up such a convincing picture of Sita that Ravan felt pleasure and pain at the same time.

Ravan was restless and unhappy and felt the urge to get Sita at any cost. He had missed the chance once in Mithila, he wouldn't again this time. His mind seethed with the idea of the conquest of Sita. Surpanakha's words lit an all-consuming fire within him. His sister knew that her strategy had worked. The end of Ravan was closer than ever.

Chapter 16

SHABARI

The entire Bhil tribe was in a joyous mode as their chief's daughter was to be married the next day. The young woman, Shabari, was watching bemusedly at the celebrations that preceded her wedding. Suddenly she saw hundreds of animals being grouped and led away.

She asked her father, 'Where are these animals being taken?'

'You know Shabari, we are all so happy that your marriage has been fixed with a good boy from a family well known to all of us. These animals are being taken to the slaughterhouse, and they will be sacrificed after your marriage ceremony is over as an expression of gratitude.'

Shabari closed her eyes in pain. She loved animals, birds and every being in nature. Though the girl was born in a tribe that hunted down animals for food, she hated the thought of causing pain to animals. She was a strict vegetarian feeding herself on tubers and fruits. She could not bear the thought of those innocent animals being slaughtered in celebration of her wedding. She sat down deep in thought, searching for a solution. Then a thought occurred to her: only if her wedding took place, the animals would be sacrificed. No sooner had she consciously decided to disappear from the wedding scene than she wasted no time and just ran deep into the forest. Leaves crackled as her feet ran over them. The teak brown primitive trees with their crunching twigs swayed in the wind providing the much-needed shade to all and sundry. The birds were orchestrating in song. On ordinary days, she would have enjoyed the magnificence of the forest, but that day nothing seemed to halt her speedy run. She kept glancing over her shoulder to see if any tribesmen were following her. She dreaded the thought of her father discovering her absence and setting his men on a manhunt.

After a few days, she reached Matangavana, the forest where the famous ashram of Sage Matanga was located. He was teaching his students about the greatness of the Supreme Lord. Shabari was enchanted with the description and teaching of Sage Matanga. She decided to serve the Sage in whatever way she could. Early in the morning, when all the students were asleep, she would take a broom and clean the entire Ashram, and while he taught his students, she would hear from a distance and go into a trance of devotion. One day, she was discovered by Sage Matanga, who recognized the greatness of her soul with his divine vision. He understood that she was from a lower caste but that did not deter him from accepting her into his ashram. Shabari was delighted. She selflessly served the Sage with the devotion of a daughter. She would clear his path of thorns and pebbles as he walked to the lake for his daily bath. She continued to clean the Ashram too. But the ascetics and high caste students of the Sage did not like this tribal woman being in their midst. They pained her with insults. But Shabari just kept at her work and grew more devoted to her Guru. He taught her just one mantra: Shri Ram. She kept repeating it as she worked and at all times of the day.

With time, Sage Matanga had grown old and weak and knew that his end was near. He called Shabari and blessed her before telling her that his time to leave the earthly abode had come. Shabari was distraught.

'Please take me along with you. I don't want to stay here without your guidance,' she pleaded.

The Sage looked at her affectionately and said, 'Shabari, you are a blessed soul. I have been reciting the stories of Shri Ram throughout my life but the Lord has not deigned to give me *darshan*. But I can see with my divine vision that the Paramatma, Lord Mahavishnu, in his Ram avatar, will come and visit you. He will be coming this way during his search for Devi Sita along with his brother Lakshman, and you will be able to host them here at this hermitage. So, continue chanting the name of the Lord and wait for that auspicious moment of darshan. Shri Ram will offer you salvation.'

He then sat in his usual meditative pose and attained yogic Samadhi.

Shabari was devastated by the loss of her spiritual guru, but his words of wisdom and his stories of Shri Ram rang continuously in her ears. She knew her Guru could not be wrong. So she firmly believed that the brothers, Ram and Lakshman, would arrive to bless her and the ashram with their divine presence one day or the other. Patiently, she waited. With unfailing devotion, she continued chanting the Lord's name, decorating the hermitage with flowers and leaves every day, as her Guru had said that Lord Ram would visit her but had not mentioned the day or time. There were plethora of delicious fruits and plants around the Ashram, each with a distinct taste. It was home to a variety of shrubs and smaller trees producing various types of berries, including jujubes, blueberries, Jamun and gooseberries. She would collect the sweetest fruits from the forest and keep them ready in a basket. There was no dearth of derogatory comments and laughter aimed at her devotion. The people and ascetics around the place called her mad. Yes. She was mad with devotion, her eyes scouring the horizon for the sight of her beloved Lord Ram all the time.

Years passed. Shabari was now very old. Her limbs were not as strong as before. But she did not give up. She took a stick for support and wandered outside to pluck fruits.

Meanwhile, Ravan had abducted Sita, and the brothers, Ram and Lakshman, were wandering through the forests in search of Sita. Ram was shouting the name of Sita, as he wandered through the verdant green forests. Lakshman could feel the anguish in his brother's voice. A wave of remorse swept through his mind.

'Would all this have happened if I had not left Sita Mata alone at the Kutir? I am the one at fault and unfortunately, my brother and sister-in-law are facing the consequences.'

Ram glanced at his beloved brother and immediately guessed the direction of his thoughts.

He tenderly put his arm around Lakshman's shoulder and said, 'Lakshman, I know what you are thinking. But understand, dear brother, it is not your fault. What is fated to happen will happen and no one on earth can prevent destiny from taking its course. So, don't berate yourself and let us proceed in our search for Sita.'

They walked further into the forest and reached the banks of Lake Pampa. The serene waters of the lake calmed down their taut nerves. The beauty of the lotus blooms and the tranquillity of the atmosphere indicated the presence of a holy place nearby. A few steps onward, they reached an ashram. Decorated with flowers and leaves, the peaceful hermitage had a welcoming look. When Shabari saw them, she ran forward to welcome them.

Shabari gazed at their handsome young faces and felt a thrill of ecstasy running through her veins. 'This surely must be her Lord Ram, who she had been waiting to see for so many years,' she thought to herself.

Yet to reassure herself, she asked, 'Am I blessed with the advent of my Lord Ram and his brother Lakshman to my humble abode?'

Ram nodded and said, 'Yes, mother. We are Ram and Lakshman, the sons of Emperor Dashrath of Ayodhya.'

Overcome with happiness at hearing their names, Shabari shed tears of joy that ran unhindered down her withered cheeks. She realized that her Guru's prophesy of the Paramatma, Shri Ram, visiting her and granting her the opportunity to feed him with the sweetest fruits of the forest was coming true.

'My Guru, Matanga Rishi, had told me before he left for his heavenly abode, that my Lord Ram would come to visit me. He asked me to wait here to receive you and that you would grant me salvation.' Shabari respectfully touched Shri Ram's feet and then went in to bring a basket of ripe and juicy red jujubes, also known as ber, which she had collected earlier during the day. She tasted each ber to test whether it was sweet enough for her Lord and then offered only the sweetest of them. Lakshman was watching this and restrained his brother from eating them saying that they were *jhoota* (already tasted). But Lord Ram admonished him and relished the berries saying, 'Anything that is offered to me with devotion, I shall accept with gratitude. Lakshman, see the good intention of the woman. Shabari wants to offer the sweetest of berries to me and keep the sour ones aside. Hence, she is tasting them before giving them to me.'

Lakshman was stunned to see the extreme devotion of Shabari and the magnanimity of his brother, Ram.

Shabari asked them about the purpose of their journey and hearing the sad tale of Sita Mata's abduction, she directed Shri Ram to visit the Rishyamook mountain.

'Sugreev is hiding from his brother Vali on Rishyamook mountain. The wise Hanuman is also with him along with some trusted monkey friends. They will surely help you in the search for Sita Mata.'

Shri Ram thanked her for her suggestion and the brothers blessed Shabari.

Shabari lit a fire and entered it, ready to join her preceptor, now that her life's mission was complete. The Lord granted her salvation, before leaving the hermitage.

The story of the tribal woman Shabari, her devotion to the Shri Ram and the Lord's acceptance of the 'jhoota ber' from her touches the very core of our hearts. There is a story of Shabari's previous life, where she was the queen of a maharaj. She did not have any attachment to worldly comforts or possessions even though she was a maharani. Once it so happened that the king and the queen had visited the Khumbamela at the Triveni Sangam at Prayagraj. Thousands of saints, holy men and rishis were assembled at the Khumb for the *shahi snans* or holy bath. The air was filled with the strains of bhajans and *namasankirthans*. This attracted the queen so much that she expressed a wish to have a darshan of the saints and enjoy their rendition. But the king refused to allow her saying that she was a queen and should keep her status in mind. She had to remain closed in her veil and confined to her quarters. The queen was dejected. She repeatedly reflected on her plight and decided that it was not worth living without participating in the bhajans in praise of the Lord. She knew that taking one's own life was a sin. So, that night, she decided to enter the holy waters of the Ganga and wait for her life to end there in the Triveni Sangam. As she waited in the water, she prayed to the Lord that in her next life, she should not be born in a royal family. She was reborn in the Shabar caste in the Bhil tribe. Thus, she acquired the name Shabari.

Though Shabari's devotion finds a mention in the Valmiki Ramayana, Kamba Ramayana, Adhyatma Ramayana and the later Telugu Raghunatha Ramayana, nothing is written about her offering tasted berries to the Lord. Even the Awadhi Tulsidas Ramayana says that Shabari fell at the feet of Shri Ram, her eyes overflowing with tears of joy, and speaks of her low caste status. Shri Ram assures her that her caste does not matter and feasts on the offering of natural fruits and tubers. It is only in the Odia Dandi Ramayana written by Balaram Das, that there is a mention of Shabari giving tasted mangoes to the Lord. But later in the Bhakti-ras-Bhodini, the Vaishnav Saint, Priyadas, elaborates on the life of Shabari. He details, how she, being of tribal origin, is subjected to ill-treatment as an untouchable by some ascetics. This was even though Sage Matanga had accepted her into his ashram.

Priyadas also writes about how Lord Ram eats the ber (jujubes) already tasted by her. He considers her to be the most fortunate of all devotees, as she is liberated by the Lord Himself.

Chapter 17

ANJANA

Maharshi Durvasa entered the Indra Sabha. The grandeur of the palace was magnified by the dance performance of the beautiful and talented celestial dancers called apsaras. On observing the advent of Maharshi Durvasa, who was well known for his anger and curses, Indra signalled to the dancers to halt their performance. They immediately stopped and went away from there.

Indra welcomed the Sage, offered him a seat and requested him to make himself comfortable. Durvasa was pleased.

He was having an interesting and serious discussion with Devendra when a tinkling laugh pervaded the atmosphere. Indra looked up uneasily. The disturbed Sage Durvasa looked around. No one seemed to be around. He proceeded to continue with his discussion. Within a few minutes, a giggling sound could be heard.

This time the Sage turned around to see a young girl looking at him and giggling away. It was Punjikastala, an amazingly beautiful young apsara. The Sage felt that the girl was laughing at his appearance. He was furious.

'Punjikastala!' he shouted. 'How dare you laugh at my countenance? Are you so proud of your beauty and youth that you feel you can mock an old sage like me?'

Indra was shell-shocked. Punjikastala was scared. But before she could open her mouth to apologize, Maharshi Durvasa rose from his seat and cursed, 'Your pride in your beauty led you to insult me. So, you shall turn into a monkey.'

Punjikastala fell crying at the Sage's feet and apologized sincerely.

'Please, Oh Maharshi! Don't curse me. I will never insult any sage again,' she begged.

At last, Maharshi Durvasa was moved by her request. He said, 'The words that roll from my mouth cannot be taken back. You will be born as a monkey. But I bless you, that by the grace of Lord Shiva, when you get married and have a son, you will be redeemed from my curse, and you will regain your original form. The son you beget will be the most powerful and divine child, the most sincere devotee of Lord Rama, and he will make you feel proud to be his mother.'

Punjikastala was born on earth as the daughter of a great monkey king, who named her Anjana. She was roaming the forests hungry and thirsty when the welcome sight of an ashram seemed to beckon her. She saw a few sages assembled at the ashram. They did not laugh or mock her monkey face. Instead, they welcomed her and gave her food to eat. This made Anjana happy.

'Daughter, can you tell us who you are?' asked one of the ascetics.

'I am Anjana,' she replied.

'You are a brave woman. You walk alone in the forest during the night, which none of us dares to do.'

'But, why are you scared to step out at night?' asked Anjana curiously.

'There is a terrible demon in this forest. His name is Sambasadan. He wants to attack and kill all of us,' said the sage with a quiver in his voice. 'And he is very powerful.'

Anjana thought to herself, 'These people are simple and kind. Moreover, they have given an unknown person like me food and shelter. They fully deserve to be protected against this demon. Why not stay on and help them in their fight?'

She followed her mind and said, 'I will stay back and help you in the fight against this Sambasadan.'

She made a Shivaling out of mud and prayed sincerely to Lord Shiva and Goddess Parvati. Suddenly she felt a voice telling her: Sambasadan can be killed only by his blood.

Concluding that it must have been the voice of Lord Shiva, she felt a surge of confidence. She then went to choose her weapons. To her surprise, there was another person already choosing his weapons.

'He looks strong and powerful. He carries himself like a king. Maybe he is a king,' she thought.

Without looking at her, the man said, 'I heard that you are going to help in fighting Sambasadan. You must be a very brave woman.'

'Well, aren't you also doing the same thing?' asked Anjana.

'I am duty-bound to protect this ashram as it falls within my kingdom,' said the man. 'But what made you decide to help in this fight?'

Anjana replied, 'These people offered me shelter and food when I needed it the most. So, am I not duty-bound to help them in return?'

He turned to look at her for the first time. She drew in her breath sharply, as he had the face of a monkey.

'I admire your thoughts, lady. Let me introduce myself. I am Kesari, the king of the monkeys here. May I know more about you?'

'I am Anjana,' she answered hesitantly.

Just then a huge roar thundered through the forest indicating that Sambasadan was approaching the ashram. Kesari picked up his weapons and prepared to fight. Anjana too lifted her weapons. They saw the gigantic demon hurtling towards them. Kesari started firing arrows at him. But the demon kept changing his form and outwitting the brave Kesari. Slowly Kesari was getting tired. Anjana was worried. She did not want Kesari to be killed. She started praying to Lord Shiva and Goddess Parvati to save Kesari from this ferocious demon.

Suddenly she remembered the words that had emanated from the Shivaling: Sambasadan can be killed only by his blood.

Anjana wondered what she could do to help Kesari when the demon assumed the form of an elephant. Kesari aimed an arrow at his chest. Blood spurted out from the wound. The intelligent Anjana quickly dipped some arrows in the fallen blood and aimed them at the demon. As each arrow pierced him, he let out a cry of pain.

'The ploy is working,' she thought. She again dipped some arrows in the puddle of blood and passed them on to Kesari. Kesari glanced at her in surprise. But seeing her serious face, he decided to use her arrows. It worked. The demon was screaming in pain as the arrows struck him. Kesari understood Anjana's ploy. He dipped his arrows in the demon's blood and aimed them quickly one after the other at the demon. Sambasadan fell to the ground with a thunderous roar. He had been vanquished at last and the forest was safe once again.

The inmates of the ashram rejoiced. They thanked Kesari and Anjana with all their heart. That evening, an aged sage spoke to Anjana confidentially.

'Daughter Anjana, you and Monkey King Kesari have saved us from sheer death. As a tradition, we offer a gift to any person who has helped us to win a battle. We wish to gift both of you something. According to us, the greatest gift we can give Kesari is you and the greatest gift we can offer you is Kesari. So, we wanted to know whether you have any objections to marrying Kesari.'

Anjana was surprised. She had been attracted to the powerful and handsome Kesari and was in awe of his strength. She knew that he was not only powerful but kind and intelligent.

She thought for a moment. 'What if he does not want to marry me?'

But she had to answer. So, she said shyly, 'I agree if Kesari is willing to marry me.'

'We have already spoken to Kesari. He admires you. He is taken with your intelligence and has expressed his desire to marry you,' said the sage happily.

An auspicious day was chosen and the marriage of Anjana and Kesari was performed much to the joy of all the inmates of the ashram. Years passed and the couple led a very happy life together. Anjana longed for a child. When Kesari and Anjana met a few holy men in this regard, they advised Anjana to pray to Lord Shiva. Being a fervent devotee of Lord Shiva, she immediately took Kesari's permission and went to do penance. Lord Shiva was pleased with her strict penance and sincere devotion. He appeared in front of her and granted her a boon. She asked for the Lord to be born as her son so that she could be released from her curse. Mahadev blessed her and asked her to continue her meditation.

Meanwhile, in Ayodhya, the Puthrakameshti Yajna was performed by Sage Rishya Shringa for Emperor Dashrath. When Agnidev offered the vessel of sacred kheer to Emperor Dashrath, he divided it amongst his queens. Valmiki Ramayan says that Kaushalya and Kaikeyi offered a portion of their kheer to Sumitra, but does not go beyond that. But, there is a story in the folk tradition that Kaushalya and Kaikeyi took their portion, but when it came to Sumitra's turn, a bird suddenly swooped down and snatched it from her hands. The other queens immediately offered a portion of their kheer to Sumitra.

The bird that took away the portion was a heavenly being. He had been cursed by Lord Brahma because of his mischievous ways. But seeing his repentance, the Lord assured him that he would be redeemed from his curse when he grabbed a portion of the sacred pudding during Dashrath's Putrakameshti Yajna. As soon as the bird sensed that the appropriate time had come, he swooped and flew away with Sumitra's portion. He was immediately redeemed from the curse and acquired his original form. The kheer however dropped from his hands, but Pawan Dev, the wind God, on the instruction of Lord Shiva, gently pushed the kheer to the outstretched hands of Anjana who was deep in prayer. Anjana was instructed by Pawan Dev to consume the kheer. She ate the kheer as instructed taking it to be the divine *prasad* of Lord Shiva. Soon, she became pregnant and delivered a baby boy called Hanuman. Hanuman is known to be the Rudravatar of Mahadev. He is called Pawan Putra, as he has the power of the Wind God, who had guided the kheer to Anjana's hands. He is known as Anjaneya and Kesarinandan after his earthly parents, Anjana and Kesari. After the birth of Hanuman, Anjana was redeemed from her curse and reverted to her beautiful original form.

Anjana's motherly love for Hanuman is well known. Since he had the power of the wind God, he could fly easily. He was mischievous to the core. He once flew towards the sun thinking it to be a fruit. A worried Indra tried to stop him by unleashing the *vajra* or thunderbolt. Little Hanuman was struck on his jaw and fell unconscious. Pawan Dev got furious at the treatment meted out to his godson Hanuman and withdrew himself from earth. With no air to breathe, the entire universe faced a huge calamity. All the gods, including Lord Indra, appeared before Pawan Dev, apologized, and transferred their powers to Hanuman. When the little boy regained consciousness, he had become stronger than anyone on earth.

As he grew up a little, he would go and play with his monkey friends. He would swing long distances between trees. He became aware of his unique powers and began using them to help his friends out when they were in trouble. Anjana got worried about Hanuman when he started troubling the rishis who were immersed in their meditation. She put him under the tutelage of Matanga Muni. Sage Matanga was well aware of the unique qualities of Hanuman and with his far-reaching vision, he knew that he was destined for great things in the future. So, he willingly took Hanuman as his student. But little Hanuman got bolder with troubling the Sages. He started hiding their ladles which they used for the yajnas, pouring water into fire, and pulling their long beards, thereby distracting their meditation. Finally, Sage Matanga cursed him to forget all his powers, till the day it was revealed to him by someone. Hanuman forgot his unique powers, and at once became an obedient and good student. Much later, at the appropriate time, it was Jambavan who reminded him of his powers, when Sri Ram required him to cross the ocean in search of Sita Mata. Hanuman was a key figure in the battle with Ravan and caused a lot of damage to the Lankan army. During the Ram–Ravan battle, it is said that Kesari, the father of Hanuman, also fought valiantly for Sri Ram.

Hanuman adored his mother, Anjana, and would do anything for her. There is a beautiful story that corroborates this fact. Once the Maharaj of Kashi was immersed in entertainment and failed to notice the arrival of Maharshi Vishwamitra. The Sage was furious. He declared that he would ask his protégé, Sri Ram, to kill the Kashi Raja. Hearing this, the King was quivering with fear. He knew that his days were numbered as the divine power of Sri Ram was known universally.

Moreover, Sri Ram respected his Guru and would never deviate from adhering to his orders. The advent of Narad Muni at that moment made the King rush to him for a solution to this problem.

Narad Muni heard the whole story and said, 'Maharaj, this is a serious problem. I can see just one solution though.'

'Please, revered Sage, tell me what I have to do.' The king was in tears.

'Maharaj, go and fall at the feet of Anjana Mata, the mother of Hanuman, and request her to protect you,' said Narad.

'But Hanuman!' exclaimed the King. 'Hanuman is the foremost devotee of Sri Ram. How will he or his mother even think of protecting me against Sri Ram?'

'They won't,' answered Narad. 'You fall at the feet of Anjana Mata and request her protection, without mentioning the name of your enemy. She is gracious and compassionate and she will offer you protection.'

The King rushed to Anjana Mata and fell at her feet saying, 'Mata, I am facing a calamity and need your protection. Please offer me protection Mata.'

Anjana felt sympathy for the weeping king. So, she agreed to protect him.

But when she came to know that the enemy of the Kashi King was Sri Ram, she was flummoxed. Now, what was the next step? She called Hanuman, who appeared immediately before her.

'Hanuman, I have given my word to protect this King and I need your help,' she said.

'Mata, your word is my word,' exclaimed Hanuman. He turned to the cowering King and asked him the name of his enemy. When he came to know that he had to fight against his Lord, Sri Ram, he was stunned. But Hanuman's love for his mother and the need to keep up her word made it imperative for him to prepare for the fight.

Meanwhile, Sri Ram, who had no personal enmity with the Kashi King, came searching for him to follow the instructions of his guru, Vishwamitra. When he saw Hanuman standing in front of the king, he said, 'Hanuman, you are standing in my way. Please move so that I can complete my Guru's order and kill the King of Kashi.'

But Hanuman refused to budge. His hands held together in prayer, he chanted the Lord's name continuously.

'Jai Sri Ram! Jai Sri Ram! Jai Sri Ram!'

Ram had no option but to aim his arrows at Hanuman. But imagine the surprise of all those present there, none of his arrows could pierce Hanuman.

Narad Muni came along with Vishwamitra and said, 'See what you have started Maharshi. Neither does Sri Ram want to fight against his beloved Hanuman nor does Hanuman want to fight against his Lord. But both of them have given their word and will keep to it. Only you can stop this unwanted war. Learned people should be able to forgive. So please forgive the Kashi Raja and put an end to this war.'

Vishwamitra immediately instructed Sri Ram to stop the war. The Kashi King fell at the feet of Vishwamitra and was pardoned.

Hanuman had succeeded in keeping his word to his beloved mother and Anjana blessed him with all her heart.

Chapter 18

TARA

A woman of courage, strength and wisdom, Tara was the celebrated queen of Kishkindha and wife of Vali. She loved her husband and would do anything for him. Vali was the scourge of his enemies. He had once defeated the mighty Ravan, and the Lankan King considered him the most powerful monkey on earth. His strength came from a boon that he received. Anyone who would come face to face in battle with him would lose half his strength, thereby rendering Vali almost invincible. Vali and Tara had a son named Angad, who was the apple of their eyes.

Once, Mayavi, the brother of Dundubhi,[1] invited him for a fight in the middle of the night. Tara tried to stop her husband from going.

'Control your anger, Nath. This is not the right time for you to go after that Mayavi,' she said.

'No, Tara,' he replied. 'I can't ignore a call for battle, be it the middle of the night or any time. I am a monkey warrior, and my valour and pride will not allow me to do so.'

Rejecting her advice and the persuasion of his younger brother, Sugreev, Vali marched after Mayavi. He asked Sugreev to follow him. Seeing the mighty Vali taking up the challenge, Mayavi ran for his life and entered a cave.

'You wait here Sugreev till I come back,' ordered Vali. 'I will kill that arrogant creature and return.'

Sugreev waited for a year but there was no sign of his brother. Suddenly, one day, he heard the war cry of Mayavi and then blood started flowing from the entrance of the cave. There was no reply from Vali. This made Sugreev think that his valiant brother was dead. To ensure that Mayavi did not trouble Kishkindha again, Sugreev closed the mouth of the cave with a stone and returned sadly to the palace.

Tara could not believe that her husband was dead. But when Sugreev led some ministers to see the blood coming out of the cave, the ministers sadly had no doubt. Though Sugreev was not interested in occupying the throne of Kishkindha, the ministers convinced him for the coronation.

After a few days, Vali returned. He was not dead as they had surmised. He had killed the cunning Mayavi and that had taken him a year. But when he saw that the entrance to the cave had been sealed, he kicked and pushed with all his might. He succeeded in moving the boulder. When he arrived at the palace, he was furious to see his brother on the throne.

Sugreev tried to explain. Tara also tried to convince her husband about the truth in Sugreev's words. But Vali was not prepared to listen to anyone.

He angrily drove Sugreev out of Kishkindha with just one garment. He also confined and usurped Sugreev's wife Ruma. There was nothing that Sugreev could do except run away to Rishyamook mountain with some of the monkeys who supported him, which included Hanuman.

When Ravan was abducting Sita in his Pushpak Viman, Sita noticed the monkeys on top of the mountain. She removed her jewellery, tied it up in a piece of her sari, and threw it down to them crying, 'Please tell my husband, Sri Ram, that this monster Ravan is abducting me. Show him these jewels and he will believe you.'

When Sri Ram and Lakshman reached Rishyamook mountain on the advice of Shabari, they came in contact with Sugreev and Hanuman. Hearing that they were searching for Sita, they were shown the jewels wrapped in a torn cloth. They were relieved to know that they were on the right path. Sri Ram and Sugreev became bound in the bond of friendship. It was then that Sugreev recited his pitiable tale and Sri Ram agreed to help him regain his wife and the throne of Kishkindha. In return, Sugreev promised to help Sri Ram find Sita and render the services of the entire monkey army to defeat the mighty Dashanan.

Knowing that Vali could never refuse a challenge, Sri Ram asked Sugreev to call his brother for a fight. Hanuman had already told Sri Ram about Vali's boon, and that only an arrow that flies through seven trees could kill the valiant monkey king.

Sugreev shouted from the entrance of Kishkindha, 'Vali, if you have the courage, come outside for a fight with me.'

Vali could not believe his ears. 'That sounds like Sugreev! Is he inviting me for a fight?'

Tara said wisely, 'Nath, yes. It is Sugreev. But he is not alone as he would not have the courage to fight you knowing well about your strength. I have heard that he had formed a new friendship with the two princes of Ayodhya, Ram and Lakshman.'

'That foolish brother of mine has the temerity to call me for a fight,' Vali exclaimed, intent on taking up the challenge.

Tara tried stopping him, but failed.

Sugreev, confident that Sri Ram was behind him, danced around, egging Vali on. The similarity between the two brothers was so confusing that Sri Ram did not want to aim his arrow at the wrong person. Hence, he waited.

Vali dealt blows on Sugreev and when he found that his brother was almost swooning with pain, he said, 'Begone from here. I have no desire to kill you.'

Sugreev ran away, while Vali returned to Kishkindha, satisfied that he had defeated his brother.

Meanwhile, Sugreev was sad at the turn of events.

'Did you send me to be trashed by my brother, Oh Ram?' he asked.

'Sugreev, my friend, it was not my fault. I could not make out the difference between you and your brother. Not wanting to strike you by mistake, I held myself back,' replied Ram.

'You go again and invite Vali for a fight. This time, you wear a garland around your neck, so that I can differentiate between both of you.'

Sugreev agreed after Hanuman also persuaded him. He wore a garland and called out Vali at the Gate of Kishkindha.

'Hey Vali!' he called. 'You thought that I ran away yesterday. I have come better prepared now. Come and fight with me.'

'How foolish can a person be?' asked Vali looking at Tara, while preparing to march outside.

Tara stopped him. 'Nath, I can't believe that Sugreev is calling you out for the second time after being trashed so badly, without some outside help. Please don't go now. Wait till you find out who is behind this call. I have heard that Ram, the elder among the princes of Ayodhya, whom your brother has befriended, is the avatar of Lord Vishnu.'

But Vali was not to be stopped. 'Tara, I am a warrior and a true warrior will never be afraid to fight anyone, be it the avatar of Lord Vishnu, himself. Don't stop me. And for your satisfaction, I assure you that I will not kill my brother. I will only defeat him.'

Tara knew that her husband would not listen. But she was really scared. She had an intuition that Vali would not return. She clasped the hands of Angad and hugged him closely.

Meanwhile, Sri Ram positioned himself behind the seven trees and this time the arrow did not miss its target. That great monkey king of incredible valour fell to the ground.

'Why did you kill me, O Ram? We had no personal rivalry, but still, you aimed your arrow from behind,' cried Vali in pain.

Ram replied, 'Oh valiant king of the monkeys! You had to be punished for ravaging Ruma, the wife of Sugreev, while he is still alive. In a kingdom, the king is supreme. He has to take care of all his subjects. Your younger brother is supposed to be like a son to you. But still, you drove him away without hearing his side of the story. His wife, Ruma, is like your daughter in law, and yet you lusted after her. Now, you tell me, is that just? Is that fair? Does it not merit punishment?"'

Vali understood his mistake and sincerely repented for it.

'Oh, Ram! Please pardon me for speaking to you thus. My wife Tara indicated that you are the avatar of Lord Vishnu, but I thought I would prefer to die by your hands if at all. Tara is a loving and wise woman. And my son, Angad, is too young to know the intricacies of life and death. When he hears about my death, he will be devastated. Oh, Raghav! Please take care of him as you would take care of Bharat or Lakshman. Advise Sugreev also. Let him not take out his anger and prejudice on Tara or Angad. They are not at fault.'

Sugreev was listening to his brother's dying words.

'Sorry brother, that I was the cause of your death. Rest assured that I will take care of Angad as my son.'

Vali looked at his weeping brother. 'Generally, siblings are the ones you share your joys and sorrows with. But somehow, during our lives, we were not fated to be friends. We were always at loggerheads with each other. But at this moment of death, I request you, Sugreev, to always heed Tara's words of advice. She is extraordinarily intelligent and had warned me against coming to fight with you. She has always had the right suggestions for the betterment of our subjects. Do not subjugate her in your anger against me. She has done no wrong.'

Sugreev nodded sadly.

Meanwhile, the message of the death of Vali reached Tara. She rushed to the field, accompanied by her son Angad and many other monkeys.

Seeing the dead body of her husband, she could not control her lamentations.

'Oh, Lord! How could you leave me and go away? You, who have been the most powerful monkey king on earth, why did you not heed my words? Why did you die, leaving me a widow? We will no more enjoy our time together on earth. Don't you know that a widow, even if she has sons and wealth, is still a widow? Bereft of her spouse, she has to live a life of loneliness. I wish to join you in death, Oh Lord of mine!'

Her words made Sugreev drown in grief. He was full of remorse. Vali had not shown any inclination to kill him, even during the last fight.

Tara, the beautiful woman, continued her lamentations. 'Oh, King! I know that all this is a result of your faults of usurping Ruma, the unfortunate wife of Sugreev and banishing your brother into exile. I tried warning you then. But you did not heed my words. How could you leave Angad alone at the mercy of his paternal uncle, whose fury is directed at us? Angad, the young prince who has always lived in luxury, who has the strength of yours in his body, who is weeping at the loss of his sire! How could you separate yourself from him?'

She turned to Ram, who was standing apart, majestically holding his bow and arrow.

'Raghav! You are all-knowing and all-powerful. You have killed my husband with a single arrow. Please kill me also, so that I can be reunited with him. And if you are hesitant to kill a woman, don't think of me as a woman. Think of me as a part of Vali and aim an arrow at my heart.'

Hearing her cries, Ram comforted Tara, 'Do not grieve. You are the wife of a hero, a great warrior! Everything happens according to God's will. The Creator ordains the balance of good and evil. No one can transgress the fixed laws of the Supreme Lord. Your son needs your wisdom and so does your country. Angad will be the heir apparent to the throne of Kishkindha. I assure you on that count.'

Tara was thus magnanimously comforted by Sri Ram and she ceased to lament.

The coronation of Sugreev took place without further delay, during which Sugreev himself announced that Prince Angad, the valiant son of Vali and Tara, would be the crown Prince, or heir apparent, of Kishkindha. It was the rainy season and so Ram and Lakshman decided to wait for some time for the monkey king to settle down in his new routine before enlisting his help in the search for Sita. They gave him four months. But Sugreev, who was enjoying the freedom and the luxury of the palace after a long time, lost himself in entertainment and pleasure with his spouse. He had conveniently forgotten about the promise he had made to Ram. Though Sri Ram was distressed, he was calm, but Lakshman was unable to control his anger at this show of ingratitude which resulted in increased distress to his beloved brother. He prepared to go to Kishkindha and confront the monkey king. Sri Ram requested him to calm down and just remind Sugreev about his promise.

When Lakshman entered Kishkindha, a beautiful city located amid caves, he was surprised to find hundreds and thousands of strong monkeys running hither thither. They were scared of the fury emanating from his eyes as he held his bow high and straight over his shoulder. The young prince, Angad, went to greet him with dignity and humility and led him to the palace.

The sound of music and laughter from Sugreev's inner abode could be heard by Lakshman. He was even more angry.

'Dear Angad, go and inform your king that the brother of Ram has arrived.'

Angad was distressed. He knew that his uncle, Sugreev, was indebted to Sri Ram and had not fulfilled his promise. He went inside immediately and caught hold of Sugreev's feet, saying, 'Saumitra has come.'

Sugreev was under the effects of wine and did not pay heed to the young Angad's words. Angad went to Tara and repeated the same words. Tara, being wise, knew the impact of Lakshman's advent. She brought Sugreev to his senses.

She told him, 'Is this the way you repay your friend? Are you not aware, that if it had not been for Ram, you would not have acquired this kingdom or regained your wife? How can you forget your promise to those great princes of Ayodhya?'

Do you even know that four months have passed and Sri Ram is waiting patiently for you to act?'

Sugreev cringed at her words. But he was so scared of the anger of Lakshman. Just then, the thunderous stringing sound of Lakshman's bow could be heard. Tara could sense the fury of the Prince. She then took it upon herself to meet and pacify Lakshman.

'Why are your eyes so full of anger, Lakshman?' she asked softly.

'Oh, wise woman, who would not be angry with what your king is doing?' asked Lakshman. 'Sugreev had promised Sri Ram that he would help in the search for Sita. Because of the rains, my brother gave him time to settle down in his new role. And that agreed time is long over. But look at Sugreev! He has conveniently forgotten my brother's distress and is enjoying himself in sensual pleasures. And you expect me to just wait and watch!'

'Oh Saumitra!' said Tara gently. 'Such anger does not become your admirable nature. We all know that we, the people of Kishkindha, owe you and your brother a lot. Sugreev has the debt of friendship to repay. None of us has forgotten that. As Sugreev had been denied all pleasures for such a long duration, he had lost his sense of time. But he has already set in motion the plans for the search. He has ordered all the powerful monkeys, who can change their shape at will, bears and others from all four corners to assemble here today. And before long, they will be at Sri Ram's service.'

Tara's gentle words pacified Lakshman. Seeing him calm down a bit, Sugreev gathered the courage to speak.

'I will be coming to meet Sri Ram today evening with Hanuman, Jambavan, Angad and others, dear Lakshman,' he said.

And true to his words, the group of monkeys went to meet Sri Ram in his cave to plan the search for Sita Mata.

Tara's advice to Angad, when he led the group of monkeys down South, was to follow the instructions of Hanuman and Jambavan and act accordingly. She was aware of the divine power of Hanuman and knew that he would protect her son from any harm.

Tara's extraordinary wisdom is mentioned in the Kishkindha Kand of Valmiki Ramayana. She is also believed to be one among the *Pancha Kanyas* (five iconic women from the Hindu epics, Ramayana and Mahabharata) along with Ahalya, Mandodari, Kunti and Draupadi whose names are extolled in a Sanskrit hymn:

Ahalyā Draupadī Kuntī Tārā Mandodarī tathā ।
pañcakanyāḥ smarennityaṃ mahāpātakanāśinīm ॥

Just remembering their names can cause a person to be redeemed of their sins. Tara was said to be the daughter of Sushena, the doctor of the monkeys in Valmiki Ramayana. Other puranic sources say that she was one of the celestial beings who appeared during the Samudra Manthan.

[1] Dundubhi and Mayavi were brothers and were sons of Maya, the architect of the asuras. Dundubhi is said to have had the strength of a thousand elephants. Ravan's wife, Mandodari was their sister.

Chapter 19

SURASA, SIMHIKA AND LANKINI

The most important part of Ramayana is said to be the Sundara Kand, which entails the search for and finding of the abducted Sita in Lanka and delivering the signet ring of Ram to Sita, thereby giving her the hopeful message of Ram coming to Lanka to retrieve her from Ravan. Her return message and Chudamani is in turn delivered to Ram to assure him of Sita's presence in Ashok Vatika. The hero of Sundara Kand is the ever-faithful Hanuman. The monkey group led by Angad had reached the shores of the ocean. The vast expanse of sparking blue waters added to their distress.

'We have covered the entire trail in the southern direction but there has been no sign of Sita Mata. Now, this ocean seems to have led us to a dead end. What do we do?' asked Angad in despair.

The wise old Jambvan and others in the monkey clan nodded in agreement.

'Jatayu's valiant fight against Ravan would mean nothing if we don't find Sita Mata,' said Jambvan.

An aged bird was sitting on a rock nearby, who was contemplating on feasting on the monkeys one by one. But he became alert as his ears picked up the name of Jatayu. The bird was none other than Sampati, Jatayu's brother.

'Did you mention Jatayu?' he asked.

'Yes,' replied Jambvan. 'But what do you know about the brave Jatayu?'

'Jatayu was my brother. From what I comprehend from your conversation, my brother died fighting for a lady's honour. And, let me inform you, I have seen the flying chariot with Ravan carrying away the lady above this very ocean. My eyes can see very far and I can spot her sitting under a tree in Lanka, the kingdom of Lankeshwar Ravan,' said Sampati.

'You can see our Sita Mata?' asked Angad eagerly. 'How can we reach her? Please tell us.'

'You have to cross this ocean and reach the island of Lanka to find her, as that is where she has been kept in captivity,' replied Sampati.

The monkey team was in a dilemma. 'Who could cross this vast ocean?'

Jambvan said, 'I could have flown in my younger days but now I am too old and I doubt if I have the strength to cross the ocean.'

He then looked at Hanuman who had been a silent spectator.

'Pawanputra Hanuman!' called Jambvan. 'Why are you so silent? You are the only one in our group who has the power, agility and wisdom to complete this job. Wake up, dear Maruti. You are the son of Marut, the wind God. I know you have forgotten your power due to a rishi's curse. But now is the time to revive your memory and use your strength to search for Sita Mata.'

Hanuman was perplexed by Jambvan's words.

'Yes, Hanuman. You have been blessed with special powers by all the gods, but because of your mischievous behaviour in your childhood, Maharshi Matang cursed you to forget your powers. But he also said that when the appropriate time comes, someone will tell you about your forgotten powers and you will be redeemed from your curse. What could be a more appropriate moment for you to recall your strengths in this hour of need of Sri Ram?'

Hanuman threw a grateful look at Jambvan as he recollected his powers and got ready to undertake the long flight over the vast blue ocean. He increased his size to gigantic proportions and jumped. His flight across the ocean from the shores of Rameshwaram to Lanka was filled with obstacles by three women, Nagamata Surasa, Rakshasi Simhika and Lankini, the guardian deity of Lanka.

Surasa was one of the thirteen daughters of Daksha who were given in marriage to Sage Kashyapa. She is believed to be the mother of a thousand Nagas, including the well-known and powerful Nagas like Adishesha, Vasuki and Takshaka. Adishesha, her firstborn, forms the bed of Mahavishnu with his coiled body, whereas Vasuki is coiled around the neck of Mahadev. When Hanuman undertook the journey to Lanka to find Sita Mata, the Devas wanted to test the extent of his intelligence and power. They went to Nagamata Surasa to request her to test Hanuman's strength and wisdom. They asked her to assume the horrific appearance of a demoness and appear before Hanuman. Surasa changed her appearance in deference to the wishes of the gods. She assumed the ferocious form of a rakshasi with terrible fangs and burning red eyes. She then leapt in the way of the flying Hanuman.

'You have been allotted as my food for the day!' screamed Surasa. Hanuman was furious at this unexpected hurdle. However, he folded his hands in salutation and said, 'Mother, I am the emissary of Ram, the son of King Dashrath. He and his wife Sita along with his brother Lakshman were staying peacefully in the wild Dandakaranya forests. But they were tricked into leaving Sita alone for a few minutes by a demon called Marich and during their brief absence, Sita was forcefully abducted by the Lankan King Ravan. Lord Ram has assigned me the significant task of finding the exact location of Sita Mata. Only then can he plan the further course of action against Ravan and save his wife.'

'I don't care what you are going there for,' replied Surasa. 'I have been given a boon by Lord Brahma that none can pass me without entering my mouth. You can proceed further only after entering my mouth,' said she and opened her mouth wide.

'Mother, I assure you that after I finish my work, I will return to enter your mouth,' said Hanuman. But Surasa could not be convinced.

'You think I am a fool!' she exclaimed. 'You will go away from here and not return. Enter my mouth first and if you are fortunate enough, move ahead.'

Hanuman could not control his anger anymore. 'I have told you that I am on an important mission for Lord Ram, but still, you are not prepared to listen. Let me also see whether you can open your mouth wide enough for me to enter then.'

Hanuman kept increasing his size. Surasa was not daunted. She too opened her mouth wider. All of a sudden, Hanuman reduced his body to the size of a thumb. He entered Surasa's mouth and came out unharmed in seconds, even before she could fathom what was happening. The son of the Wind God had outwitted the dangerous Surasa.

'Oh, mother of Nagas! Oh, daughter of Daksha! My respectful salutations to you,' said Hanuman. 'I have fulfilled your request. I have entered your mouth. Now allow me to proceed on my journey.'

Surasa at once assumed her original form and bowed before him. 'O Hanuman! O mighty son of the Wind God! I was requested by the gods to test your intelligence and capability. You have passed the test with flying colours. You are the only one who could have undertaken this mission with such aplomb. May you fulfil your objective and help Rama reunite with the princess of Mithila.' Hanuman accepted the blessings of Surasa and moved ahead.

The next hurdle on his flight came in the form of a demoness called Simhika, who could take any form. This gigantic demoness could catch her prey's shadow and reduce his speed. All her life she had been catching the shadows of birds that were flying in the sky and pulling them down to eat them. That's exactly what she did with Hanuman. Seeing Hanuman flying like a luminous Garuda, Simhika thought to herself that she had found the perfect meal for the day. She caught the shadow of Hanuman and pulled it down towards her. This reduced his speed drastically.

Hanuman wondered, 'Why am I slowing down as if I am a ship caught in a wind blowing in the opposite direction? There must be some reason for this.'

He looked around to see who was causing this new obstruction. He could not find anyone in front, back or above. Looking down, he found the gigantic form of Simhika immersed in the sea with her mouth wide open trying to pull him towards her mouth through his shadow. Hanuman had heard of this demoness from Sugreev. Sugreev had called the demoness 'chayagrahini' . To counter her, he tried to use the same trick he had used against Surasa. He increased his size enormously. But the grip of Simhika was too strong and she refused to let him move forward. He then turned himself into a needle-sized being and entered her mouth. Before she could close her mouth, he started growing in size within her. This made her uncomfortable in the beginning, after which she began writhing in pain as he mutilated her internal organs and killed her.

There are stories in folk renderings that Simhika was the daughter of Sage Kashyapa and Diti. She had once caught hold of Chaya, the wife of Suryadev and mother of God Shani. It is believed that Hanuman and Shani fought and defeated her. At Shani's request, Hanuman had let her go free, with the stern warning that if she obstructed him at any point in time, he would kill her. Simhika had not forgotten her defeat at the hands of Hanuman. She wanted to avenge her defeat and hence she obstructed him on his way to Lanka. And she was finally killed by Hanuman. There is another story in the folk tradition that Simhika was the mother of Rahu, one of the Navagrahas.

After overcoming Simhika, Hanuman flew over the ocean and reached the shores of Lanka. The view of the city from the mountain peak was magnificent. Imposing gates, palatial houses, beautiful gardens and deep blue lakes added to the splendour of Lanka. However, Hanuman could see that the city was almost impenetrable because of the scores of soldiers guarding it from all sides. It seemed to be a veritable fortress. He jumped down from the mountain and entered the splendid city of Lanka. Lanka-Sri or Lankini was the guardian deity of Lanka. She had seen the monkey who had assumed a miniature size trying to enter the city and called out to him.

'Hey, monkey! Who are you and what are you doing here? Speak the truth if you want to save yourself.'

Hanuman looked at the angry woman and said calmly, 'I will tell you the truth. But before that, I would like to know who you are. Why are you looking at me with such anger and threatening me?'

'You impudent monkey!' she exclaimed. 'You have the temerity to ask me who I am! Well! For your information, I am Lankini, the guardian deity of this city built by Vishwakarma. I am following the orders of Lankeshwar Ravan, who is presently the all-powerful King of Lanka. I am protecting the city under his orders. As you are ignoring me and trying to enter the city, I am going to kill you in a moment.'

Hanuman was not frightened. He stood boldly in front of Lankini and said, 'I came here just to have a look at the beautiful city of Lanka. After seeing the city's wonders in its forests, gardens and buildings, I will leave as I came in.'

'You cannot enter the city without fighting against me!' screamed Lankini angrily, delivering a huge blow on Hanuman's cheek. Hanuman's anger was now truly fuelled. He clenched his left fist and punched her, though not with full strength as he knew that she was a woman.

Lankini fell on her face. Her limbs were shattered. She got up slowly. Her fear was visible on her face as she folded her hands in salutation to Hanuman. Brahma's words came back to her mind.

'O great monkey!' she said in a voice tremulous with anxiety. 'I am the soul of Lanka. You have overcome me with one blow. O leader of monkeys! Hear now the truth about what Brahma said when he offered me this boon of being the guardian deity of Lanka. He said that the day I was overpowered by a monkey, bad times were in offing for the rakshasa clan. You overcoming me with one blow is an indication that the time has come. On account of his lust for Sita, the wife of another man, Ravan and the rest of the Rakshasas are going to be destroyed.'

She then showed Hanuman the way into Lanka saying, 'I will not stop you now. Be free to see what you want. I know that you have a mission in mind. Go ahead and complete it. Find the pure and chaste Vaidehi and fulfil your mission. I am leaving for my original abode and will report this to Brahma.'

Hanuman went forward and entered the city of Lanka to search for Sita Mata.

The flight of Hanuman to Lanka is vividly described in the Valmiki Ramayana and all the subsequent Ramayanas that have been written. His use of cunning and shrewdness in handling Surasa, his use of brute force in killing Simhika and his brief yet significant encounter with Lankini, increase his appeal as the destroyer of all evils.

Chapter 20

TRIJATA

Ashok Vatika was the scene of utter chaos. The kidnapped princess Sita had refused to enter Ravan's opulent palace. Hence, she had been imprisoned in the Ashok Vatika, where she sat woefully under an Ashoka tree, keeping a Durva grass with her for protection.

'Sita, you don't realize what you are missing by refusing to be my wife,' said Ravan. 'I am captivated by your appearance, even though you are devoid of jewels and adornments. I have so much wealth that we can live happily together roaming around the world. Your Ram has been banished. He is a poor prince. Why do you waste your thoughts on him? Marry me and you will lord it over all others in this kingdom.'

He started boasting about his conquests and his expanding kingdom. But Sita was unmoved by his haughty words.

'You fool Ravan!' she screamed. 'Is there no one here who can give you the right advice? Think about the family I come from. Think about the family I got married to. How can you even dream of marrying me? You don't understand what you have invited by bringing me here forcefully. My Lord, Ram, will not let you go unscathed. He will kill you and everyone who supports you.' Her angry words resounded across the open-air garden.

This conversation continued for some time but eventually, Ravan had to leave in a huff. He had tried his best to convince her to marry him, but the frail yet strong-willed Vaidehi had refused vehemently.

Ravan had appointed Trijata to oversee Sita's captivity. There was a cordon of more than three hundred rakshasis who had been assigned the task of convincing the adamant princess. They had surrounded Sita and were continuously harassing her. Already, separation from her beloved husband was troubling her. Finding herself abducted and imprisoned in an unknown land had taken its toll. Now, the crude and abusive behaviour of the rakshasis only served to increase her fear and grief.

Seeing her in this plight, Trijata, the daughter of Vibhishan, felt sympathy. She was won over by the soft-spoken princess and her single-minded devotion to her husband.

'Stop!' she shouted. 'What are you all doing? Don't you know that you are so many against one? Is this the way you treat an unfortunate woman? Do not lay your hands on this pure woman. Do you even know who she is? She is the daughter of the great ruler of Mithila, King Janak. She is the wife of Ram, and the daughter-in-law of the mighty Emperor Dashrath.'

'But we are only doing what we have been ordered to do,' said one of them.

'I know,' answered Trijata. 'But think! So many of you against one woman! Do you think it is fair?'

She continued, 'And let me tell you about a dream I had yesterday. It was terrible and I saw it during the wee hours of the morning. Generally, dreams seen at that time could come true.'

'What did you see Trijata?' asked one.

'I saw a beautiful ivory chariot drawn by a lot of swans. They were moving in the sky with Ram and Lakshman seated royally dressed in silk clothes and adorned with flower garlands. On a pure white snow-clad mountain surrounded by the azure blue sea, I saw Janaki, clad in dazzling white clothes getting reunited with her Lord Ram. And would you believe it! I saw another dream where Ram and Lakshman were mounted on a celestial elephant with four tusks. Brightened by a radiance that glows from heavenly beings, they approach Sita who was dressed in pure white robes and adorned with flowers. Ram lifted her gracefully from the mountain into his embrace. Mounted on the elephant, she rose to touch and gently wipe the sun and the moon with her hands. That celestial elephant stood over Lanka with all three of them astride.'

'Then another dream followed,' continued Trijata after a pause for breath. 'I again saw Ram and Lakshman astride a beautiful chariot drawn by eight white bullocks. The next dream was interesting. I saw Ram seated on a throne and he was being bathed with the waters of the holy rivers by sages. All the Devas, Gandharvas, Rishis and Vidhyadharas were there saluting and praising Ram's qualities. This very same Sita, dressed beautifully and adorned with wonderful jewels, seated next to him. It was then that Ram appeared as the supreme Lord Mahavishnu with a *shanka* (conch), *chakra* (discus), *gada* (Club) and a Lotus flower. After that, I saw Ram and Lakshman accompanied by Sita climbing onto a flower-bedecked vehicle and moving away towards the northern direction.'

Trijata paused. The other rakshasis continued to wait for her to continue.

'The next dream was the most terrible dream I had ever seen. Ravan's head was shaven, and he was dripping in oil. He was intoxicated and yet he continued drinking wine. He was falling from the Pushpaka Viman (chariot of flowers) down to the South and I could see the mad panic in his eyes. I saw him being dragged by a woman towards the region of Yama, the lord of death.

Dashanan was incoherent, speaking, laughing and weeping at the same time. At Yamalok, I saw him joined by his brother Kumbhakarna, his favourite son Indrajit, and all his other sons. All of them had their heads shaven and were bathing in oil. They were stinking. It looked like hell. I saw Ravan riding on a pig, Kumbhakarna on a camel and Indrajit on a crocodile moving towards the southern direction. Only Vibhishan, Ravan's youngest brother, was not with them. He was standing on the chariot in the sky with four ministers, protected by a white canopy. I also saw Lanka burning because of a monkey whose tail was set on fire by your cruel emperor.'

'Trijata, you are trying to scare us,' said one of the rakshasis.

'No. I am not trying to scare you all. I am scared myself, as I feel that most of the people of Lanka are going to die and our king is going to be the cause of our death,' said Trijata. 'Do you think he is right? He is lusting after another man's wife and expects her to leave her divine husband and marry him. Is he right? You tell me.'

'Even though he is not right, he is our king and we have to obey him,' said another rakshasi.

'You can do what you like, but I will not allow all of you to terrorize Janaki like this,' stated Trijata.

'I want to also show you something. Look at Sita. Her left eye is twitching indicating good times for her as she will reunite soon with her beloved husband. More good omens can be seen as her left arm and leg are quivering. And can you all hear a bird cooing on the branch of a tree close by? Can you feel the joy in its cooing? Do you know what it foretells? It indicates the arrival of a close friend or protector. So, as soon as possible, I would advise all of you to ask for Sita's forgiveness and seek her protection. Her all-powerful husband and his brother are about to reach Lanka. Once they are here, they will defeat Lankeshwar and his huge army. Janaki will be rescued and if Ram comes to know that you have troubled her like this, he will not forgive you all. Only Janaki can protect you.'

This dream of Trijata is an important part of every version of the Ramayana, including the Valmiki Ramayana, and is said to have brought solace to Sita in her captivity, as it was the only supportive voice amidst enemies in an alien land.

'If your dream does come true Trijata, I will always be your protector,"' said Sita, tears running down her cheeks.

Though Trijata was first sent to guard Sita in her captivity, she was drawn by her simplicity, purity and divine nature. She decided to help Sita in every possible way and thus became the first true friend of Vaidehi in Lanka.

Trijata also played an important part in bringing news about the advent of Ram's monkey army into Lanka. She informed Sita about the bridge that the monkey army was building across the ocean to reach Lanka.

In another subsequent instance, Ravan brought an illusory head of Ram to convince Sita that her husband had already been killed. Sita believed it and panicked. She wanted Trijata to prepare a funeral pyre for her. Trijata consoled her. She informed her that Ravan had magical powers and the head was an illusion. Sarama, another rakshasi, confirmed the message and assuaged Sita's fears. Again, after Indrajit struck Sri Ram and Lakshman with the Nagpash, and when they were lying still and bound by the Nagpash, Ravan ordered Trijata to take Sita and show her the battlefield.

Seeing the brothers lying unconscious on the battlefield, Sita cried out loud. She was not able to bear the sight of her Lord lying in that condition and wanted to commit suicide.

'Dear Sita,' said Trijata gently. 'I don't think your husband and his brother are dead. Look at their faces, calm and still bright with life. Please don't take any hasty action. Let me confirm their status with my father Vibhishan, and then we can take further steps.'

Trijata then came back with the news that both the brothers were alive and well and back on the battlefield. Sita was relieved.

The next day, when Lakshman was struck by the Shakti Astra of Indrajit, Sita became inconsolable. Trijata again came to her rescue with the news from the war front. She assured her that Sri Ram would never allow anything to happen to his younger brother. Her continuous relay of information about the heroics of Hanuman and the recovery of Lakshman with the Sanjeevani medicine comforted Sita to a great extent.

Trijata was also instrumental in bringing the news of Indrajit's death to Janaki, who heaved a veritable sigh of relief, as she was aware of Indrajit's power and strength.

The death of his son came as a lethal blow to Lankeshwar. He could not control his grief, and raised his sword to kill Sita, whom he believed to be the main cause of Indrajit's death. But he was stopped in his tracks by both Trijata and Mandodari, who asked him whether he had lost his sense of pride and bravery to such an extent that he was in the process of attacking a helpless woman.

After Ravan was defeated by Sri Ram, again it was Trijata who conveyed the happy news to Sita. Thus, Trijata was a constant companion to Sita throughout her tenure of captivity in Lanka. She brought the hope of a silver lining to the dark situation in which Vaidehi found herself in Lanka. In various versions of the Ramayana, including the Aranya Kand and Yuddha Kand of Valmiki Ramayana, Trijata has been mentioned as a constant companion to Sita. Though Valmiki describes Trijata as an aged rakshasi, later versions of Ramayana describe her as Vibhishan's daughter.

When Sri Ram wanted proof of Sita's purity, it was Trijata and Sarama who vouched for Sita's *pativrata*. It was another matter that Sita underwent the Agni Pariksha and came out of it unscathed thereby providing proof of her purity.

It was a fitting tribute to Trijata, that she and Sarama accompanied Sita back to Ayodhya. But realizing that Trijata would not be welcomed in Ayodhya, because she was a Rakshasi, Sita asked her to go to Varanasi and seek *moksha* (salvation) from Lord Vishwanath. There is a temple to Trijata at Varanasi near the Kashi Vishwanath Swami temple, where she is worshipped as a goddess of fertility by the locals.

Chapter 21

SULOCHANA

Sulochana, the beautiful princess of Nagalok, was enjoying the company of her friends. Her father, the all-powerful Adishesha, whose coiled body forms the couch for Mahavishnu, came in with a smile.

'Sulochana dear, Indradev has come here for protection,' he said.

'Protection against whom, father?' asked Sulochana.

'Oh!' exclaimed Sheshnag. 'Indra, the king of the gods, was defeated by Meghnad, the warrior prince of Lanka, and the proud son of the mighty Ravan. Indra ran away and has come here seeking my protection.'

'Are you going to protect him?' asked Sulochana.

'Of course, I will,' replied Sheshnag.

Who was this powerful Meghnad who had pushed Devendra into a corner?

Meghnad had been so named because he gave a thunderous roar after his birth. His father, the powerful Ravan, had ensured that all the constellations were in perfect positions at the time of his birth. Except for God Shani, everyone obeyed him. The boy became very powerful. On hearing about the power and might of Meghnad, Indra sent some gods to attack him. But Meghnad defeated them and threw them out. He made a vow to fight against Indra, then and there, and later he managed to defeat and imprison him. Finally, Lord Brahma had to intervene and ask for Indra to be released.

In return, Lord Brahma gave him the title of Indrajit (one who won over Indra) and offered him a boon.

Meghnad asked for immortality, but Brahma could not grant that. Hence, he asked for a boon that he would be killed only by a person who had not slept for fourteen years. The person had to practice celibacy too for those fourteen years. Lord Brahma was glad to grant him that boon and in addition also told him that once he completes a yajna to his Kuldevi, Nikumbala Devi, nobody would be able to defeat him. But if that yajna is not completed, he would be killed by the person who had stopped the yajna.

When Indra rushed to Nagalok to seek the protection of Sheshnag, Meghnad followed him. There his eyes fell on Sulochana. His heart skipped a beat. He fell head over heels in love with her. Sulochana happened to glance upwards at that moment. She looked at the handsome prince.

'I am Meghnad, the son of Lankeshwar Ravan,' he introduced himself.

Sulochana was attracted by his good looks and baritone voice. She looked away shyly and said, 'I am Sulochana, the daughter of Adishesha.'

'What an apt name! Your eyes are expressive!' exclaimed Meghnad.

Meghnad was smitten by her beauty and he could infer from her expression that she too was attracted to him.

'I love you,' he said. Sulochana shyly lowered her gaze.

Just then, they were interrupted by a messenger from Sheshnag.

'Princess, your father wants you to meet him at once,' he said.

Sulochana went to meet Sheshnag in excitement. She knew her father adored her. She wanted to tell him about her newfound love for Meghnad.But before she could say anything, her father announced, 'I have fixed your marriage with Indra, the king of gods.'

Sulochana was stunned. Being a woman with strong views she immediately refused. Her father was furious. But she was adamant.

'Father, I have fallen in love. I love the man who has earned the name of Indrajit from none other than Brahma, after defeating Indra,' she stated. 'How can you expect me to marry someone other than Indrajit, and that too, Indra, whom he has defeated?'

Adisesha could not believe his ears. His beloved daughter was speaking to him in a tone of refusal for the first time in her life. He glowered at her and said, 'You dare to argue with your father! You don't deserve to stay in Nagalok anymore. You can marry your Asura prince, but be sure your husband will meet his end at my hands, even if I have to incarnate on earth to carry it out.'

Sulochana went away with a heavy heart. But the ensuing battle saw Indrajit fighting against Adishesha and winning.

They got married and returned to the palace. When Ravan heard of his son's exploits, his heart swelled with pride. Sulochana was welcomed in a traditional manner by Mandodari, Indrajit's mother. The couple lived happily for some time. But within a few months, Sulochana realized that her marriage was not going to be a bed of roses. Being the daughter of Adishesha, Sulochana was, by instinct, a staunch devotee of Lord Vishnu. But her father-in-law hated Vishnu. Carried away by his statements, Indrajit refused to allow his young wife to continue her daily worship. She was torn between her faith and devotion to her God, Mahavishnu, and the orders of her husband, whom she loved. Her confidant was Mandodari, who understood her plight but was helpless as both her husband and son were all-powerful and stubborn.

In Ayodhya, Ram and Lakshman, who were incarnations of Lord Vishnu and Adishesha, had been exiled for fourteen years. Ram's wife Sita accompanied them. In an unfortunate sequence of events, Sita was abducted by Ravan and held captive in Lanka.

Sulochana was virtuous by nature. She was aghast at the treatment meted out to Sita. Not being able to bear the injustice, she spoke out. She warned her father-in-law that Sita was not an ordinary woman. And disrespecting a woman's honour would ultimately lead to his defeat. She was not the only one to warn Ravan. Mandodari, his primary queen and mother of Indrajit, also warned her husband. But the egoistic Ravan had no intention of listening to any of them. He brushed aside their warnings and imprisoned Sita at the Ashok Vatika, where she was guarded by a horde of rakshasis.

Sulochana felt sorry for Sita and wanted to help her. She did try a few times. But her angry husband told her in no uncertain terms that any help she rendered to Sita would not be tolerated. She could do nothing but obey.

However, when she got to know that an unknown monkey was destroying the fruit gardens of Lanka, she was worried. Next, she heard the news of the death of one of Ravan's sons at the hands of the same monkey. She knew her husband well. He would not tolerate this. And as expected, she heard that he had caught and tied the monkey with the Brahmastra. The monkey had been brought to the palace and its tail tied with cloth and oil poured on it. The tail kept extending and, in the end, there was no cloth and oil left in the city. Lankeshwar and his men laughed as they set fire to the tail, but in no time the monkey swished his tail all over the place. This led to the entire Lanka burning.

Sulochana knew in her mind that the monkey was no ordinary one. This was confirmed when she heard that Hanuman had arrived in Lanka as a messenger of Rama.

Within a few months, Ram, with his monkey army, arrived in Lanka via the Rama Setu that they had built across the ocean. Sulochana's heart knew that this forbode bad tidings for Lanka. Rama was on the side of justice. He had come to fight a battle and take back Sita who was lawfully his. Sulochana was aware that justice always prevails. She was not the only one. She tried to convince her father-in-law that Sita was the lawfully wedded wife of Ram and he should return her honourably. Mandodari also voiced her views in the same vein, but Lankeshwar was not willing to listen to any of them. Vibhishan, the younger brother of Ravan, tried counselling him but to no avail. Additionally, he was ousted from the palace. He went and surrendered at the feet of Lord Rama, who accepted him. It was Vibhishan who played a vital part in the ensuing battle as he knew all the secrets of the Lankan army and their generals.

Every day some brave warrior and general met their end. After the mighty Kumbhakarna's death, Indrajit decided to head the Lankan army. He came to Sulochana to apprise her of his decision. Her heart was beating fast. She knew victory could not be theirs as they were on the wrong side of justice. But solemnly, she performed the aarti and applied the battle- tilak on his forehead, with no show of emotions. After he proceeded to the battlefield, she retreated to her prayer chamber and started her *vrat* for the wellbeing and victory of her husband.

Indrajit fought an intense battle with Lakshman. His magical powers and his bravery ended the lives of many monkeys in the monkey army. His Nag pash struck both Ram and Lakshman, who fell unconscious as the poison spread through their bodies. Indrajit went back to Lanka with a victory smile. But Garud, the *vahan* of Mahavishnu, helped them recover by removing the snakes and their venom. This surprised Indrajit. Then he used his powerful Shakti Astra on Lakshman. Lakshman fell unconscious. Indrajit was sure that by the next morning, Lakshman would be dead. Again, he led a victory procession into Lanka. Ravan was thrilled with his son's heroics and the whole Lankan army celebrated.

Ram was weeping, holding his brother in his arms. Vibhishan suggested that they get Lakshman treated by the Lankan Vaidya, Sushena, without any further delay. He mentioned that the person who had been struck by the Shakti arrow would not live beyond the next dawn. Hanuman approached Sushena, convinced him about the primary duty of a doctor to attend to a patient and brought him to treat Lakshman. After examining the unconscious Lakshman, Sushena said that only the medicinal Sanjeevani leaves could save him. Hanuman flew in search of the Sanjeevani but not being able to recognize the plant, he brought the whole mountain before dawn. This resulted in Lakshman being treated with the Sanjeevani in time, and he was revived. Ram was relieved. Lakshman got ready to face Indrajit again in the battle.

When Indrajit heard that Lakshman had survived the effects of the Shakti Asthra, he was stunned. No man could survive it. He understood that Ram and Lakshman were divine.

Before going to war again, he went to meet his father. He tried telling Lankeshwar about the enemy's divinity, but

Ravan asked him whether he had lost his famed courage and was trying to back out of the war.

Indrajit was sad when he heard these words. He said, 'Father, you have completely misunderstood what I am trying to convey. It was my duty to inform you that I have realized the divinity of the enemy and that's what I did. That does not mean I am a coward and will shy away from doing my duty towards you and my motherland. I am proceeding to the Nikumbala Devi temple and I am going to perform the yajna. Please ensure that no one knows about my plan and on no condition should I be disturbed. If I finish the yajna successfully, I will be invincible.'

Ravan laughed happily.

Mandodari was listening to the whole conversation and she could only bless her beloved son with a heavy heart.

Indrajit then went to Sulochana to take her leave.

He said, 'I am going to our Kul Devi temple and performing the yajna. No one knows the place except our family members. After the yajna, I will proceed to the battlefield. I don't know whether I will return. If I happen to finish the yajna successfully, I may.'

Sulochana looked at him with steady eyes. She bravely bid him farewell and encouraged him to do his duty as a son. She stared at his departing figure till he was out of sight and then continued with her vrat.

When Vibhishan came to know of Indrajit's plan through his spies, he informed Ram about the significance of the Nikumbala Devi Yajna. If the yajna was completed, a celestial carriage would arrive and, after that, there would be no way Indrajit could be defeated. Understanding the danger of such a situation, Hanuman and Angad accompanied Lakshman to the hidden cave temple. Vibhishan, being one of Lankeshwar's brothers, knew the way to the cave and he led them there. They succeeded in disturbing the yajna, despite Indrajit's dogged perseverance, after which he left the yajna and returned to the battlefield. The valiant prince knew that his end was near. But he gave his best and continued fighting with all his might. Surprisingly, something was protecting him from being struck by Lakshman's arrows.

Sulochana continued her vrat with devotion. It was the strength of her Pativrata Dharma that was protecting her husband on the battlefield. Sri Ram mentioned this to Lakshman.

'Lakshman, you are a great warrior, and there is no doubt that you will vanquish Indrajit. But there is something you should know. Indrajit is married to Sulochana and both of them love each other dearly. He has only one wife and that wife is a great Pativrata Stree. So, ensure that when Indrajit is killed, his head does not fall on the ground.'

Meanwhile, Ravan happened to see Sulochana performing the vrat. His pride in his son's strength made him disrupt Sulochana's vrat in anger. At that very moment, Sulochana realized that her husband would not come back alive from the battle. She was right. Lakshman had struck Indrajit with his powerful arrow and the valiant warrior's head was cut off from his body. Lakshman caught the head of Indrajit and carried it safely to the tent of Sri Ram.

Sulochana's anger against Ravan could not be contained. She went to the palace, hugged her son and said, 'You will be properly cared for by Vibhishan, dear son.'

This was her way of predicting that Ravan would die at the hands of Ram and Vibhishan would be the future king of Lanka.

She then marched into the durbar hall and boldly accused Ravan. 'You are the sole cause of my husband's death. Are you happy? None of your sons is alive anymore. All the ladies of Lanka are becoming widows. Their wails are being heard everywhere. Are you satisfied now?'

She then turned towards Mandodari, 'Mother, you have lost your son too. I have lost my husband. My son has lost his valiant father. And the root cause of all this is the lust of your husband after another man's wife.'

So saying she marched away before anybody could retaliate.

Ram ensured that the body of the great warrior, Meghnad, was accorded the dignity it deserved and his people left the body at the gates of Lanka. Ravan could not believe that his beloved son was no more. When the final rites of Indrajit were being performed, Sulochana arrived there with a calm and composed expression and jumped into the funeral pyre. She performed Sati, uniting with her beloved husband forever. And true to his word, Adisesha, the father of Sulochana, had killed her husband by reincarnating on earth as Lakshman, Ram's younger brother.

Chapter 22

MANDODARI

'Come what may, I am not allowing a grieving woman to enter my house. Take her away, anywhere I least care. This is my house. It is for me and my children. I am the landlady and master of the house,' said a defiant Mandodari.

Ravan couldn't believe his eyes and ears. Was she the same soft-spoken Mandodari whose eyes were spitting sparkles now?

'Let me see how you stop me from taking her inside the palace,' threatened her husband.

Ravan was a known philanderer. He knew many women—celestials, mortals, Gandharvas and asuras—but Mandodari never resisted so violently in the past.

Today, she confronted him like a rock, with her arms stretched to her sides. Her husband held a struggling Sita in his vice-like grip, ready to take her inside.

'Stop right now, don't compel me to call Indrajit and Kumbha and order them to throw you both out of the palace,' said the queen.

'O the queen of the rakshasas, I have heard about your virtues and righteousness. You are like my mother. Please help me. Your husband abducted me against my wish in the absence of my husband and brother-in-law. Please send me back to my husband.'

Mandodari looked at her husband with contempt, who said defensively, 'I have brought her to Lanka on the strength of my arms. She is my hostage. I brought her here to get Ram and Lakshman to Lanka and seek revenge for the humiliation of my sister Surpanakha and the death of the cousins Khar and Dushan. Let them surrender before me.'

'What will you do with Sita after killing the princes?' asked Mandodari

'I haven't thought about it.'

'That's not an answer, be specific,' demanded Mandodari

'Listen Mandodari, Sita was wasting her youth and beauty in the forest with a weak and deprived mortal. She deserves better. But I can assure you, I will not force her into becoming my queen. Let her stay in the luxury of our palace and enjoy the splendour of Lanka. After a few days, she will agree to marry me.'

'He is a coward and a liar. Your husband approached me when I was alone in my cottage and my husband Ram went hunting. Disguised as a Brahmin seer, he came seeking alms. When I came out with the offerings, he revealed his original form and forced me onboard his chariot. He acted like a petty swindler and not as a mighty king of the rakshasas,' said Sita.

Mandodari said to Ravan, 'Is she right? How could you take a woman against her wishes? Did you forget the curse of Rambha?'

'You don't have to remind me all the time about that wretched apsara. I have not ill-treated Sita and brought her to

Lanka only to make her the empress. You are not allowing her to enter the palace knowing it well that one day I will win over her. You are simply jealous of her youth and beauty. Come what may, I have decided to make her my samragyi. If you don't cooperate, I'll make sure you became her chief maid,' said Ravan in a stern voice.

'The kingdom of rakshasas is not your personal fiefdom. They have created it through the blood, hard work and sacrifices of your mother's family and her people. Sita is a human and not an asura. The rakshasas will never accept a mortal as their queen-consort. Don't forget to ask Kumbha and Indrajit whether they were agreeable to make me the slave of a mortal only to satiate the concupiscence of a lascivious person.'

'That is outrageous. You are trying to pitch my brother and son against me. Aren't you ashamed of your utterances?' Ravan thundered. He was angrier than she had ever seen him.

'I am not objecting to your taking another woman. I am aware of rakshasas taking more than one woman at a time. My only concern is she must give her consent. I am giving you one year to win over her. If you could, I will welcome her in the palace like any other woman in the past, but certainly not as the Samragyi. The Samragyi is and will always remain an asura princess,' said Mandodari in a grim and defeated voice and started walking away from the scene.

'Don't challenge me, Mandodari. You are underestimating my charm. Have you forgotten how I won over your favour in no time?' said Ravan sarcastically, without looking at his wife or Sita.

'Before the end of one year, Ram will find me and take me back after killing you. Think about your death instead of winning over me. Your days are numbered,' said Sita, and looked at the tense and scary face of the queen.

As Mandodari, her eyes brimming with tears, was leaving, Vibhishan entered the palace. She confided in her younger brother-in-law about Sita's abduction and her subsequent refusal to allow Sita into the palace.

'Bhabhi is right,' Vibhishan agreed. 'It's considered inauspicious to keep a weeping woman in the house, especially a home blessed with happily married women and children. The presence of such sorrow can bring misfortune to the household. The negative energy of a constantly grieving woman could potentially weaken even the strongest walls. If we want to protect Lanka, we must ensure that Sita remains outside the city limits.'

At the advice of Vibhishan, Ravan agreed to keep Sita in the Ashok Vatika or the garden of Ashoka on the outskirts of the city. They constructed a strong impregnable wall around the garden guarded by the fierce rakshasis round the clock. No male demon could enter the Ashok Vatika. They employed well-trained demonesses to work inside the garden. Trijata, the daughter of Vibhishan, headed the team of the rakshasis.

Ravan was not exaggerating when he said how, within no time, he charmed the young and exceptionally gorgeous Mandodari. Ravan was not yet a great emperor, but he was on his way to becoming one. One day, he went to see Mayasur, the chief architect of the asuras and the king of Mayarastra. Ravan and most asuras, except for Prahlad, who worshipped Vishnu, were devotees of Lord Mahadev. So was Mayasur, who built a beautiful Shiva temple near his palace in Mayarastra. The temple was a marvellous piece of architecture designed like the Mount Kailash. An artificial freshwater lake, the same as the Mansarovar, was at the base of the temple. Like the Mansarovar, this lake too remained placid and cold irrespective of the weather. Maya created the Kailash and the Mansarovar with such an illusionary perfection that, from a distance, it gave the impression of Shiva's real abode. A Parad Shiva Lingam was installed within the sanctum sanctorum of the temple.

Mayasur had heard of the Brahmin boy's remarkable deeds, particularly how he, with the aid of his asura maternal grandfather had reclaimed their lost island of Trikuta. Maya had originally built the golden city of Lanka at the Trikuta hills. However, Kuber, the son of Sage Vishrava defeated the asuras and made Lanka his capital. Thus, born of the same father but two different mothers, Kuber was the stepbrother of Ravan. The asuras' aim in arranging the marriage of the demon princess Kekashi with the eminent Brahmin scholar Vishrava was fulfilled when their son, Ravan, reclaimed Lanka for the asuras.

By the time Ravan was twelve, living in the ashram of his father, he mastered the four Shrutis, six Shastras and other scriptures. He was a great astrologer and an expert ayurvedacharya. He learnt music, fine arts and statecraft from his father. To please Lord Shiva, he practised Rudra Veena for hours sitting in solitude in a cottage. The veena named after the Great Lord was designed by Shiva himself. Ravan's intelligence and learning capacity was ten times that of an ordinary person; hence, his father named him Dashanan. After completion of the academics, the three brothers—Dashanan, Kumbhakarna and Vibhishan—went to the netherworld to get trained in weaponry, horse riding, charioting and occult sciences with their asura relatives under the supervision of their maternal grandfather.

Mayasur had meticulously planned to entertain his esteemed guest. In the morning, Ravan joined the two princes, Mayavi and Dundubhi—the elder brothers of Mandodari—for a hunt. As evening fell, a musical concert featuring the celestial Gandharvas was arranged. Before the event concluded, Maya requested his guest to play the Rudra Veena, to which Ravan readily agreed.

Ravan seated himself in the yogic vajrasana pose, bowing respectfully to the veena. The instrument, with one resonator slightly lower, touched the ground on his right side, while the other end rested near his left shoulder. With the precision of a yogi in deep meditation, Ravan used his controlled breath as a modulator. Closing his eyes, he began to pluck the strings of the veena, and the air was soon filled with melodious notes. The enchanting music spread like the delicate fragrance of Parijat flowers, stirring the hearts of all who listened.

Yet, amidst this musical splendour, a young and beautiful girl found herself captivated more by the performer than the performance. She was Mandodari, the youngest child of Mayasur and his wife Hima, an apsara, and her gaze was fixed on Ravan.

Mayasur and his wife Hima were blessed with two mighty sons, but they longed for a daughter. For many years, Hima fervently prayed to Mother Parvati, and her prayers were finally answered with the birth of Mandodari. As the daughter of an apsara, Mandodari possessed divine beauty. Following her mother's guidance, Mandodari began worshipping Lord Shiva from a young age, praying for a husband who embodied the qualities of the Lord Himself.

In response to her devotion, Shiva promised her a husband who would be the most powerful man in the three worlds—greater than Indra, Varun, Shani, Marut, and all others. He would also be the greatest devotee of Shiva ever known.

When the music of the veena had stopped and people enthusiastically cheered and clapped, Mandodari was still lost in the musician. Ravan had a well-built body, broad shoulders, a lion's chest and long arms. His forehead was smeared with three horizontal lines of sandalwood paste or tripund, showing his Shaivite leanings. A cotton holy thread or *yagyopavit* hung from his left shoulder towards the right side of his waist across the chest. His eyes were large, bright, and penetrating. He wore diamond earrings in his earlobes and a necklace with nine large crystals, each mirroring his head. It gave the impression that the performer had ten heads. He was draped in an ocean-blue silk dhoti with a yellow border. An indigo-blue stole with crimson-red borders adorned his forearms and shoulders. Blue and black were the favoured colours of the asura men. Mandodari couldn't take her eyes off the man. He was the man Lord Shiva wanted her to marry, thought she.

Mayasur and Hima discussed the marriage proposal with their daughter. Next afternoon, Ravan was to return to Lanka. Like most asura parents of young girls, they too considered Ravan the most eligible bachelor. They saw how mesmerised their daughter was with the aura of Dashanan. Before leaving Mayarastra, Ravan must meet their daughter. Maya had arranged for Ravan to stay in their palace and not the royal guest house, as was the practice. The parents wanted them together for some time before they decided their daughter's marriage. They arranged their meeting in the dining hall during breakfast.

Mandodari eagerly waited for the honoured guest and her parents at the family dining hall. She watched him enter the room elegantly. He bowed before the princess like a perfect gentleman. Mandodari, rising from her seat, paid obeisance to him. They were engaged in small talks when a maidservant came and announced that the king was busy preparing drawings for the proposed temple in Lanka and the queen didn't feel well. Mayavi and Dundubhi had left the palace early for some urgent royal work.

Mandodari was alone with Ravan. He told her about his recent exploits and grand designs. He wanted to be the emperor of the three worlds. Ravan promised that if she married him, he would make her the queen consort or the Samragyi of Lanka. Before the breakfast was over, they had bonded so well that Ravan, before leaving Mayarastra, asked Mayasur for his daughter's hand. They were married within three months. The marriage was solemnised in the presence of the great rulers of the three worlds. Shukracharya, the guru of the demons, presided over the marriage ceremony. Mandodari riding the Pushpak Viman left for Lanka through aerial route leaving the home of her birth. In a grand ceremony attended by all the relatives and other demon kings, they ceremonially crowned Mandodari, the impress of Lanka.

Ravan, Kekashi, and the family members were overjoyed when Mandodari informed her husband and mother-in-law about her first pregnancy. Sumali and Malyavant were eager to welcome their fourth generation. Without knowing whether it was a boy or a girl, they discussed his education and training. Ravan, as an eminent astrologer, knew after the calculations that the child would be a boy. He would be a great warrior and remain undefeated by the mortals and gods. But he was heartbroken when he found that the life of his son was short, and he would die young before the eyes of his father.

The birth-cry of the child of Mandodari sounded like thunder. He was, therefore, named Meghanad. The prince was a handsome boy, an ultimate warrior, and an extremely knowledgeable person. Since his childhood, he was an obedient son who was like god to him. Two other sons, Atikaya and Akshaykumar, followed the birth of Meghnad. Ravan, in the meantime, married hundreds of women by the Rakshasa and Gandharva way of marriage. Wherever he saw a beautiful young woman, he brought her to Lanka by killing or imprisoning her family. No woman considered herself safe from Ravan and his goons. One day, when celestial nymph Rambha was going to meet her lover, Ravan molested her. She cursed him that in future if he abused any woman against her will, his head would rupture.

Ravan faced the first major humiliation of his life when he went to take part in Princess Sita's Swayamwar. Janak, the King of Videha, was holding a wedding competition for his daughter Sita, who was not only extremely beautiful but also possessed the greatest of the womanly virtues. The participant must string Shiva's legendary bow, Shiva Dhanush. Mandodari was not happy with her husband's decision to queue up as an ordinary contestant to win the princess of a small and insignificant country. After all, he was the one and only Lankesh. But Ravan pleaded with his wife, 'Do you seriously think I am after that mortal girl I have never seen before? Don't you see I have the apsaras, Gandharvas and Yakshanis waiting for my command. I want to prove to the world that I am the most powerful person and the greatest devotee of Lord Shankara. After winning the contest, I want to bring the Shiva Dhanush, his bow to Lanka.'

'What would you do with the princess you won in the swayamvar?'

'I have given no thought to it. My focus is only on the bow of my lord,' replied Ravan.

When Ravan returned to Lanka empty-handed without the Shiva Dhanush or Sita, he did not come out of his palace for one week. Meanwhile, the news received from Mithila further rubbed salt on his wounds. A teenage Kshatriya prince from Ayodhya who attended the swayamvar with his guru, Vishvamitra, and younger brother Lakshman not only could string the bow but also broke it into pieces. Ram married Sita and took her to

Ayodhya. Mandodari repeatedly tried to cheer Ravan up and bring him out of the seclusion, but he wouldn't listen to her.

Surpanakha's miserable condition broke Ravan's heart. How mercilessly the younger Kshatriya prince mutilated her nose, ears and breasts. When his sister told him about Ram, Sita and Lakshman, he resolved to take revenge for his humiliation that happened almost thirteen years ago. He never forgot about Sita; his heart longed to meet her. In the name of taking revenge on his sister's insult and restoring the asura pride, he would abduct Sita and bring her to Lanka.

Mandodari asked, 'How are you planning to seek revenge on the princes of Ayodhya?'

'I know only one thing: we must take revenge without delay. I'll seek advice from Marichi, who had earlier met them in the Tatak Forest.'

'Yes, he is the right person to consult. But never forget Ram is the prince who effortlessly shattered Shiva's bow, you couldn't even move. The two brothers have killed mighty warriors like Tataka, Subahu, Kabandh, Khar, Dushan and many others who were almost as powerful as brother Kumbha or our son Indrajit.'

'Mandodari, have confidence in the prowess of your husband. I am Dashanan, the lord of the three worlds. Killing mortals is below the dignity of great asura warriors. It's like hunting deer and rabbits and not a tiger or wild boar.' He embraced his wife closely, stroking her back softly. She didn't remember when he did that last. Was he nervous or was there something he didn't want to reveal?

After sending Sita to Ashok Vatika under tight security, Kekashi and Mandodari made their way to Dashanan's palace. They found him pacing restlessly in his bedroom, his drink untouched, and the maids dismissed. Kekashi recalled her husband's warning—a prophecy foretelling the annihilation of the asuras at the hands of humans, monkeys, and bears. Did her son know of this prophecy? Mandodari doubted it, for she had seen this behaviour many times before. When Ravan desired a woman, he would find no peace until he possessed her.

The two women implored Ravan to return Sita with due state honour. They suggested that Vibhishan and his wife Sarama accompany Sita, believing that this would settle the matter. They promised to persuade Meenakshi not to insist on seeking revenge. Finally, Kekashi reminded her son of the prophesy of his father, Sage Vishrava.

'Mother, don't believe him. He never uttered a single word of appreciation for me. He has only one son, and that is Kuber.'

'You must not speak about your father's prophesy so lightly. He is the grandson of Lord Brahma. He has taught you astrology. Tell me what your calculations have to say?'

'Like father, Brahma too has become old and cynical. He has written on my forehead that a mortal shall kill me. Is that possible, mother? Can a mortal stand and face the mighty sword Chandrahas of your son?'

'I know your father more than any other person in the world. He doesn't nurture prejudice against anyone, least of all against his son. You seem to have lost your mind, desire overpowering your senses.'

'You are my mother. That doesn't mean you will speak in favour of those homeless urchins,' said Lankesh.

Of late, Mandodari had observed that the relations between the mother and son were not so cordial. Ravan was everything his mother wanted him to be. But his love for women was not to her liking. It always brought infamy, death and destruction. It did not surprise the queen when her mother-in-law, without uttering a single word, left the palace of Lankesh.

After leaving Ravan's palace, Kekashi met her other two sons and grandchildren. Then she changed into the attire of a rishika and returned to the ashram of Vishrava, taking Meenakshi with her. That was the last time she would see her son.

Mandodari remained undeterred by the harsh words her husband had spoken to his mother in her presence. Ravan's overwhelming lust had blinded him, making him deaf to reason. But as his wife, it was her duty to stand firm and oppose his sinful ways, guiding him back to the right path. She was worried about her husband's life and the looming threat of widowhood.

'My lord,' she began, 'you are the most intelligent person on earth. Must I remind you that you are about to embark on the most senseless and immoral war you've ever fought? The sigh of a chaste and virtuous woman is deadlier than the Brahmastra. Sita's husband is no ordinary Kshatriya prince. He has already defeated you once in Mithila. Khar, Dushan, Tataka, Subahu, and Kabandha fell before him like ordinary soldiers. No matter the outcome, you shall be the loser. Even if you could somehow win—though that is impossible given the ominous planetary positions—you cannot have Sita against her will. You will be left standing exactly where you are today.'

'Mandodari, don't speak the language of a coward. You are the queen of Lankesh. The ten digpals or the masters of the directions attend the daily chores of my palace. You are talking about the planets and their relative positions. The planets stand in my court with folded palms, bowed heads and lowered eyes. I can change their routes and locations at will. And Sita, where will she go after I behead Ram and Lakshman? She will fall at my feet and beg for forgiveness.'

'Sita doesn't care about the luxuries of a palace. She gave up all that in Ayodhya and volunteered to exile with her husband because she loves Ram. You know you can't change the position of the planets. They have given that illusion to please you. Their movement is a part of the expanding or contracting brahmanda. No one, not even Lords Brahma, Vishnu and Mahadev, could alter their position.'

Lanka waited with bated breath for the retaliation from the exiled princes. During this tense period, more troubling news arrived: Ram had killed Ravan's greatest ally, Vali, the King of Kishkindha, with a single shot. Vali had been so powerful that he had once defeated and imprisoned Ravan himself. Vali's younger brother, Sugriv, had become the new king of the vanara and bear tribes. He pledged his full support to Ram in the quest to find and rescue Sita.

Tara, Vali's wife and a close friend of Mandodari, now faced a difficult situation. Her decision to marry Sugriv deeply unsettled Mandodari. As a devoted wife, Mandodari couldn't fathom how Tara could remarry so quickly. However, soon realized that Tara's primary concern must have been the safety and future of her son, Angad. The duties of a faithful wife and a chaste woman, Mandodari reflected, had become secondary to Tara's responsibilities as a mother.

Immediately after the four months of the rainy season, something unprecedented occurred. A vanara—a tribal man dressed as a monkey—managed to circumvent Lanka's security and infiltrate the impregnable fort of Trikuta. He met Sita and conveyed Ram's message with ease. However, he wasn't content with just delivering the message; he wanted to challenge Ravan's might. To make his presence known, he wreaked havoc in Ashok Van, uprooting and plucking trees right in front of the guards. This vanara, as they later learned, was Hanuman, the son of the wind god Pawan.

Hanuman's rampage was ferocious; he defeated, maimed, and killed the soldiers who tried to confront him. Ravan then ordered his son Akshaykumar to capture this unruly monkey and present him in the court. Hanuman killed Akshaykumar in a one-sided battle. He then defeated Ravan's invincible eldest son, Indrajit, and forced him to use the infallible weapon of Brahma—Brahmastra. Mandodari learned of her son's death from the maids and rushed to the royal court. Despite her grief, Ravan, Meghnad, and others were more focused on punishing Hanuman than mourning the loss of the young prince.

A crestfallen Mandodari immediately returned to the palace, overwhelmed by the greatest agony a mother could endure—the loss of her child. Akshaya was only a young boy, not yet a seasoned warrior. His death was not one of valour on the battlefield; instead, it was abrupt and brutal. The vanara had uprooted a massive tree and brought it crashing down on Akshaya's head, killing him instantly.

Mandodari spent sleepless nights, refusing food for days, consumed by grief. She knew this was just the harbinger of a greater tragedy. A single vanara had infiltrated Lanka, killed the mighty Lankesh's son, and burned the city to ashes—yet returned unharmed. Ravan promised his wife that he would avenge their son's death, but deep down, she knew that no vengeance could ever bring back her beloved Akshaya.

Nine days of mayhem and bloodshed passed, wiping out the entire rakshasa army and all their greatest warriors with no major casualty to the aggressors. Except for one day when Indrajit grievously injured Lakshman, victory remained one-sided. After the first five days of the battle, Mandodari stopped watching the proceedings from the watchtower. Angad killed her two brothers—Dundubhi and Mayavi—who came with their army to support their brother-in-law. Kumbha couldn't face Ram's arrows even for half a day. Within hours of him entering the battlefield, Ram sent him to Yama's abode.

Mandodari went to see his wife Vajrajwala but had no words to console her.

On the tenth day, Lakshman killed Meghnad. His adversaries were so impressed by his valour, and devotion to his father and motherland that Ram asked Lakshman to personally supervise handing over of his body to the Lankan authorities with the honour of a myrtyr. Mandodari was fully awake when she heard a soft knock at the door. Meghnad's wife Sulochana, with a three-year-old son sleeping in her arms, entered the chamber.

Ravan sat in his favourite yogic posture before Shiva Linga playing the Rudra Veena in complete solitude, his eyes closed. Mandodari stood in the temple built by her father that laid the foundation of their marriage. Without opening his eyes, Ravan said, 'Come, Mandodari, sit near me. I was waiting for you.'

'Yes, my lord.'

'Do you want to listen to something in particular, your favourite hymns or the Shiva Tandava Stotram.'

'I'd rather sit and listen to whatever you played.' replied Mandodari.

Ravan stopped playing the veena after some time. He said, 'Mandodari, when I pray before the Lord, I enter in a one-on-one conversation with Him. He told me that the Lord wanted me to reach Kailash at the earliest as my days on earth were numbered. He promised to make me his favourite *gana*. Do you think, my dear, it is right for me to make Him wait?'

'My Lord, you must not think about your brothers and sons who have gone away. You are mighty Dashanan who conquered the three worlds at the strength of his arms. None of them were around except brother Kumbhakarna when you won the world for us. I repeatedly told you to return Sita. But you preferred waging a war instead. Once you have taken a decision, I am with you under all circumstances. Lankesh, you are and will ever remain undefeated on the battlefield.'

'Mandodari, promise me you will agree to my last wish.'

'Yes, I will.'

'No, not like this. Take my hand in your beautiful palms and in the presence of Lord Shiva promise you will agree.'

Mandodari's heart sank. She did not believe the disappointing words spoken by her husband. How could he speak the language of a surrendered soldier? Her Lankesh will return victorious after killing the two princes. She would once again take her place by his side on the throne. Together they will make a new beginning. Lanka will thrive and a new empire shall come up stronger and larger.

'Tomorrow morning, I leave the fort to return only at the end of the battle, victorious or dead. I'll camp outside the fort gates. You have a great responsibility coming your way. After my death, you must preserve all that I have achieved. To achieve that you must marry Vibhishan, who is the next king of Lanka.'

'No, my lord, please don't seek such an indecent and offending promise. I'll, like Sulochana, commit sati if anything happens to you.'

'No Mandodari, you must live and occupy the throne of Lanka. We must counter tactfully the nefarious designs of the Aryan sages. They want to destroy our rakshasa culture so dear to us. The golden era of the rakshasa's reign will end with my death. Promise me, with the help of Malyavant, my maternal grand-father, you will bring our glory back. You will not leave Lanka or this world before making our grandson, the son of Meghnad, a great emperor. This empire belongs to you as much as it will belong to the victors. You have a responsibility towards your people to lead and guide them.'

Ravan held Mandodari close, gazing deeply into her eyes. She shook her head, a soft whimper escaping her lips. Throughout the night, they spoke of the days of their youthful romance, the joys of parenthood, and the countless sweet memories that had bound them together. Their love was evident in every word, yet they deliberately avoided any mention of Sita or the impending battle.

The spell was broken by the sound of a trumpet, heralding the dawn. To Mandodari, the blare of the trumpet sounded like the wail of a grieving woman, desperate and aggrieved.

'It's time to take leave, Mandodari. Bring me my sword, the Chandrahas, and fetch my bow. Today, they will know why this devotee of Mahadev is the greatest warrior in the universe.'

A hero perished; a culture was obliterated. The Vanara and Reechh tribes, forced to surrender their natural habitats and abandon their ancient ways of life, transformed themselves into humans. With the fall of the southern peninsula, the Aryan conquest of Bharatvarsha and sages' dream of the Akhand Bharat was realized. Kaikeyi's misunderstood boon elevated a prince to godhood, yet patriarchal society offered no forgiveness to either Kaikeyi or Mandodari. Kaikeyi was cursed for banishing Ram to secure the throne for her son, while Mandodari was condemned as a power-hungry woman who, instead of following her husband to the funeral pyre, married her brother-in-law in her later years.

Mandodari kept her promise to her husband. She wed King Vibhishan to become the Empress of Lanka, but she would never truly be his wife.

Acknowledgements

A literary venture can succeed in its primary mission of reaching, informing and entertaining its readers only if it has the visionary support of a great publisher. We wish to express our heartfelt gratitude to Ajay Mago of Om Books International for reposing confidence in us and entrusting us with this significant project.

A special note of appreciation goes to Shantanu Ray Chaudhuro and Ayan Dawn for their remarkable editorial contributions.

We wish to thank our literary agent, Suhail Mathur of The Book Bakers, for connecting us with the wonderful team at Om Books International and also creating a magnificent cover for the book.

We offer our humble respect to the countless authors, composers, and singers who have brought the timeless tale of the Ramayana to life, continuing to inspire generations.

Above all, we are deeply grateful to the devotees of Shri Ram for their unwavering faith and devotion in the Lord.